IC ALE

D1626305

# The Playwrights Speak

# *The Playwrights Speak*

## EDITED BY WALTER WAGER

WITH AN INTRODUCTION BY
JOHN RUSSELL TAYLOR

 LONGMANS

LONGMANS, GREEN AND CO. LTD.
London and Harlow

Associated companies, branches and representatives
throughout the world

SBN: 582 11784 4

Printed in Great Britain
by Ebenezer Baylis and Son, Ltd.
The Trinity Press, Worcester, and London

*This book is dedicated to*
*Jessie and Max Wager*

# Contents

# Acknowledgements

MANY INDIVIDUALS have provided helpful advice, information or assistance that contributed to this book. The editor wishes to register his debt and gratitude to the following: For arranging the interview with John Arden, Peter Bellwood of the Establishment Theatre and Walter Alford of John Springer Associates; for setting up the Arthur Miller interview, Barry Hyams, press agent for the Repertory Theatre of Lincoln Centre; for arranging the meeting with Tennessee Williams, David Rothenburg; for scheduling the talk with William Inge, Samuel Lurie; for setting up the Peter Weiss interview, Merle Debuskey; for help in finding the Dürrenmatt interview, Richard Schechner; for discovering the interview with Albee, Stanley Kauffmann—and for aid in collecting the data for the introductory note, David Roggensack and Howard Atlee; for helping find and clear the Osborne interview, J. R. T. Hopper, overseas publicity officer for the British Broadcasting Corporation; for assistance in setting up the interview with Arnold Wesker, Mort Nathanson and Dorothy Ross; and for assistance in finding and clearing rights to the Harold Pinter interview, George Plimpton, formerly Number 'o' of the Detroit Lions and still editor of *The Paris Review*.

The editor owes a special debt to Arthur Miller for teaching him how to operate a tape recorder.

Thanks are also extended to John Freeman, Horst Bienek, Professor Rosette Lamont (and Charles Mee), Laurence Bensky, Michael Nardacci, Walter Chura and Reverend Amadeus Fiore. In addition, it would be unfair not to mention the person who first suggested that such interviews might be interesting and useful, Gilman Kraft, former publisher of *Playbill*.

Finally, the editor is pleased to express his appreciation to

Arthur Miller, Harold Pinter, Tennessee Williams, Edward Albee, John Arden, Eugene Ionesco, Friedrich Dürrenmatt, Arnold Wesker, William Inge, John Osborne and Peter Weiss.

w. w.

# Introduction

## BY JOHN RUSSELL TAYLOR

OPINION IS FREE, but fact is sacred. A sentence of fact is worth a bookful of comment. Such brusque formulations do not necessarily denigrate the critic's role, but they do serve to remind us that critical study, like everyday audience enjoyment, must start from the facts: the particular play, the particular book, the particular painting. Unless there can be some measure of agreement about the fundamental nature of the thing itself, most comment is useless. And an important way to the facts of the case is via what the creator himself can tell us.

Not that this is necessarily 'fact'. Once a work of art is finally separated from its creator, it must lead an independent life of its own, embodying in itself its own standards of judgment. And when this has happened, we can fairly say that after all, the creator's views of it are just one man's opinions, no more and no less to be accepted without question than anyone else's. But this is not quite true. A creator's intentions cannot make anything what it is not: if a man writes what he takes to be a comedy, and the world at large agrees to see it as a tragedy, then there is nothing that his pronouncements can do about it. But it often happens that if some special knowledge (such as only the playwright can give) of the circumstances in which a play was written, or of what the writer had in mind when he wrote it, cannot make it seem better or worse in our eyes, at least it can make it more interesting.

And this sort of interest is the foundation of criticism, The critic's business is largely the making of connections, the providing of contexts. For though each work has to be judged on its own merits, as a more or less satisfactory evening in the theatre or whatever, the critic can often show audiences the way to enjoyment by *placing* a play, explaining how it fits into the pattern created by the writer's previous work, or how it continues a particular line of development in the drama of the day. If we take a spectacular success story like that of Harold Pinter, who progressed in public estimation from the complete disaster of *The Birthday Party*'s first production in 1958 to the triumph of *The Caretaker* only two years later, we can see at once how this works.

The main trouble with *The Birthday Party* in 1958 was nothing inherent, but simply its lack of a context. The sort of play it was, and the way that it worked in theatrical terms (particularly what it did and did not choose to tell us on the basic level of plot), were unfamiliar to the theatre-going public, and to the critics. What they expected then of a play—any play—was far different from what Pinter gave them. And by the time that they had adjusted to the facts before them—the real nature of this play as distinct from that of any other play they had seen—it was too late to enjoy it. Two years later, time, another production of *The Birthday Party* on television, and some knowledge of what the dramatist himself thought he was doing and had set out to do, all these had changed expectations and had created a context in which *The Caretaker* could at once find its audience and become a major commercial success.

This happened, not of course because the explanations and the background information had made *The Birthday Party* itself any better, but because they had helped audiences to approach Pinter's writing in the proper terms. And this is what, with luck, we may hope to get out of interviews, such as those contained in this book, with the men primarily responsible for what we see in the theatre. The personal details are not just gossip; by knowing more about admittedly advanced and difficult dramatists like Peter Weiss and John Arden, or even quite conservative dramatists like William Inge, we can come to their plays not necessarily in a more indulgent, less critical frame of mind, but certainly more prepared for the very special experience each can give us if we are ready for it.

The interviews in this book are with a widely varied group of dramatists from widely varied backgrounds. Any attempt at a neat classification of them rapidly breaks down. Ionesco, Pinter and Albee can be vaguely related to the Theatre of the Absurd, but each of them in his more recent works has been growing away from it, radically in the case of Albee. Beyond that, what can one say? The three other American dramatists, Tennessee Williams, Arthur Miller and William Inge, are the leading representatives of the middle generation, and all of them are, in the broadest possible terms, exponents of theatrical realism. But their temperaments and their interests separate them much more forcibly than these facts bring them together. The same might be said of the other three British dramatists, John Osborne, John Arden and Arnold Wesker. They are very much of an age, and all of them have shown some sort of concern with social problems and the present condition of England. But it would be hard to think of three plays less alike in their style and emotional climate than, say, *Inadmissable Evidence*, *Roots*, and *The Workhouse Donkey*. As for Dürrenmatt and Peter Weiss, they are right out on their own, belonging to no school and following no bent but their own.

Hence, perhaps, the usefulness of the direct, personal approach in each case. One thing that nearly all the writers interviewed have in common is their doubt about the extent to which they have been influenced by others, about the closeness of their relationships with others. Arden sees a relationship with, rather than a direct influence from, Brecht; Inge thinks he is closest to Synge and Chekhov; Ionesco thinks he has been influenced more by works of philosophy and some novels than by other plays. And so on. All of them, despite their greater or lesser degrees of personal involvement in the theatre, concentrate mainly on telling us about their own interior development apart from and largely outside the theatre, their childhoods, their reading, their family circumstances, how they go about the business of writing.

And that is as it should be. They provide the raw material, we make the judgments. Dürrenmatt says at one point 'I hope I am interpreting myself correctly. We're often our own worst interpreters.' Albee remarks 'You get into these conceptual terms and I'm on very shaky grounds. I don't know what I'm talking about half the time.' Again and again in these interviews we find the dramatists drawing back from any too direct discussion of what they meant, preferring not to think too 'critically' about their work, perhaps in fear of murdering to dissect. Partly, of course, this is the practical pride of the writer who knows that if what he has written does not, sooner or later and given a reasonable amount of careful attention, explain itself, then it has failed and there is little point in his trying to tell us what it ought to have said. But more importantly, the reticence of those interviewed comes from a very real sense of the mystery of their calling. Technically many of them know exactly what they are doing, they could explain their texts in terms of working theatre down to the last comma. But when it comes to capsulating what they had to say, explaining purposes and messages, they are often genuinely at a loss. As far as Pinter is concerned, *The Caretaker* is just a play about two brothers and a tramp in a room: he prefers not to dig deeper into its analysable meaning, simply because what he was creating was a dramatic action which cannot be completely paraphrased but must speak only in its own strictly dramatic terms.

The dramatist, in fact, seems to be the perfect type of the man who cannot tell what he is going to say until he has said it, and even then will explain himself only with the greatest hesitancy and circumspection, as though he is merely the fallible interpreter of an oracle. And if one would not hold that this necessarily should be so, there seems from experience to be every reason why we should mistrust the playwright whose extra-dramatic explanations are too ready. Among the playwrights treated in this book, the crucial instance is Arthur Miller. Miller has always been a terrible explainer of what he is doing and saying in his plays. As Albee remarks rather cattily, he 'keeps telling us he's writing tragedies all the time'; it is tempting to go along with Albee's other comment on Arthur Miller: 'If he'd shut up, he might write better.' But I wonder. For me the failure of all

Miller's plays (with the possible exception of *The Crucible*) is precisely that he knows too exactly what he wants to say, what point he wants to make about Life, Death and other such grandly cosmic concepts. If he stopped telling us all about it on every conceivable occasion he would probably be even more determined to make his statements crystal-clear in his plays, whereas he is even now over-ready to preach to us in the plays, using his characters merely as so many mouthpieces for his ideas or as aunt sallies for him to knock down.

Perhaps the reason that *The Crucible* does not qualify for this stricture is that it is the only one of Arthur Miller's plays in which, as he says, the plan really does 'open the way to the passion'; it is the only one in which he seems to be saying more than he meant, and something other than what he consciously intended. It is the play of his which sends one out of the theatre feeling one has been taught least, and experienced most. I am rather afraid, though, that it is the didactic Miller that his great British admirer Arnold Wesker most approves of. Again in Wesker's work we are offered theatre with a message: its faults are the same as those of Arthur Miller's drama, but fortunately Wesker, a far more emotional man where his pet causes are concerned than Miller, is less consciously intellectual in his attitude to drama, and his plays are likely every so often to go off at their own sweet will, in directions quite different from those first envisaged by the author. It is at these moments, usually when the drama moves beyond words to express itself entirely in action—Beatie's ecstatic dance in *Roots*, the raid on the coal-store and the final parade in *Chips with Everything*—that Wesker's writing takes on a properly dramatic richness and complexity, far removed from any cut-and-dried messages he may feel honour-bound to deliver.

If it is possible to doubt whether the drama is necessarily Miller's or Wesker's natural means of expression (whatever they may have to say on the subject) all the other dramatists in this book are certainly of the theatre, theatrical, to their fingertips. Dürrenmatt agrees with Ionesco that 'theatre doesn't have a didactic purpose, *mustn't* have a didactic purpose,' and in all his plays has been content just to develop a situation, to tell a story in lively dramatic terms, and leave it to his audience to figure out a meaning and a message if they want to. As he very acutely says, they will do this anyway: 'The audience actually creates the connection between theatre and reality; it finds its own world in ours, whether we like it or not.' And if we take a characteristic Dürrenmatt play, like *The Visit* or *The Physicists*, we find that it works like a confidence trick: it all seems to be saying something, to be making a quasi-philosophical point about the nature of the world we live in, but the more closely we examine the suggestions of deeper significance, the more shadowy and inconsistent they appear. Each play is, as it were, a do-it-yourself kit, providing the materials (quite deliberately, I think) for all sorts of profound interpretations, but finally refusing to be confined absolutely to any single reading. Does this necessarily make Dürrenmatt a less serious dramatist than Arthur Miller? I don't think so: he may even perhaps be a more serious dramatist, even if a less serious man.

Ionesco's description of his beloved 'club' the Collège de 'Pataphysique, might also be applied to his plays: 'One can say anything about 'Pataphysics. Everything is true.' Though for convenience's sake Ionesco may be fitted into the Theatre of the Absurd along with Beckett, Adamov, Genet, Pinter and others, he really belongs much more evidently with an earlier generation of Dadaists and Surrealists. His plays mirror the absurdity of man's situation in the universe less by embodying a philosophical view in appropriate action (as Beckett's do, for example) than by constructing their action in such a way as to reflect a view of things in which causes and effects are disconnected and words drained of all meaning and of all use as a means of communication. From the series of simple, striking images of anarchy and topsy-turvydom in Ionesco's early plays one might go ahead to construct a philosophical system which would explain and contain them: but that is quite different from starting with the philosophy before you write the plays. The interview in this book gives us quite a vivid picture of Ionesco himself, and of what sort of person he is.

Unfortunately it was done some time ago, while Ionesco was still working on *Exit the King* (*Le Roi se Meurt*), so it throws little light on his striking change of style in his later full-length plays (starting with *Rhinoceros*), or why they are so much less memorable and effective than his earlier work. But then on such subjects, delicate as they are to approach, the creator is probably just as uncomfortably at a loss as everyone else.

Two interviews in particular have rarity value. Both Tennessee Williams and John Osborne, enormously successful, extravagantly well publicised, seem to be quite shy of talking to anyone directly about their work and themselves. Possibly this is because both are very conscious of being instinctive writers, with generous, flamboyant, rather hit-or-miss talents. The Osborne *Face to Face* interview tells us, not surprisingly, a lot more about Osborne's personality and his personal background than about his plays as such, in fact not one of his plays is specifically mentioned by Osborne in the whole interview. This too is fair enough, though one would like to know how Osborne would fill in the background of his stylistic evolution from *Look Back in Anger*, with its straightforward naturalistic approach, to *The Entertainers*, with its ambitious, possibly Brechtian structure of overt comment on the central matter of the plot. Or for that matter, whether Osborne sees the hero of *Inadmissible Evidence*, a sort of Jimmy Porter twenty years on, as a psychiatric case, or as the only one in step while the world goes wrong.

Tennessee Williams is a little more forthcoming about his work, but not much: the self-portrait he paints is that of an artistic recluse who has found his 'own way of writing which has crystallised for me and nobody influences me anymore'. On the other hand, he proves to be considerably more interested in what is going on around him politically and socially than one might imagine from his plays, with their obsessive private world. Obviously he is in this the direct opposite of, say, Arthur Miller, for whom a man's concerns must necessarily be made the subject-matter of his drama. Williams can conceive, since this is how it works for him, of being a political man, with a vote to use and opinions on the state of society in general, and yet finding that little or nothing of that slops over into his work, which draws rather on a deeper, more elemental and certainly more personal level of experience and interest. For him the concern over civil rights and so on is the prose of his life; drama is the poetry.

Somewhere between Williams and Miller comes William Inge, while Edward Albee can perhaps most usefully, now, be regarded as the Tennessee Williams of the younger generation. Inge is a lot less well known in Britain than he should be, at least as far as the theatre is concerned: none of his plays has had a professional London production, though the cinema has filled the gap with film versions of *Come Back, Little Sheba*; *Picnic*; *Bus Stop*; *The Dark at the Top of the Stairs* and *A Loss of Roses* (*Woman of Summer*). Perhaps this is all as it should be, for his work depends so much on its precise placing in a particular American context, that of uneventful small-town life in the Middle-West, that it is hard to imagine a British cast doing it anything like justice (though this may in itself be a reflection on its strength and lasting value).

Albee is a far more cosmopolitan, far more eclectic figure. Significantly, he gained his reputation mainly from his first short pieces, with their discreet touches of Theatre of the Absurd (*Zoo Story* especially), but hit the commercial bigtime with *Who's Afraid of Virginia Woolf?*, a tremendously vital realistic comedy-drama which drew heavily on Strindberg and Tennessee Williams and could hardly have been further away from advanced modern theatre practice. Not that it matters. Adroit theatrical craftsmen are these days far more difficult to come by than wild untaught geniuses, and undeniably Albee, the virtuoso manipulator of well-made-play machinery, is a far more prepossessing figure than Albee, the humble follower of Beckett and Genet.

The two other dramatists interviewed in this book, John Arden and Peter Weiss, have perhaps one thing in common: their political involvement and their powerful yet indirect way of expressing it in their work. Weiss would probably agree with Arden when he says 'I think it is impossible to avoid being a political playwright or a sociological playwright. I think that man is a political animal, and everything we do is to some extent political. . . .' Perhaps not every spectator would see in *The Marat/Sade* precisely the political message that Weiss himself sees. Apparently he had some reservations about Peter Brook's famous Royal Shakespeare Company production because it did not make it clear enough that Marat and revolutionary Socialism were in the right. But that, enthusiasts for the production might reasonably reply, only goes to show that even if the play rises out of a definite Marxist point of view, in the event Weiss has gone beyond his conscious intentions and written a play in which it is impossible to see one faction as entirely right and the rest as entirely wrong.

This sort of ambiguity—or dramatist's fair-mindedness if you will—is the hallmark of John Arden's plays. Also their most puzzling quality. For theatregoers in general are used to seeing plays which are either clearly message-pieces or clearly not. You may be willing to accept both, but you expect to be told pretty clearly which kind is before you in any particular instance. Arden breaks the rules by writing plays which are social in their subject-matter, and therefore ought to have clear messages, but treating these subjects with such scrupulous fairness to everybody's point of view that even when we know (from outside evidence such as this interview) where his own personal sympathies lie, we would be hard put to it to decide from the plays themselves.

As yet, no play by Arden has achieved anything like a commercial success, though understanding seems to be coming with closer acquaintance, especially when productions of his work are sponsored by such eminently respectable bodies as the National Theatre, which carries its own guarantee of seriousness and integrity. And once we do become acclimatised to Arden's steadfast refusal to take sides within his plays, to give us clear pointers for our sympathies, we appreciate that his method is the most truly dramatic. All we need is the context; we have to be able to go into the theatre with some idea of what we should expect, rather than just about managing to work it out by the time we leave. If the interviews in this book can help to bring that about, they will have served their purpose well.

# *Preface*

TWO YEARS AGO I warned a novelist friend that it was time for
him to publish another book if he wished to remain a social and
literary lion. If he did not do so soon, all the pretty young girls
would lose interest in him, for he would be 'last year's novelist'.
I am reasonably confident that none of the dramatists treated in
this volume is 'last year's playwright'. Whether or not they have
had successful productions of new works during the past twelve
months, they have all contributed something significant and
distinctive to the world of theatre and must be numbered among
the men whose dramas are part of the standard—the basis for
comparison.

This is not to say that every one of them is a genius, a great or
an immortal. But they are all important playwrights, and it is
no exaggeration to predict that at least three—perhaps five—have
created works that future generations will enjoy. There are several
other dramatists whom I would have liked to include. Samuel
Beckett does not choose to sit for interviews, the only comprehensive interview with Jean Genet is not 'available' and space
limitations preclude the expansion of this book beyond its present
number of pages. A second volume is contemplated, however,
and it would certainly include more of the French playwrights
plus some deceased greats. This present book is restricted,
perhaps erroneously, to the living.

As you will notice, each interview is preceded by a brief
biographical sketch. The variations in the lengths of the sketches
and/or interviews do not represent any editorial judgment as to
the rank or importance of the playwrights, but rather reflect the
nature of the material that I have been able to find. It has been a
pleasure to look for it, a rewarding delight whose results I hope you

will find equally stimulating and satisfying. Of course the interviews are not all complete or wholly comprehensive, and indeed they raise as many questions as they answer. But that is part of the challenge and the pleasure for the thoughtful or even the semi-informed or the curious, is it not?

Part of my challenge in preparing this book was meeting the playwrights. Each is an individual, of course, but as a group they are men of great style, have an understandable gift of language, are often witty and almost always just a bit guarded in the presence of a stranger who may distort their words or betray their ideas or confidences. They are a bit theatrical but still very pragmatic, with few of the pretensions that some generals, actors and politicians reflect when facing a journalist with a tape recorder. Like anyone else, they don't always tell the same story exactly the same way twice, they resent being confronted with quotes from past interviews, and they are quick and adept at dodging delicate questions about sexual, political or family problems. These summary remarks about the dramatists—comments which are, hopefully, neither overgeneralisations nor oversimplifications—are meant to apply primarily to those writers whom I interviewed. At the risk of sounding sanctimonious, it should be implicit that the interviews were chosen because each seemed the best for this book rather than because of the person who asked the questions.

One reason that these interviews may be fairly rewarding is because the writers are thoughtful men who have all been questioned many times. The public and press care about playwrights today. Although there may be doubts as to the depth and solidity and profundity of the so-called 'cultural explosion', it does seem clear that we are enjoying a substantial growth in 'live theatre'—perhaps a hungry reaction to the meagre nourishment of broadcast and film fare. Campus and resident repertory theatre groups are booming on both sides of the Atlantic, government support is growing and the 'permanent' shortage of talented playwrights that seems to trouble all nations is now being met—at least in part—by an increasing number of writers turning to the stage.

It is hoped that young playwrights and would-be playwrights may find some cheer, inspiration, wit and wisdom in this book, for it is the writers who are the key to any theatre.

They are men—and women—of courage and determination—or is it stubbornness?—for writing for the stage is very hazardous indeed. It is perhaps ironically fortunate that television drama has not fulfilled what seemed to be its promise a decade ago and that film production costs have escalated so immensely that movie companies rarely will risk hiring a young or new script writer. As an odd result, the living theatre—which is plainly growing more adventurous and open to experiment and original creative talent—may be just about the only place where a creative dramatist can go. If this seems to be the trend, let us keep in mind that it can be reversed quite easily. It would be naïve, unrealistic and dangerous to think otherwise. As the Twentieth Century Fund's November 1966 study of the economics of the performing arts indicated, only a very small percentage of Americans attend live theatre—which is hardly a broad healthy base to support the development of new writers and ideas. This same limited 'middle class and intellectual' urban audience is also a reality in British theatre, but less so because of government support. In the United States we have already seen such a trend—the encouragement and production of fresh new works—develop, flower and die in New York's often moribund Off-Broadway world.

The challenge is there for the writer, the producer and the audience. It is pointless and sophomoric merely to belabour Broadway and the West End; that answers nothing and most of the perceptive critics, theatre professionals and scholars have abandoned that dreary ritual. We can no longer say that genuinely creative playwrights cannot get a hearing or a production; this book is in part a testament to such writers' recognition and success. Something more than rote anti-Establishment denunciation of commercialism will be required, and perhaps the dramatists and the producers and the audience will rise to the challenge.

A lot of new writers are certainly trying. Remember my friend whom I warned to do a new book lest he become 'last year's novelist'? He had strange other ideas. Ignoring all hazards, he went to Europe and quite compulsively wrote a play—a wild, 'crazy' piece of 'black humour'. It opens on Broadway next month.

WALTER WAGER

# Arthur Miller

THIS INTERVIEW was tape-recorded in Mr Miller's suite in the Chelsea Hotel, New York City, on 10 November 1964. The questioner was the editor of *Playbill* and of this volume. Arthur Miller, a lanky, bespectacled, earnest and good-humoured man, had come from his home in Connecticut for the final rehearsals before the Lincoln Centre Repertory Theatre production of *Incident at Vichy*.

Arthur Miller was born on 112th Street (Manhattan) in New York City on 17 October 1915. A good friend and working colleague of the playwright, director-critic Harold Clurman, has described the dramatist's parents as 'unequivocally middle class and Jewish'. Miller has often commented that while he did not become a devout practising Jew he did absorb 'a certain viewpoint — a commitment to the continuity of life and the need to go on even though there is tragedy in the world'. Miller's mother was born in the United States. His father, Isidore, whom the play-wright has described as 'a much more realistic guy than Willy Loman'—the tragic protagonist of *Death of a Salesman*—was a clothing manufacturer who emigrated to the United States from Austria-Hungary at the turn of the twentieth century.

The dramatist completed elementary school in Harlem, and then achieved a mediocre academic record at a Brooklyn high school. He wanted to go to the University of Michigan because he was attracted by its theatre programme. As a boy Arthur Miller was a baseball fan who had seen only two plays in his life, both commercial melodramas, but he had read enough Ibsen and Shakespeare and other playwrights to know what theatre could be. But by the time Arthur Miller was ready for college, business reverses made it impossible for his father to pay the tuition, so the young man worked a year in a warehouse to earn the tuition. He persuaded Michigan that his talents surpassed his high-school grades, was admitted and at Michigan wrote several plays which won Hopwood prizes. It was also at university that he met his first wife, Mary Grace Slattery, whom he married in 1940.

He wrote his first play in six days in 1935, during a school vacation, but worked harder on another drama which won him a $1,250 prize in a Theatre Guild competition. After his graduation in 1938, the prize money and $22.77 a week from the Federal Theatre Project permitted Miller to exist in Patchogue, Long Island, while he continued to write. Although a number of his early works were submitted to the Group Theatre and other producing units, none was staged. To help support his wife and two children, he wrote several radio dramas.

In an excellent interview with Olga Carlyle and Rose Styron published in the Summer 1966 issue of *The Paris Review*, Miller recalled that 'We had twenty-eight and a half minutes to tell a whole story in a radio play, and you had to concentrate on the words because you couldn't see anything. You were playing in a dark closet, in fact. So the economy of words in a good radio play was everything. It drove you more and more to realise what the power of a good sentence was, and the right phrase could save you a page you would otherwise be wasting. I was always sorry radio didn't last long enough for contemporary poetic movements to take advantage of it, because it's a natural medium for poets.'

Miller himself was writing a good deal of verse in his early plays, and later the initial draft of *The Crucible* was done in verse, as was much of *Death of a Salesman*. He 'broke it up' because he was afraid of the effect of verse upon American actors. In these early years Arthur Miller also wrote two books—*Situation Normal*, a diary of his work on a film about Ernie Pyle, and *Focus*, a novel about anti-Semitism that was published in 1945.

It was in 1944 that Miller saw the first professional production of one of his theatre works. *The Man Who Had All the Luck*, a drama about a conflict between a socially conscious son and a father whose business was facing a strike, ran for four performances on Broadway. One critic, Burton Rascoe, saw Millers' powerful promise, and several producers asked to see his next script. That work, which opened on 29 January 1947, to critical acclaim, was *All My Sons*. The Clurman-Kazan-Fried production was honoured as Best Play of the Season by the Drama Critics' Circle and brought Miller his first national recognition.

It also brought him the first substantial and steady income of his life, for *All My Sons* was a popular success that ran 328 performances. In 1949 *Death of a Salesman* started a run that was to last 742 performances and bring Miller both the Pulitzer Prize and another Drama Critics' Circle award. Years later the playwright was to reflect that the haunted fantasy-ridden central figure, the agonised father who pursued the seductive but unreal 'bitch goddesses' of popularity and success, was based on a salesman whom he had known rather slightly and briefly. This was a play that touched many people, and disturbed quite a few others. Some oddly viewed the protagonist's work as the key issue, and one Japanese theatregoer is reported to have commented that 'If a salesman fails to make sales, he deserves to lose face.'

*Death of a Salesman*, like the two preceding Miller plays, involved a father in conflict with his son on a moral issue. 'Miller is a moralist,' Harold Clurman wrote in Volume One of *Theatre*, the annual journal of the Repertory Theatre of Lincoln Centre. 'A moralist is a man who believes he possesses the truth and aims to convince others of it. In Miller this moralistic trait stems from a strong family feeling. In this context, the father as prime authority and guide is central. From *The Man Who Had All the Luck* through *Death of a Salesman*, the father stands for virtue and value; to his sons he is the personification of Right and Truth.... The shock which shatters Miller's dramatic cosmos always begins with the father's inability to enact the role of moral authority the son assigns to him and which the father willy-nilly assumes.... Both may be innocent, but both suffer guilt.... Woman in Miller's plays is usually the prop of the male principal without whom man falters, loses his way.'

Miller's focus on father and family began to become somewhat less prominent in the dramas that he wrote after *Salesman*. The next play was *The Crucible*, the 1953 work on witch-hunting in the Puritan era that was admittedly based on the then current Red-hunting of Senator Joseph McCarthy and his allies. Miller has twice said that *The Crucible* may be his favourite among his own works, and that is understandable in light of the political and professional ordeal that he himself endured. Arthur Miller, who had been so conservative as a youth that he had favoured Hoover over Roosevelt in the 1932 election, was known to be somewhere left of centre and to be an articulate critic of what has come to be called McCarthyism. It may well be that *The Crucible* was not among the favourite plays of right-of-centre Congressmen, and it is possible that some of Miller's essays and public comments angered those legislators most committed to purging America of Communists. In 1956—the year that he divorced Mary Miller to wed Marilyn Monroe—Miller was found guilty of contempt of Congress for refusing to tell the House Un-American Activities Committee the names of individuals who had attended a meeting of Communist writers eight years earlier. The playwright has publicly suggested that he was being punished for the refusal of the famous second Mrs Miller to pose for a photograph with the Committee's publicity-hungry chairman.

Whatever the facts about this grotesque incident, Miller was cleared of the charge by the U.S. Court of Appeals in 1958. Shortly before his trouble with Congressman Walter, Miller's *A View from the Bridge* had been produced in 1955 and it was not then a success in New York. Subsequently it has fared better both outside America and Off-Broadway. During the nine years that

4

followed *A View from the Bridge*, Miller—beset by personal problems and troubled by the effects of McCarthyism on many 'friends'—appeared to reach a dead end, writing little until 1955 when he wrote *The Misfits* as a novel and film. His second marriage ended, and in 1962 he wed Austrian photographer Inge Morath. This marriage produced a daughter and also helped move Miller back towards work that he himself regarded as acceptable. *After the Fall*, which the dramatist insists is not entirely autobiographical despite the bitter protests of friends of the late Miss Monroe, was staged in 1963. In 1964 *Incident at Vichy* followed.

Miller is writing again, and he has recently stated his goal quite succinctly. 'Günter Grass has said that art is uncompromising and life is full of compromises,' Arthur Miller said in the spring of 1966. 'To bring them together is a near impossibility, and that is what I am trying to do.'

W. W.

🔲🔲🔲🔲🔲🔲🔲🔲🔲🔲🔲🔲🔲🔲🔲🔲🔲🔲🔲🔲🔲🔲🔲🔲🔲🔲🔲🔲🔲🔲🔲🔲🔲🔲🔲🔲🔲

*I have been reading a collected edition of your plays and I notice one play,* The Man Who Had All the Luck, *is not included. Why?*

MILLER: I never felt I really finished it; I had written it when I was very young, and I thought I was writing a perfectly realistic play. It turned out that it really wasn't altogether that. It was a kind of a myth, and when it was produced it was produced as a completely realistic play, and it made very little sense that way. It has one foot in both camps; it has a foot in each camp. And I think it should be rewritten to take on a consistency which it doesn't quite have now and as a result, can't come to a true climax.

*Do you ever go back to a play that's finished and rewrite it?*

MILLER: I could with that, because I know the solution to it, but the subject doesn't interest me anymore.

*That was what I had in mind; you seem to move on to new subjects. But the introduction to your collected plays has one recurring reference that intrigues me. That's the question of reality and realism. This is a major occupation of yours?*

MILLER: It always has been, yes. My aim is to deliver up the symbolic meaning of what I see, what I feel, and I've never been able to do it through a naturalistic technique. And yet I don't think that the solution is a completely symbolic drama. In other words, I am trying to account as best I can for the realistic surface of life as well as Man's intense need to symbolise the meaning of what he experiences. There are numerous methods of trying to accomplish that, and I think from one play to another of mine there have been different attacks on the same problem of delivering up the meaning of what the experience is.

*When you go to write a play, do you decide in advance what your technique is going to be? Have you carefully evaluated what sort of style you want, what would fit the subject best?*

MILLER: In the most general way, yes. Actually, any play I finish and produce has had a tendency to create its own laws. I can attack some material with a firm plan in mind, but generally speaking, after five or six minutes of playing, it lays down its own form.

*It has its own natural inner structure?*

MILLER: Yes, that's right.

*Yes, I would suspect that this would be true, because going back to the introduction to this most interesting book, you make frequent references to the need for passion in playwriting, which means that you have not meticulously planned your plays as, say, certain types of modern musicians might write almost mathematical music.*

MILLER: I plan as far as it is possible to plan—that is, I plan up to the point where the plan is there in order to open the way to the passion. It's not there for its own sake. I have no special admiration for any formalism in itself. I can write in numerous ways, but there's no point in doing that. And I'm seeking for the key to whatever material is at hand.

*You have mentioned that some people have felt your work was negative or nihilistic, and yet it seems quite clear that those are not your views at all. You say life has meaning. You refer to the fundamentals of life and man's relation with man and with God. Are most people aware of the fact that you are concerned with God?*

MILLER: I think most people aren't aware of anything. We have trained the audience in America to go to the theatre. It's a convention that they go to the theatre to have, so to speak, the glands of emotion exercised, and what the play's really about, aside from its story, is taken to be an embarrassing excrescence implanted by the author. The fact that a whole structure, all the emotion and all the observations in it, are to throw light on a certain mystery is rather beside the point. These elements are rarely, if ever, discussed by anybody.

*As I walked out of* The Representative *which is obviously less than a perfect play, I was astounded and quietly infuriated to find people strolling out as if they'd seen* Hello, Dolly! *They're saying, 'Hello, Gertrude, where're we going to eat, where'd Charlie park the car?' They had not participated in the play. They had seen it, but it had not really reached them.*

MILLER: Well, I think that's partly because of the training this audience has to regard the theatre as the most superficial kind of entertainment in the way that, oh, the circus or a Western is, is always thrown into one pot.

*Where's the responsibility for that? How has that happened?*

MILLER: Well, in general the Anglo-Saxon mind flees from any objectivity about what it's looking at. It's more French, Middle European to ask the question of 'What is this really about? What lies behind this? What symbol of meaning is the author attempting to throw light on?' With the English and with us,

7

there is a terrific resistance to any knowing what you are doing in an objective way.

*And that would create a problem in regard to another comment you made—the goal of drama is the creation of a higher consciousness. That would make a dramatist face a rather difficult problem with our Anglo-Saxon audience.*

MILLER: Oh, it is difficult. Very, very tough. But it has its compensations only in one respect, and that is that it forces our drama into concreteness—which is a good thing. It makes the American writer prove with immense evidence, concrete evidence, what he's driving at. However, it is defeated finally by the unwillingness and the inability of this audience to consider what he's driving at, over and beyond the overt story. After all, most reviews of most plays are retelling the story of the play, the overt story of the play.

*Is that why you took your most recent plays from Broadway to the Lincoln Centre Repertory group?*

MILLER: Well, one reason is that I had hoped, and I still believe, that the first order of business in this theatre is to open the theatre to a wider audience, an audience of students, of people who are not totally oriented to the most vacant kind of entertainment. After all, the audience is half of the production, and I think that one way or another that audience must be broadened, and it must be given a new environment in which to be an audience. I think over the years, whether it be Lincoln Centre or it and other such companies, a new kind of attitude will develop towards plays, an attitude which does take into consideration and is in fact basically interested in what underlies this structure that they're looking at. It is an audience, finally, not of strangers. You see, this audience today is totally strange to the aims and the preoccupations of the artists.

*This is an audience that's seeking a social experience, to a large degree.*

MILLER: I don't think they're seeking an experience so much as an escape from experience, and they're at odds with serious writing so much of the time. And I think that's the problem.

*Speaking of serious writing, one question that must be asked of any playwright or creative writer many times is exactly how do you write? Quite literally, where do you write, and how do you write?*

MILLER: At home, in Connecticut, where I've lived for many years now. I've always worked in the country, even twenty years ago when I had to rent a house for $75 a year. I can't write in this city, possibly because I was born here. And I work generally in the morning. On good days I can work all day. On most days three or four or five hours, on the typewriter. And the writing is a series of thrusts and sharpening of those thrusts and discarding of false issues and a purification of the image that originally impelled the play to seem like a play. Consequently, there's normally either literally on paper or for years before in the mind a series of revisions taking place. I have written plays in a matter of two weeks, six weeks, five weeks.

*Since you became a recognised playwright?*

MILLER: Oh, sure.

*What plays did you write in five or six weeks?*

MILLER: *Death of a Salesman.*

*Really?*

MILLER: But by the time such a thing gets written, it has been in effect written and rewritten a thousand times in the head. There are other ways of doing it. *The Crucible* was seven months; *All My Sons* was two years; *A View from the Bridge* was three weeks.

*Speaking of* The Crucible *and* A View from the Bridge, *those were made as foreign films?*

MILLER: Right, French. For a long time I was *persona non grata* here in the movie industry. They wouldn't do anything of mine after *Death of a Salesman* because I had left-wing connections and was in effect blacklisted. That's the main reason.

*That seems incredible today looking back on it. Of course, that whole period seems almost as incredible as the subject matter of* The Crucible.

MILLER: Well, it's not incredible to me.

*No that's a real experience that you will not ever leave.*

MILLER: It's a fact, and that's the only reason why that happened.

*I see. Now your newest play,* Incident at Vichy. *What brought you to that subject matter?*

MILLER: Well, I have always felt—and as the years go by I feel even more strongly—that the period of the Nazi occupation of Europe was the turning point of this age. I think as time goes by we'll be seeing more and more it is that. Not only in the political sense, but in the whole attitude of Man towards himself. For example, we discovered after the war—seemingly independently —that there was an immense social pressure to conform, a chilling of the soul by the technological apparatus, the destruction of the individual's capacity for choosing, an erosion of what used to be thought of as an autonomous personality—all this was carried to its logical extremes by the Nazi régime, which ended up by controlling not only Man as a social animal in his job and on the assembly line or in his office or in the Army but in his bed, in his relationships to his children, who were taught to carry any expression of opinion by him to the authorities as a patriotic act, until you had created a nation of people who could be said to have lost or given up or been robbed of what for two thousand years was supposed to have been the—their human nature. They now existed to carry through a social programme. In my opinion we have inherited this. Whatever else it was, it was a total development of industrial psychology. We are struggling with the same incubus. But we, by virtue of different tradition—I hope by virtue of having learned something from the past, although I doubt it—we are struggling against that and still trying to keep an efficient technological machine going. There is unquestionably a contradiction between an efficient technological machine and the flowering of human nature, of the human personality. It's for that reason that I'm interested in the Nazi machine, the Nazi mechanism.

*Is that why you went to the war-crimes trials in Germany?*

MILLER: When I went there I had no idea why I was going there. I happened to have been in Austria, and I read in the paper that these trials were going on in Frankfurt. They had been going on for a long time, and I had been vaguely aware of them because certain small articles had been published in the press here. But I had never seen a Nazi. Simple as that. And I had certainly never seen a mass murderer, and I was near enough to go, and without too much difficulty. And when I went there, I discovered that these trials had been going on for nearly a year, that some of the Nazis had been in jail as long as three or four years, and that, as an avid newspaper reader, I had noticed hardly anything about it. And so when I got there the newspapermen who were covering this for the wire services—there were four of five of them—asked me to write something about it in order to draw public attention to it, because it was of immense importance not only to Germany but to the whole world. And I did. I'm glad to say that, as a result of that, the amount of space given this trial increased immensely from that time. It became an interesting story finally. But in going there and travelling in Germany a good deal, I became reminded again of what I had been thinking about that time for twenty years. I know a good deal more about it than I ever did then, before this last few years. The basic story of *Incident at Vichy* I had known at least ten years ago, but I hadn't really known how to make a play out of it.

*You had heard of a factual event or incident which, with the playwright's art, you have developed and expanded into a statement of the nature of Man?*

MILLER: That's right, yes. It usually needs only some turn of a phrase sometimes. Sometimes it's one action that can set off, that can trigger a play.

*You must catch your passion before you can communicate it.*

MILLER: Yes, I can't manufacture a play just because it's a good idea. There are numerous great stories that I know that I could never make into a play because they don't match some personal preoccupation of my own.

*Now there was a period of a number of years, as the press has pointed out rather repeatedly, in which you did not write. Or is it that you didn't write anything that you wanted to produce?*

MILLER: That's it. I wrote as much if not more than I had before, but I have an immense respect for the dramatic form, and if I can see holes through something I can't go on with it. And if I can't account for the action I'm putting on the stage, I don't expect anybody else is going to be able to, and it just didn't seem dramatically whole or true enough for me to produce what I had written.

*Then we were misinformed, in fact. What you wrote was not up to your standards.*

MILLER: It just wasn't capable of being completed satisfactorily. That's all.

*Do you think you might go back to that, or are you moving on to new projects?*

MILLER: I can never go back. It's impossible. I've never been able to do it. I wouldn't go back.

*A play such as* Incident at Vichy *presents certain fundamental problems about mankind even though it's set twenty years ago.*

MILLER: Well, that play applies. Put it this way—the occasion of the play is something that happened twenty years ago. The play is about tomorrow morning. There's a difference between the occasion of a play and what it is about.

*I'd like to quote from something you wrote which is, I know, a very treacherous thing to do, 'A play cannot be equated with a political philosophy, at least not in the way a smaller number of multiplication can be assimulated into a larger. I do not believe that any work of art can help but be diminished by its adherence at any cost to a political programme, including its author's, and not for any other reason than there is no political programme—any more than there is a theory of tragedy— which can encompass the complexities of real life.' Now that I have made this elaborate preamble, the question of politics as such is not really one that concerns you nearly as much as the question of Man and his nature. Is that right?*

MILLER: It concerns me as a citizen because politics is the way we regulate our destructive instincts. Without politics we would be at each other's throats more than we are. But as a dramatist, politics is one very important expression of the human dilemma, and it's the human dilemma which I'm interested in. I don't think a great many people know who ran for Vice-President eight years ago when everybody might have been excited about one man or another, but the impulses that create political conflicts are my business. They are the human impulses, the human contradictions. And those are the ones that I think a drama has to deal with.

*You have said that drama and its production is an expression of profound social needs. What needs do you have in mind?*

MILLER: Well, there are many. One—drama is one of the things that makes possible a solution to the problem of socialising people. In other words, we are born private, and we die private, but we live of necessity in direct relation to other people, even if we live alone. And dramatic conflict of significance always verges on and deals with the way men live together. And this is incomprehensible to Man as a private person. He is always trying to find out where he stands in his society, whether he uses those terms or not. He always wants to know whether life has a meaning, and that meaning is always in relation to others. It is always in relation to his society, it's always in relation to his choices, to the absence of his choices, which are dominated by other people. I think that when we speak of dramatic significance we're really talking about, either openly or unknowingly, about the dilemma of living together, of living a social existence, and the conflict is endless between Man and his fellows and between his own instincts and the social necessity.

*That was, I think, expressed quite vigorously in* After the Fall.

MILLER: Yeah, sure.

*Which seems to me to be one of the more profoundly misunderstood plays of our time, by the critics anyway.*

MILLER: Well, in this country. But in Europe it isn't. It has opened in twenty-three different theatres in about eleven countries, and the reviews I've gotten so far deal with it as a play. In that sense, it fared no differently than almost anything else I have written. *Death of a Salesman* was taken to be a play about an old salesman. *A View from the Bridge* was taken to be a play about an incestuous longshoreman. What underlies these plays is not discussed, but, as I say, it's part of a long tradition that they wouldn't be discussed that way.

*Then you would say our critics are more reportorial than analytical or critical?*

MILLER: For the most part that's true. I don't see how it can be much different when you have to write a review in twenty minutes or half an hour. You are bound to be driven back to retelling the story and saying whether or not you were affected by it. I don't know how you would reach any further in that given time, but again I say that, as things stand now, the bulk of the Broadway audience is not interested in any more than that. And I think they will someday be made to be interested when they find that it is interesting. It's a process of maturation, that one should ask not only what is the story or what happened, but what it signifies.

*One could say there are only one or two critics in New York who could understand what anything signifies.*

MILLER: Well, that may be so. I don't really know.

*Or who really care, go that deeply into the question.*

MILLER: That may be so.

*The style of the most recent play,* Incident at Vichy, *would you call that a realistic style?*

MILLER: No, but I don't have a ready label for it. The style of that play is commanded, so to speak, by the situation; it is dealing with the literal situation as well as the moral and ethical situation. It deals with a group of people who are faced with the need to respond to total destruction, and when that is the situation, you are not in what can normally be called a realistic situation.

*They're facing death?*

MILLER: Yes. Or the possibility of death. And totally senseless death. Death with no reason. And when that happens, you can't imagine people behaving as they would in any other circumstance so that the intensification of all reactions creates a kind of symbolisation of people, just when one faces a sudden emergency you act in ways you never dreamed you could act. And those actions go to imprint themselves on others who observe you— a personality which is quite possibly strange to your ordinary personality so that you automatically adopt what you could call a style of behaviour. It's that style that this play is written in.

*Survival style?*

MILLER: Well, you could call it that.

*Now before, when you spoke about the failings or lack of maturity of Broadway audiences, is that something you think is limited to the Broadway audience, or is it common with theatrical audiences throughout the country?*

MILLER: I find it's less so outside New York. Principally because outside New York the convention is different in theatregoing. Outside New York the theatre would attract those culturally starved people, the schoolteacher, the doctor, even the trade-union man who finds that there's nothing much interesting in his environment and wants to see something which might perhaps throw some light on his earthly career. My own experience with those out-of-town audiences in general is that they tend to try to dig deeper. A large proportion of them regard the theatre as not merely a way of wasting two or three hours.

*Or as entertainment.*

MILLER: Yeah. Well, of course, the most entertaining thing I can imagine is the most interesting thing, and I think one of the most interesting things we can consider is embodied in one word —'why', not 'what'.

*That is the clue to your definition of reality, too.*

MILLER: Sure.

*A play which has realism is why people do it, not merely the account of what happens.*

MILLER: That's right. A play's an interpretation. It is not a report. And that is the beginning of its poetry because, in order to inter-pret, you have to convince, you have to distort towards a sym-bolic construction of what happened, and as that distortion takes place, you begin to leave out and overemphasise and consequently deliver up life as a unity rather than as a chaos, and any such attempt, the more intense it is, the more poetic it becomes.

*You are aware that there is poetry in your plays?*

MILLER: Well, to be precise, there is poetry, and there is verse. I'm not a poet in the sense of being a versifier. That is something else entirely.

*No, but there are great bursts of lyricism, which are as specifically identifiable of you as a hatband which says 'Arthur Miller'.*

MILLER: Well, yes.

*That pleases you.*

MILLER: Well, it pleases me if it's anything that tends to forcefully set forth the vision behind the play. And it could be a silence, it could be a gesture, it could be one character handing to another a cigarette case, and it can be a speech, or a series of speeches. The metaphor is everything, the symbolised action, the action which is much greater than itself and is yet concrete is what we're after, I think. I think the structure of a play should be its essential poem—what it leaves out and what it follows to a real climax. Before there can be the other poetry, there must be that.

*Do you go to the theatre very much yourself?*

MILLER: I go very rarely. I read plays more than I see them. I go mostly when I'm about to cast a play to see the actors that are working and to refresh myself with the fact of the theatre. But not ordinarily.

*I didn't realise that you took an active role in the casting and the actual production.*

MILLER: I do as far as is possible for somebody who is not aware of everybody who's working and who is around. I wish I knew more about them, and from time to time I make sporadic attempts to find out. But to really cast well you should obviously know who is around and what they can do. I find I have to rely on others too often.

*Now in the course of a production, is there likely to be some rewriting before opening night?*

MILLER: It depends. Some plays I hardly touch at all. Others I do some work with.

*This is an intimate association with the director, right? Well, do you have any comments on the general state of our playwriting, compared to, say, the British playwrights? Do you feel they're moving in different directions?*

MILLER: I don't see a direction, to tell you the truth. That's not a statement of criticism; it may be just as well. We don't have enough new plays of any significance produced to speak of any direction.

Since I've been around, there's been a group of individuals who work at the same time in many different directions, and I suppose the most obvious trend is what's called 'theatre of the absurd', which is a meaningless category because you can't put Albee in the same box with Beckett, who, of course, is not an American. Albee is essentially much more concrete in terms of behaviour and is much more realistic and is much closer to the realistic tradition in this country. I don't see a trend. As a matter of fact, I never have. We often talked about trends in the Thirties, when plays so often had some open social protest involved with them. But there again you couldn't put Odets and Lillian Hellman in the same box because one was much more involved with lyricism than the other, and one was closer to Ibsen, the other possibly to Chekhov, who are very opposite poles, and yet they were all thrown together because they were both interested in social protest. I wouldn't have any over-all comment to make about it. I don't see one unity.

*Let me ask you one final question. In addition to your plays, you have written two films, one for the Army during the war, right?*

MILLER: Well, I wrote the original screenplay for *Story of G.I. Joe*, which was never used.

*I see.*

MILLER: It was the basis of the final picture.

*And you did one novel.*

MILLER: Yes.

*Which I think I read before I ever saw any of your plays.*

MILLER: *Focus.*

*Yes.*

MILLER: I've written about fifteen short stories, which will be collected soon, and a number of essays.

*But do you think you may ever go back to novels or are plays your business?*

MILLER: I would doubt it very much. I have too many plays to write, and I'm more at home in the medium, I love it more, and I can do it better.

# Edward Albee

THIS INTERVIEW was conducted in Mr Albee's handsomely furnished town house in New York's Greenwich Village on 20 October 1965, and was first published in the Winter 1965 issue of *Beverwyck*, the literary magazine printed at Siena College, Loudonville, New York. The playwright was questioned by two editors of the undergraduate quarterly, Michael Nardacci and Walter Chura. Their description of this important, controversial, existential dramatist is certainly as good as any. After identifying him as '*the* playwright of the 60's,' the young men added that 'Albee himself is a quiet, intense person, a darkly good-looking man who could pass for twenty-five instead of his real age of thirty-seven, and who talks very much like George in *Who's Afraid of Virginia Woolf?*: a low, cultivated, almost brooding speech with a flair for sudden wit or a mildly cynical comment on present states of affairs.'

There are a few more adjectives that apply: slim, alert, precise, courteous, careful and cool. Albee has the manner and style of the wealthy Eastern gentleman; he dresses and lives the part for which he was raised. He is a successful dramatist because of his intelligence, perceptions, talent and willingness to treat questions that few American playwrights examined before him; he wears his success as comfortably as his Ivy League uniform of button-down shirt and grey flannels. He is a serious, sophisticated person of considerable charm, a widely travelled bachelor interested in art, literature, and music but most of all theatre. He is often a frank and articulate man, and while he does not seek personal publicity —which he certainly does not need—he is usually willing to answer journalists' questions on almost every subject except his private life.

And there is another relevant adjective: tough.

In his polished, controlled way Albee is so much tougher than most of those who denounce him as 'decadent' that it is no contest.

There is a story, perhaps apocryphal, about a woman walking up to Edward Albee at a party and gushing that she knew his mother. 'I wish that I did', the dramatist is reputed to have replied. It is a matter of record that the baby who was to be christened Edward Franklin Albee was born on 12 March 1928; that is set down in *Who's Who* in America. No other shred of personal information is included in his self-written biography in that reference book, only the names of his plays. It is as if he either wanted to forget the rest or nothing else but the works mattered. He has said, 'I had a good home and a good education, none of which I appreciated'—but little more.

Edward Albee does not know where he was born, and it is not clear whether he knows who his parents were. The baby boy was in Washington, D.C., very soon after his birth, but at the age of two weeks he was brought to New York City, where he was quite clear on the night of 22 September 1966, when *A* son of tycoon Edward F. Albee of the Keith-Albee vaudeville circuit, a highly profitable theatre chain. His wife, Frances, had been described by her playwright-son as 'an expert horsewoman and a remarkable person'. The adopted boy was the only child of the Reed Albees and was raised in luxury in their splendid home in Larchmont, a fashionable Westchester suburb of New York City. There is little information readily available on the dramatist's childhood, but his adolescence was plainly brisk if not stormy. He was something of a 'problem', so he was sent to boarding school at eleven. He was expelled from Lawrenceville, spent a fairly short time at Valley Forge Military Academy, which failed to tame him, and finally graduated from a third private preparatory school, Choate. 'I didn't write *Catcher in the Rye* and *End as a Man*; I lived them', he reminisced not so long ago. He completed only a year and a half at Trinity College in Hartford before terminating his formal education.

After Trinity he drifted comfortably to Manhattan, where he worked off and on as a copy boy at an advertising agency, a record salesman, counterman in a lunchroom and a writer of radio continuity. Since he has mentioned 'working for nothing' for WNYC, the New York City public station, it is possible that this was his script experience in broadcasting. A bit later he took a job delivering telegrams. 'It was a nice job because I walked and didn't have to concentrate on the delivering of the telegrams,' he told interviewer Sidney Fields. 'Except I didn't like delivering the collect wires from the city hospitals telling people about the death of a relative. I got to the point where I'd tell them to read it without paying for it, and then I'd run off to escape the wails of grief.' Somewhere between Trinity and his first play, Albee served in the Army, where he studied Russian in a language school.

He was writing irregularly, mostly poetry of no great merit, during this period—something he could afford to do because his affluent Albee grandmother had left him a $50-a-week income upon his attaining the age of twenty. He had written several abortive novels in his teens, was not satisfied with the poetry and turned to writing for the stage at twenty-nine and a half. He was—at that time—tense, frustrated, 'isolated' and drinking 'a lot'. His initial drama was a remarkable one-act play that he named *The Zoo Story*, which was produced in Germany (28 September 1959) before being staged Off Broadway at the Provincetown Playhouse in New York on 14 January 1960. It immediately attracted attention in academic, intellectual and *avant-garde* theatre circles, and the dramatist received enough confirmation so that he could easily proceed to write two more short works.

In 1959 he completed *The Death of Bessie Smith* and *The Sandbox*. The former was inspired by Albee reading on the jacket of an LP album an account of how the great coloured singer perished when denied admission to a 'white' hospital in the South, and it is believed to be the only Albee play based on actual events or containing some social 'message'. *The Sandbox*, designated 'a brief play in memory of my grandmother' who had recently died, had its first performance at the Jazz Gallery in Greenwich Village on 15 April 1960. The world premiere of *Bessie Smith*, a play in eight scenes 'For Ned Rorem'—the handsome and literate young composer—took place in the Schlosspark Theatre in Berlin on 21 April 1960. It was staged in New York, Off Broadway, not long afterwards. This was the so-called Golden Era of Off-Broadway theatre, full of creativity and imagination, inexpensive to produce or attend and challenging to observe. The initial New York production of *Zoo Story*, for example, saw it on a double bill with Samuel Beckett's *Krapp's Last Tape*.

The critics were already talking about Albee as a new and different voice; to most conventional daily newspaper reviewers his work was interesting but strange, while members of the *avant-garde* such as Martin Esslin, were beginning to rank Albee as a gifted American spokesman for the Theatre of the Absurd and compared *Zoo Story* to the plays of Pinter. An intelligent middle-of-the-road reviewer such as Richard Watts of the New York *Post* recognised Albee as 'an important and unhackneyed voice of his generation', and the first interviews began to multiply. In one of these the wry dramatist told Henderson Cleaves with apparent sincerity that 'I'm just a normal, healthy American boy.'

If anybody believed this, Albee's next play must have caused some second thoughts. *The American Dream* opened at the York Playhouse in New York on 25 January 1961; it was a brilliant but unabashed assault upon sentimentality, togetherness, the American sense of national mission, notions of progress and optimism, prudish and euphemistic talk and the other 'square' weaknesses that diverse critics have chivvied for a long time. Albee's deliberate use of clichés was compared to that of Ionesco by more intellectual critics; other observers, journalists, patriots, and those contented with the 'pure entertainment' of the Broadway theatre were less impressed.

The grotesque game of comparisons flourished, now it was John Osborne, who had been labelled Britain's 'Angry Young Man'. Without reflecting on the dynamic author of *Look Back in Anger*, Albee made it clear that he preferred to go it alone and that such tags bored him anyway. 'I'm not ostentatiously angry,' he told one journalist, 'but I'd be a clod not to be annoyed by the non-thinkers, their attitudes, cruelty, insensitivity, wanton and intentional stupidity, their deliberate insulation against other people. And I meet it the best way I know how. I write about them.' He explained to another interviewer, Mary Pangalos of *Newsday*, that he did 'not think that we live in an ideal society, and my plays express, more or less, a dissatisfaction with the *status quo*. I will write about whatever bugs me at the time I am writing it.' A few years later, in 1964, he was to explain to the editor of this book that he writes about things that concern or move him to such a degree that 'it is less painful to write about them than not to.'

By the end of 1961 Edward Albee had—to paraphrase the lyric from *Oklahoma!*—gone about as far as he could go with one-act or short plays done for Off-Broadway audiences. Of course, he wasn't writing with any audience in mind, but Albee and his friends—who were also his producers and are now his partners in Theatre 1967—had reckoned that Broadway audiences were not yet ready for his sort of provocative 'black drama'. However, his next play was a full-length one and its obvious power, coupled with the writer's already substantial reputation, convinced them that the new work would succeed on Broadway. It went first to Boston, where some of the dialogue troubled the local censor; straightening this out was simple and the publicity generated didn't hurt either.

On the evening of 13 October 1962, the curtain at the Billy Rose Theatre on West 41st Street rose on a play that was to stun, arouse, thrill and fascinate much of the world—*Who's Afraid of*

*Virginia Woolf?* Instantly—well, within a week—Edward Albee was deprived of his status as the private property of the *avant-garde* theatre and converted into a controversial but lauded internationally-known dramatist. With only a few exceptions the New York critics acclaimed the play and the writer. Some, years later, in a 1966 interview with Joan A. Rubin, Truman Capote announced that he pays little attention to theatre reviews written by critics other than Walter Kerr, since the others 'are all written by potheads'. One cannot say what the critics smoked when they saw *Virginia Woolf* that October in 1962, but the reviews were euphoric.

The play was a tremendous hit, and talk about its characters, relationships, view of marriage and pungent dialogue spread out from New York in billowing waves. There was a good deal of speculation—in taxis, living-rooms and in print—as to whether the dramatist wasn't attacking marriage and heterosexual relationships altogether, with criticism pouring in from both the ultra-'square' and the ultra-intellectuals for various reasons. 'I almost got married when I was eighteen,' the playwright told one journalist. 'I've nothing against marriage. I think it's a perfectly passable way to live.'

This did nothing to still those who saw Albee's plays as anti-female if not subtly homosexual, and they continued to contend that this was supported by the 'unsympathetic' way in which he presented his female characters. At a 1965 luncheon in the Overseas Press Club in New York, the playwright answered a question on this at length.

'Are there any female characters in my plays who are worthy of love or sympathy? Well, I would be hard pressed to think of an author who has written any character in any play, male or female, that he would bother to write about if he didn't think the character was worth some degree of exploration which suggests love and sympathy—and certainly in a Christian sense. So many people have always asked and are always asking, "Mr Albee, why are all the women in your plays terrible?" They're not. I found the character of Martha in *Who's Afraid of Virginia Woolf?*, for example, one of the most complete female women that I had experienced in the theatre in a long time. I found her quite worthy of sympathy, affection even and love. In *Tiny Alice* the character of Miss Alice, performing rather unpleasant tasks as she has to, as is her assignment, is not an unsympathetic character as far as I am concerned.

'In *The American Dream*, which is, I suppose, sort of an attack on a number of our mores, the character of Grandma certainly is an enormously sympathetic character, worthy of a good deal of affection and love.

'The dramatist is always commenting on people, and the problem is to comment effectively and make art out of it. You're making a critical comment when you create the life of somebody. You can only make propaganda out of it if you think somebody is entirely bad, entirely good. You must expose both attributes. A character totally unworthy of sympathy or love would be totally unworthy of attention—the author's attention or the audience's, I would think.'

As might be expected, that statement satisfied some, left others discontented and left most of those who had criticised his vision of women unconvinced. It is, of course, unrealistic to try to judge a dramatist by what he writes about one sort of character or nationality or age group. This is not to say that a playwright's attitude towards something as basic as the man-woman relationship is irrelevant, but it is certainly not the sole standard to be applied in considering the works of a writer as interesting and powerful as Edward Albee.

To return to the chronology, *Virginia Woolf* had a long run and was still one of Broadway's reigning hits on 30 October 1963, when the next Albee play opened at the Martin Beck. This was a dramatic adaptation of Carson McCullers' novella *The Ballad of the Sad Cafe*. It was ably directed by Alan Schneider, who has staged all the Albee plays and is a good friend of the dramatist, and performed by a gifted cast—but it failed. Reviews were polite but unenthusiastic, audiences grew smaller week by week and after a few months it closed. This was less than a year after *Virginia*

*Woolf* had won the New York Drama Critics' prize as the best new play of the 1962–1963 theatre season and collected five Antoinette Perry 'Tony' awards. The two respected theatre authorities who recommended which play should receive the Pulitzer Prize had both proposed *Virginia Woolf*, but the committee—in a really pitiful display of prudery—rejected the recommendation because some members thought it was 'dirty'.

A year to the day after *Sad Cafe's* premiere, *Tiny Alice* opened at the Billy Rose. A number of critics and theatregoers expressed uncertainty as to what the play was all about, and speculations on *Tiny Alice* became one of New York's most popular indoor sports. This began to annoy the dramatist.

On 22 March 1965, Albee walked across the stage of the Billy Rose Theatre to try to explain to the assembled journalists what *Tiny Alice* was all about—the reason he had convened this extraordinary press conference. 'It is a fairly simple play and not at all unclear, once you approach it on its own terms,' the dramatist announced. 'A lay brother, a man who would have become a priest except that he could not reconcile his idea of God with the God which men create in their own image, is sent by his superior to tie up loose ends of a business matter between the church and a wealthy woman. The lay brother becomes enmeshed in an environment which, at its core and shifting surface, contains all the elements which have confused and bothered him throughout his life: the relationship between sexual hysteria and religious ecstasy; the conflict between the selflessness of service and the conspicuous splendour of martyrdom.

'The lay brother is brought to the point, finally, of having to accept what he insisted he wanted . . . union with the abstraction—whatever it be called: God or Alice—and in the end, according to your faith, one of two things happens: either the abstraction personifies itself, is proved real, or the dying man, in the last necessary effort of self-delusion, creates and believes in what he knows does not exist.

'It is, you see, a perfectly straightforward story, dealt with in terms of reality and illusion, symbol and actuality. It is the very simplicity of the play, I think, that has confused so many. . . . My thesis for *Tiny Alice* emerged from the body of the work rather than preceding it. But it is this: it is an examination of how much false illusion we need to get through life and also the abstraction of the deity as man needs it. . . . I wasn't trying to write a thesis play. It is sort of a dream play.'

*Tiny Alice* lingered through the spring, died. The next Albee play had an even shorter life in its initial New York production. *Malcolm*, a dramatisation of a short novel by James Purdy, opened at the Shubert on 11 January 1966. Nobody seemed to find much of merit in the play, and the performance of the actor in the title role apparently did little to help the production. Albee took the defeat with excellent grace and some wit; he was not shaken and he retained his urbane youthful 'cool'.

He returned to his house at Montauk to write another play. Some of his friends thought that it might be a drama called *The Substitute Speaker*, a play that he's been 'thinking' and promising to do for several years. Instead, he delivered to his capable partners-and-producers, Richard Barr and Clinton Wilder, the script of *A Delicate Balance*. 'You can get nice tensions going on the stage,' Albee once told a *New Yorker* interviewer, and that was quite clear on the night of 22 September 1966, when *A Delicate Balance* opened at the Martin Beck. Critical reaction was generally positive; one newspaper reviewer went so far as to state that this was Albee's best play.

Most recently, Edward Albee completed a new 'book' for David Merrick's ill-fated musical version of Capote's *Breakfast at Tiffany's*. If he follows what appears to be a pattern of alternating 'originals' with 'adaptations', then another new drama should be ready by autumn 1967. Despite his occasional jests about the possibility of his 'retiring' early, Edward Albee, has many more plays to write.

w. w.

*First of all we'd like to start off with a few basic questions, for the benefit of those of our readers who may not be familiar with your background. Could you tell us something of your education, and about any writing you might have done before you became an established playwright?*

ALBEE: I started writing poetry when I was six years old, so I didn't have much education before that. I started writing novels when I was fifteen years old, and I don't suppose I had much education up until that point either. I stopped writing poetry when I was twenty-seven, I stopped writing novels when I was eighteen. I had a certain amount of formal education, ending with a year and a half at Trinity College in Hartford . . . which I suppose is a perfectly good college. And then . . . I started writing plays when I was twenty-nine and a half. There's really not much of any interest between the ages of zero and thirty. I wrote a three-act sex farce called *Aliqueen* when I was twelve or twelve and a half. But it did get lost, and I suspect it was thrown away, which is probably just as well.

*Have you considered doing any more poetry?*

ALBEE: Good God no. It was getting better between the time I was six and the time I was twenty-eight, but not as much better as it should have been getting. I don't think I'll inflict any more of that on anybody.

*One of the literati at Siena claims to have seen some of* Alice in Wonderland *in your play* Tiny Alice. *He also noted that Lewis Carroll's novel, in addition to having a character named Alice, also has the Red Queen. 'Ali-queen.' Do you think there was any resemblance between the two—*Tiny Alice *and* Aliqueen?

ALBEE: I wish there were! I've found usually that the best thing to do is to read over criticism, essays, and term papers that people write on my work . . . and I usually end up taking the symbols and the points and intentions that make me seem most intelligent . . . and then I pretend that those are the ones I meant. In the question of the case of *Tiny Alice*, of course, the majority of the criticism was so opaque and . . . absolutely stupid . . . that I've had to follow along and stay with my own interpretation of the play as the most intelligent one.

*You do have a single interpretation of the play then?*

ALBEE: I have an interpretation of the play . . . it's a perfectly simple and straightforward play that doesn't need any interpretation.

*Hmmm. Well, getting on to something a little more specific, in regard to your actual technique in writing a play, do you begin with a situation and try to examine it for its implications, or do you try to impose some significance on it?*

ALBEE: The process goes like this: I discover that I have gotten an idea somewhere. I never *get* an idea—I discover that I *have* one. Then over the next six months or a year or two years, it gradually, slowly develops—I think about it occasionally. The characters are forming at that time, and eventually after a certain period of time when the idea seems both vague enough and clear enough to start working on, and the characters seem three-dimensional enough to carry the burden of work by themselves, then I go to the typewriter. So the actual writing time is very short—anywhere from a month to three months. But the pre-writing process—which is a form of writing, I suppose—takes a good deal of time.

*Do you find the final job of getting a play on paper very difficult?*

ALBEE: It's fairly exhausting. I start getting a very bad headache after three or four hours and I have to stop. It's pretty tiring . . . mentally. . . . But then again, that's my weak point.

*Do you make many revisions while writing?*

ALBEE: I usually make some pencil corrections on my first draft; then I make a second draft, not making very many changes. I find myself making fewer changes each time. Some people are of the opinion that I should change *more*.

*What about your characters? Do you use actual models—that is, people you have seen or known? Or do they come out of nowhere? That is, are you conscious of their origin?*

ALBEE: One of the nicest things a writer's got is both a conscious and an unconscious mind. Now naturally any character which a writer creates, or supposedly creates—puts down on paper, at any rate—is an amalgam of people and attitudes seen, a distortion of those people and attitudes, plus a certain amount of invention to put them into a situation. It's probably best not to try to figure out the writer's point of view—how much of which is involved.

*But you don't usually consciously model a character after someone in particular?*

ALBEE: Oh no. I never do that.

*While your plays are in production, do you find it easy to get along with your cast and director and so forth?*

ALBEE: I find it very easy to get along with the cast. . . . I don't talk to them. I talk through the director. I get along with the director fairly well. We have most of our arguments before rehearsals start. A few large ones during rehearsal. But not too many. I've gotten to the point now where I don't care whether a play goes into production or not; the experience for me is completed when I've written it. I just don't *care* whether it's produced. I do have to *eat*. So the results are I have to have the plays produced . . . but that's the only reason.

*Again with characters—do you find yourself putting them in a situation outside the play?*

ALBEE: All the time. I find it's the only way I can discover whether they have enough of their own identity. If I know that they can function in a situation outside the play, then I know it's time to start writing them down.

*Let's get on to some of the specific plays. Now, in regard to* The Zoo Story—*how old were you when you started writing it?*

ALBEE: Uh ... twenty-nine. It was sort of a thirtieth-birthday present to myself.

*How long were you at work on it?*

ALBEE: I don't remember on that one. I didn't have to start answering these questions until after I wrote *The Zoo Story*, so I didn't keep it in memory. I don't know. I must have been thinking about it awhile. Probably the same length of time as the others.

*How long did it actually take you to put it on paper?*

ALBEE: Three weeks.

*And from there we gather it was some time before it was produced in New York.*

ALBEE: Well, before it got produced in New York it was produced in Berlin. Then about six months after that it was produced in New York.

*How did the Berlin production come about?*

ALBEE: Quite circuitously. A friend of mine in New York sent it to a friend in Italy, who sent it to a friend in Switzerland, who sent it to a friend in Germany.

*If we could, we'd like to move on, then, to* The American Dream *and* The Sandbox. *Many people have seen a number of similarities between the two plays—of course, they involve some of the same characters. Others see connections between* The American Dream *and* Who's Afraid of Virginia Woolf?

ALBEE: They do? I've never noticed that. Well, except perhaps in one case the nonexistent son, and the other, two parts of an existent son. I mean, symbols recur, but the similarities are certainly not stylistic. Nor are the people at all the same. So the similarity could only be in the symbolism.

*Did you have* Virginia Woolf *in mind when you started working on* The American Dream?

ALBEE: I doubt it.

*You've made a good deal of use of Grandma in both* Sandbox *and* American Dream. *She's probably the most likeable and certainly one of the most hopeful of your characters. Do you envision using her again— in an advanced form, of course?*

ALBEE: I don't think so, I can't imagine it—she's tired, poor thing. No, she's found a nice Van Man,* she's okay.

*We'd like to return to the subject of* Tiny Alice. *In looking over the tremendous amount of commentary do you think that many people seem to have understood it—that is, deciphered what seems to be a very difficult play—or do you think people have taken what is essentially a simple play and tried to cloud it over with symbols and double meanings?*

ALBEE: The second, of course. The critics were almost to a man, as I said before, unanimously stupid about this particular play— trying to make it a great deal more difficult than it was. Hunting symbols. 'Finding the allegory.' Approaching a basically emotional atmosphere from an intellectual point of view. Now I'm not trying to suggest that the play was terribly simple; metaphysics never is. But there was a curious attempt made to misunderstand. Whether it was conscious or unconscious, I don't know.

*How do you view the interpretations? Are you amused, do you find yourself getting angry? Or are you indifferent?*

ALBEE: One can't do any of the three, really. One can be a little amused, but amused rather sadly because unfortunately the majority of our audiences take their cues from what the critics say. For example, with *Tiny Alice* at the previews before the critics slept through it, the audiences were quite alive and alert. There were both lots of boos and a lot of cheers at the end of each of the preview performances. And so the critics got at it and wrote that it was too difficult to understand, and from then on the audiences came in and they were puzzled until the minute they

*See *The American Dream* for explanation.

got out. I think that if our audiences thought for themselves a little more we could be more amused by our critics. You could get angry, I suppose, and hope that all the critics would grow up, or get some brains, or drop dead. But they won't, and, it would seem, they keep getting replaced by their juniors, with exactly the same attitudes. I have to be indifferent, finally, because one isn't writing for the critics or for an audience, for that matter. One is basically writing for—when I say for one's self I mean for one's self in relation to the historical continuation of the theatre, which has nothing to do with the response of any particular critic or any particular audience, in any given year. Again, unfortunately, the theatre is set up in the United States, at least in New York, in such a way that success is equated with longevity and critical approval. The indifference has got to be sort of an internal resource. One of the desperately bad things that happens to so many playwrights is that they try to accommodate themselves to the *status quo* . . . to what the critics want, and to what the critics tell the audiences they want. And the audiences in turn think that what they really want is what the critics tell them they want. And it's this accommodation to the *status quo* that I've seen ruin the talent of more playwrights than I can mention.

*Do you think this applies to the other arts in America?*

ALBEE: Not quite as much, because playwriting has an extraordinary immediacy. I don't think you can kill a novel or a piece of music—well, people are indifferent to music anyway, so that doesn't matter. You can't kill a novel or destroy a painting that easily. No, it's mostly in the theatre. 'Show biz!'

*Well, leading from this subject, perhaps a loaded question: Why do you write?*

ALBEE: It's what I do.

*Do you feel any, shall we say, compulsion to write?*

ALBEE: Well, one does like to do something. I must have decided to be a writer when I was very young, since I started writing poetry when I was six. I suppose I thought it would be easier than working. It's not, and it's a great deal more time-consuming, alas. As I say, it's what I do. It's the only thing I've ever done that I've enjoyed doing. And being something of a hedonist, I suppose that's why I do it.

*Do you think you'll ever go back to other forms of writing?*

ALBEE: I doubt it. And then again, I don't know how much longer I'll continue writing plays. I've got ideas for about another five or six years, but after that—who knows?

*We understand you did complete part of a novel.*

ALBEE: Well, yes, I made a stab at it a couple of years ago. No, I don't think I'll finish that. As a matter of fact, *Esquire* called up one day and said, 'We're publishing beginnings of novels by people.' So I wrote five or six pages and sent it in to them. One of the shortest novels ever published. I left it open for further development, but I don't think I was very serious about it. I mean, *Esquire* isn't very serious about things; why should I be?

*A recent article in the* Educational Theatre Journal *by Thomas B. Markus called 'Tiny Alice and the Tragic Catharsis', is the latest in a long series of commentary on the play. His most notable comment was that* Tiny Alice *is the only dramatic tragedy to be written in over a hundred years, and that this fact, producing an unfamiliarity with the genre, might be the reason that so many people have been unable to understand it.*

ALBEE: Hmmm. Isn't that nice! I don't know whether it's the only tragedy that's been written in the past hundred years—Arthur Miller keeps telling us he's writing tragedies all the time. I'm glad Markus saw the play as a tragedy . . . it is. *You* know . . . it's nice to have a *few* people friendly.

*His own particular interpretation goes something like this: first of all, the play must be viewed in its religious sense. Brother Julian is sent to Miss Alice's castle, and there is presented with three abstractions called, 'Alice,' but is unable to reach out for the essence beyond it. He must also reject his own private abstraction of God. He proves unable to do this, and brings condemnation upon himself. At all close?*

ALBEE: Well, that's in the right direction. It isn't particularly the *abstraction* that he wants to reject—he wants to hold onto the abstraction. It's the *personification* of the abstraction that he keeps rejecting. And at the end of the play, he accepts the personification. At the end of the play he doesn't say, '*God*, I accept Thy will,' he says, '*Alice*, I accept thy will.' Alice being another personification of perhaps a *different* abstraction. But Mr Markus is at least aware of what was going on in the play, which is nice.

*Many people see elements of* Faust *in the play.*

ALBEE: Oh, I suppose probably it's there. The only way you can avoid having any of these things creeping in is to be a self-conscious illiterate. Not having read anything.

*Since you've mentioned it yourself, could you tell us something of your own reading habits?*

ALBEE: As Peter said in *The Zoo Story*, 'I have considerable catholicity of taste.' I read a lot. Sporadically. Sometimes three or four books at a time, sometimes ten books in a week, then sometimes nothing for a month. I don't like to read fiction when I'm writing. Right now I'm reading all the books I can find on . . . apes.

*Apes?*

ALBEE: I suspect there is probably going to turn out to be a play there, eventually.

*Do you read philosophy as philosophy?*

ALBEE: I'd rather not, I'd rather read it as . . . somebody like Unamuno wrote it, in the form of novels. I suppose I get philosophy more through fiction than through philosophical tract. Being a writer, I don't think very clearly.

*We wonder if we could have some comments on your work in progress.*

*We've heard through your secretary and others that you're planning a play on Attila the Hun.*

ALBEE: Yes, I think I'll write a play on Attila. He seems like a nice guy. And then I have a play that I'm working on right now called *A Delicate Balance*. And there's another play that I've been putting off for three or four years called *The Substitute Speaker*. Then I'm going to do an adaptation of Jack Knowles' book *A Separate Peace*. And as you know I've finished *Malcolm*\* . . . that goes into rehearsal in a couple of weeks. So as I say, I have enough stuff for four or five years . . . I suspect. Unless I write too fast.

*Have you done any recent work on* The Substitute Speaker?

ALBEE: No, I'm putting that off. I've just finished the first act of *A Delicate Balance*. *The Substitute Speaker* is going to be terribly tough . . . for me, not for the audience, necessarily. Well, it will be tough for the audience, too, because . . . hopefully they won't be able to take it. But it's not obscure, it's much too clear. They won't be able to take it, because it's clear. But I want to get a whole six- or eight-month period ready so I can work on that one very hard.

*We understand there are rumours that the second act will consist of a single monologue.*

ALBEE: Primarily, I think . . . almost totally a monologue. The play will only be in two acts.

*Why is it that the characters in your plays seem bent on tearing each other apart?*

ALBEE: I suppose the characters in my plays are interested in teaching other characters about self-knowledge.

*How about the audience?*

ALBEE: Yes, the audience, too, eventually. . . . After all, it isn't

---

\* A stage adaptation of a novel of the same name by James Purdy.

the parcel of communication between the playwright and the audience, sometimes. It's the battle between the playwright and the audience, and the degree of communication that's going to take place. Now, I'm not a didactic playwright . . . and I don't sit down and write a thesis play in order to teach an audience something. If the audience wants to sit there and learn something and become a part of the experience, that's fine with me. But I think writing a thesis play, unless you're somebody with a mentality like Brecht's, is going to get you in very serious trouble. It's got Arthur Miller in serious trouble all of his life.

*You say you are not a thesis playwright, and that you're going to give the audience something they won't be able to take. Do you consider this 'entertainment'?*

ALBEE: Yes, I do indeed. Entertainment, I've always held, is not being taken out of oneself . . . being removed from one's reality. It's *partially* that, it *can* be that, but it should also be engagement, putting oneself into reality and into one's environment. Entertainment is that which is different in one fashion or another from one's own apprehension of reality. It doesn't have to be elevating —well, everything is elevating in one sense or another. A lot of plays are being written today that people wish weren't written . . . well, I say that's all to the good. If society changes, then the plays won't be written any more.

*Would you consider yourself a social playwright rather than a philosophical playwright?*

ALBEE: All plays are social comment to one extent or another. Even plays fashioned as escapist entertainment are a comment on the view that society has of itself and of its needs. Some playwrights are conscious social critics, intentional social critics . . . some do it more intuitively. But as for being social or philosophical . . . I don't see how you separate the two. We've gotten past the simplistic social-attitudes days before the Soviet purge trials in '35 and '36. Can't have that sort of stuff anymore. No, the *Waiting for Leftys* and all that was being done in the early Thirties. . . .

It's impossible now. People realise that you can't divorce social from the philosophical ... without writing fairy tales.

*In regard to political attitudes, a recent article in the* Tulane Drama Review *quoted the following excerpt from* Who's Afraid of Virginia Woolf?, *George speaking*: '*You better watch those yellow bastards, my love ... they aren't amused. Why don't you come on over to our side, and we'll blow the hell out of them?*' *In view of the situation, political comment would seem unlikely. But the author contends that in this statement you are calling for the bombing of Red China.*

ALBEE: It would sound like that, wouldn't it? After all ... George and Martha are very much like George and Martha Washington. *Nick* is very much like the gentleman who used to run the Soviet Union. And indeed ... the joining of the Soviet Union and the United States against the 'dread yellow peril'. Of course! But this comment on geopolitics was thrown in half seriously. For those who saw it and for those who didn't, it didn't matter.

*Now that it's come up, what are your opinions on the relations of the academic community to politics? And what do you think of Arthur Miller's recent refusal to come to the White House because of his disagreement with the President's policy in Vietnam?*

ALBEE: Oh, if he'd shut up, he might write better. The only thing that bothers me about all these student demonstrations that are going on now is that they don't seem to be *for* anything. They're *against* things. There was a time when social and political protest used to be in favour of something, not just in opposition. The artistic community isn't as bad as the academic community ... in the academic community I include not only teachers but students. Of course, the artistic community seems to come out in favour of more general things ... like 'world peace' ... and 'cleaner streets' ... and ... John Lindsay. You know ... nice, clean, healthy American things like that! But not enough specifics like 'Get out of Vietnam'. We'd all like to get out of Vietnam, would we not? If everybody would get out of Vietnam it would be very nice. Max Lerner was saying a couple of weeks ago that one thing the American kids can't learn is that since the United States has decided to be a world force, it's going to have to get a little ugly. World power is ugly. There's a little validity to the protest that's going on, because the depersonalisation of government has gone a little bit too far, of course. The control of news. There's just a little . . . tinge of fascism in the government of the United States these days. I don't think it's intentional . . . nor even conscious. But . . . it's not a thing that can be changed by putting a bunch of John Birchites in . . . at all. It has something to do with geopolitics again . . . the stakes being high as they are. There's a certain lack of communication between government and the people these days . . . and that might be what's being commented on by the demonstrations. But I'm just concerned that they take such particular acts as uniformed recommendations that we get out of Vietnam. The particularisation seems to be uniformed . . . the reaction is probably pretty good . . . in a generalised way. And I'd rather see people protesting and marching and carrying on than sitting around like a bunch of D.A.R. members.

*Before we get too far from it . . . this idea of tearing things down and never building. Now . . . certain people, critics, columnists and so forth, have made the same statements about your plays. How would you answer these people?*

ALBEE: By saying that you can't build on the previous structure, you can't build on rubble. You've got to build on level ground. You've got to *raze* something before you can *raise*.

*You do think, then, that once society has cleared away the rubbish, it can rebuild?*

ALBEE: I'm not sure about that. But it seems to me the only important thing to do is . . . for example, maybe it's impossible to live without false illusions. It may well be. But I think the responsibility is to be aware they *are* false illusions and then go on living with them. No answers. Only questions . . . But I'm not a philosopher, I'm a writer.

*In a sketch in* Current Biography *you were quoted as saying you were a great admirer of Jean Genet, as well as other French playwrights. Do you still find this is true?*

ALBEE: I've been influenced one way or another by every play I've ever read or seen. It's a question of selection . . . acceptance or rejection. Now . . . you read a play by Scribe and you say, 'Uh huh, that's very interesting. Well, I'll never do that.' You read a play by Racine and you say, 'I admire Racine very much. I don't like him at all.' You read Sophocles. 'That's pretty good.' Conscious influence is that idea . . . that one is influenced one way or another by everything one comes in contact with. It's a matter of selectivity.

*Do you believe that you are working now on what might be called a theory of art?*

ALBEE: Let's put it this way: It's very dangerous for a writer to become so self-conscious that he thinks about himself in the third person, and examines the body of his work and then considers the implications of it. That's very dangerous . . . insanity lies that way. Most writers have a certain element of insanity in them, but it's controlled. If it stops being controlled, then communication stops. But at the same time . . . one can't help, I suppose, thinking occasionally about the effect one's work has on people, and the relationship of it to the whole historical continuum of the art form. And one notices things—best not to think about them too much—because then you start trying consciously to do them, and that's not a good idea, either. . . . So I'm not going to say what they are.

*What do you think of the cinema as an art form?*

ALBEE: It could be one some day.

*Have you seen any motion pictures which you would call works of art?*

ALBEE: I don't know. You get into these conceptual terms and I'm on very shaky grounds. I don't know what I'm talking about

E

half the time. I've seen a few good movies, sure—ones that I thought were interesting. But for the most part, and especially in the United States, the film is in *terrible* shape. Very bad. After all, you're dealing with a much more artificial medium than you are on the stage. And to be able to persuade anybody that what's going on on film has any reality, has anything to do with anything at all is very tricky. It's so much easier to escape into a film and lose oneself in it than it is on the stage.

*What do you think of the forthcoming film version of* Who's Afraid of Virginia Woolf?

ALBEE: I don't think anything about it. I haven't seen it. Am I satisfied with the casting? I don't know . . . I'll have to see the movie. I'll be fascinated to see it.

*Have you been following the advancement of the filming?*

ALBEE: Only what I read in the papers. I wasn't even allowed to see the script. But then again, I haven't asked to see it either.

*We have heard that you originally had wanted to write the screenplay.*

ALBEE: Well, I tried for a year and a half to get all the controls I wanted. I wanted to cast it myself, choose the director, write the script, have cutting-room control. They . . . laughed. They laugh in Hollywood a great deal. So finally I just got weary and let greed get the best of me and sold it to the movies, being promised by Warner Brothers that Bette Davis and James Mason would do it. Which I think would have been very nice. If they wanted to put Hollywood-type people in it, they're two pretty good Hollywood-type people. And then all of a sudden James Mason and Bette Davis turned into Richard Burton and Elizabeth Taylor. Movie magic, But you know, it might possibly turn out to be a very good picture. If it does I'll be delighted. If it doesn't . . . well, maybe one could make a movie out of the play.

*Of course Martha imitates Bette Davis at the beginning of the play— what effect might that have had with Miss Davis playing Martha?*

ALBEE: Oh, I think that would have been marvellous. Yes . . . I think . . . No . . . I won't say that . . . No, I won't . . . Wouldn't be very nice. . . .

*Are there any proposals for filming* Tiny Alice?

ALBEE: I don't know. The Chinese might want to do it! But nobody else has asked me.

*Have you ever thought about doing any film work yourself?*

ALBEE: I've thought about it, but I haven't come to any conclusions about it yet. I find that everything I think about belongs on stage. But I will say there are sections in *Tiny Alice* where I wish I'd been able to use film. Like in the entire last monologue. I think it would have been nice if the entire stage could have been filled with just a big close up of Julian's face.

*In connection with the theatre, you mentioned you were interested in music. Have you ever thought of doing a musical?*

ALBEE: Oh, I'll probably get around to that one day. I do want to do a musical. I don't know what it's going to be about yet. A very different musical—from anything that's ever been done before.

*Would you have in mind doing the same thing to your audience as you've done in the past: that is, would you set out to upset it?*

ALBEE: I don't *set out* to upset audiences, mind you—it's not the reason that I write the plays. I notice that audiences *tend to be* upset. . . . I don't know. I don't know what anything's going to be like until I've started the play . . . . It won't be *Oklahoma!* when I do it.

*No. . . . We understand you are working on an opera.**

ALBEE: Yes, I've got that about half finished. Nice, depressing little opera, about totalitarianism, free society, and sanity and insanity. Lots of laughs.

*Libretto by Mr Albee; music by William Flanagan.

*We understand a portion of it is to be presented some time in the near future?*

ALBEE: Just what we laughingly call the 'love duet'. It's really an argument between two people . . . . It's supposed to be done next spring. I don't know. . . sometime in the next year and a half. I have to finish the libretto first.

*Could you tell us something about* Malcolm?

ALBEE: Well . . . it's about the necessary destruction of innocence. That's all I'll say about it. Except, it's sort of nice . . . in a terrible way.

*Black humour?*

ALBEE: That's the term these days.

*What do you think of the present situation on Broadway in relation to art?*

ALBEE: How can you use the two words in the same question?

*Yes, well that answers it. Then what about Off Broadway?*

ALBEE: Better. Certainly every year more good plays are done Off Broadway than on Broadway. But Off Broadway isn't so interested in accommodating itself to the *status quo*. Some of the things people see on Broadway aren't plays at all but manufactured *artifices*. They confirm and put to sleep rather than disturb and keep awake. Every year one or two plays of some serious pretension are allowed to survive on Broadway but never more than one or two. The whole theory is that Broadway is a buyer's market and art is always a seller's market.

*Could you tell us something of how you got involved with Theatre 1966?*

ALBEE: That was sort of inevitable, I suppose, working with the men that I did—the co-producers. We decided that we'd like to produce plays, produce the plays we want to see, the way we think they should be done. The natural extension of that was to start the entire Playwrights Unit so that we could gather a group

44

of playwrights whose work we thought was interesting so that we *could* put it on . . . and in the way we wanted. So the whole thing has mushroomed, perhaps a little bit too much. I don't know.

*Has your work with this group made you optimistic about the future of the American theatre?*

ALBEE: I wouldn't say it has made me optimistic about the theatre of the future, no. It suggests to me that there are a certain number of young playwrights who, with some nourishment, might *possibly*, if they've got the talent and the guts, make a go of it in the commercial theatre.

*Which do they need more?*

ALBEE: Both in equal parts, I think. On Broadway more people get by with . . . not with guts, certainly, but with a certain kind of awful *grit*. But if you put together talent and *guts*, you can get a fairly good and serious playwright surviving the entire massacre.

*Is there any play on Broadway at the present time that you would consider worthy of intelligent playgoers?*

ALBEE: Right now there is not one play playing that is worth anybody spending a nickel to see.

*What do you think of* The Subject Was Roses?

ALBEE: I share the opinion of one of the most influential daily drama critics in New York who told me: 'Look, we all know it isn't a very good play. It's a tiny, small, little play. But I think if we encourage him, he might be able to do something.' ['He' being Frank Gilroy, author of the play—ED.]

*About two years ago, when* Virginia Woolf *and* The Ballad of the Sad Cafe *were playing at the same time, someone remarked that there were only two plays on Broadway worth seeing and they were both written by the same person.*

ALBEE: Did he say who it was?

*No, he didn't but . . .*

ALBEE: Well, there might have been somebody else with two plays on Broadway that year. I think Anouilh had two plays that year. I don't know if they ran concurrently.

*At any rate, have you seen anything on Broadway within, let's say, the last two years that you think has been—*

ALBEE: Worthwhile? Oh, sure, a few things. *O What a Lovely War* . . . Anouilh's *Poor Bitos*. Occasionally some fairly interesting things come along that shouldn't be slaughtered as quickly as they are. The good plays tend to be killed pretty quickly. But for the past couple of years nothing has really *stood out*. Much more interesting work done Off Broadway. Now two of Brecht's plays have been done on Broadway in the past two years—both of them done badly: *Mother Courage* and *Arturo Ui*. Both are very important plays but they were done badly so they went away very quickly. You see, one of the great problems with the structure of our theatre is this: It is the responsibility of critics not to judge a play only on how well it succeeds to its intention but also on how important that intention *is*. Now a critic can say that . . . *The Odd Couple* is a *fairly* successful example of its genre. But at the same time it is the critic's responsibility not to make *The Odd Couple* a play that's going to run for seventeen years, when a play like *Poor Bitos* is ten times more important a play. And I'm sure Neil Simon, the author of *The Odd Couple*, would agree with this. But the critics, because they didn't think Anouilh succeeded totally to his intention, didn't give him as high marks as they gave Neil Simon for succeeding to *his* intention. Nevertheless, the Anouilh play remains infinitely more important than the Neil Simon play. And it is the critical responsibility to encourage people to see the plays that have a great deal more to do with the history of the theatre.

*Have you seen any musicals in the past couple of years that might have even approached art?*

ALBEE: No, not one. They're big and bloated and imitative and dull.

*Has there ever been a musical which, shall we say, has 'satisfied' you?*

ALBEE: No, I don't think so, really. But then again I'm a bit of a grouch.

*Do you think pure comedy, whose sole purpose is to make one laugh, has any place in the theatre?*

ALBEE: Oh, sure! Of course. I think all the cumbersome musicals and all of the escapist comedies should continue, naturally. But I do think there should be a certain coexistence—more than has been tolerated. No, I'm not trying to turn Broadway into anything as lugubrious as the new season at Lincoln Centre, you understand. Nothing as terrible as that. No. Coexistence.

*What do you think the chances are for a young dramatist getting anywhere today?*

ALBEE: Well, that depends on the two things we were talking about before—the degree of his talent and the extent of his guts. If he's very talented and is willing to hold out for what *he* wants, why . . . he may get his reward in heaven and he may just possibly get it on earth. Otherwise he will sell his soul and be very happy.

*The latter being the ultimate sin?*

ALBEE: Ah. . . . You keep hoping for a utopian situation and maybe you can get both. But the terrible thing is, you can never tell about self-deception—whether you're doing it or not.

*Was there ever any point where you doubted that you could make it on your own terms?*

ALBEE: Let me answer you this way: Before I wrote *The Zoo Story*, I didn't know how one wrote a play; before I saw rehearsals of *The Zoo Story*, I didn't know how a play was rehearsed; I had *no* expectation of the critical response to that play.

*Were you ever surprised by the success you have had?*

ALBEE: I haven't been *surprised* by the degree of what we term 'success' in this country that I've had. This doesn't mean to suggest that I think I've deserved it or haven't deserved it. But I find that very little surprises me. Sometimes the stupidity of critics surprises me, but very little else. I doubt that I'd be surprised if I stopped writing plays five years from now. Very little surprises me. A great deal *interests* me but very little surprises me.

*You said that writing is 'what you do'. If, then, you did stop writing, plays, what would you 'do'?*

ALBEE: I'd probably start writing music. That's what I wanted to be when I was eleven—a composer. I hope I keep on writing plays. I suspect I'll keep on writing them as long as I enjoy doing it. But not after that point.

*It has been said that the American family would seem to be a recurring theme in your plays. It seems to follow through* Sandbox *and* Dream *and* Virginia Woolf . . .

ALBEE: Well, there's a relationship, of course, between *Sandbox* and *Dream*. But each of the plays are stylistically a little different. I suppose there is *thematic* relationship but not in any didactic sense. One's preoccupations don't change all that much.

*How about the theme of parents who in one way or another are murdering their children, and children, at least symbolically, killing their parents?*

ALBEE: That occurs in two plays—*The American Dream* and *Who's Afraid of Virginia Woolf?*—but then again I've written eight plays, so it's hardly a *recurring* theme.

*Some claim to see it in* Tiny Alice. *They maintain that Brother Julian becomes a symbolic child of Miss Alice and the Cardinal—*

ALBEE: Becomes the father? Shame on the Church? People are often eager to make neat packages. But I think one of the most preposterous things in the world is to examine a body of work that is growing and come to conclusions about it. If I were to drop dead I could understand an evaluation being made. Having written

48

eight plays out of the thirty or forty I'm supposed to write, it all seems a bit premature. This whole thing may be merely a preparation for something entirely different.

*Is it possible that an artist may not be able to see all the implications of his own work?*

ALBEE: That's the argument given by the critic. It's immaterial of course.

*Might you ever consider sitting down to write out your own interpretations of your plays?*

ALBEE: No, no. I do think for the most part the plays are pretty clear. They *say* what they're about. I've also felt that any play that you could tell what it's *about* in a sentence or two, that should be the length of the play. The play has got to be an entire reality. And if it's only a thesis, it's not going to work.

*People were first confused by* Virginia Woolf *but gradually they seem to have come to realise just what it means. Do you think this will happen with* Tiny Alice?

ALBEE: Oh, sure. As soon as they stop thinking and react to it emotionally, sure. Even that one.

*Last year a symposium was given at the College of Saint Rose in Albany on your work, at which all the main speakers were priests and Sisters—*

ALBEE: I don't know what this fascination is that my work has for our robed ones. I really don't know. The priests and Sisters are always carrying on about my work. It's nice. The Church is trying to involve itself with art and reality and everything. But I've never understood it exactly. What went on?

*Well, one Sister said she thought* Tiny Alice *would have as much impact five hundred years from now as it does today.*

ALBEE: Hmmm! Very sweet lady.

*At any rate it seems to be a general consensus that the play deals with universal human problems.*

ALBEE: Well, I'd like to think that but I don't know whether it will be around *five hundred* years from now or not. Maybe somebody will think about it again in *five* years.

*A person from the audience offered the idea that perhaps Julian was a representation of the Second Person of the Blessed Trinity; the Cardinal represented the Father; and the gigantic thing that comes through the doors at the end was the Holy Spirit.*

ALBEE: You see, that person was particularising too much. A play that is meant to be taken into the unconscious almost directly without being filtered through the brain cells can't be approached that way because you get stuck in specifics, stuck in allegory, stuck in symbols, and then you don't get the intended emotional impact.

*Could you tell us something of the effect that your interest in music has on your plays?*

ALBEE: I do think there is a relation between dramatic structure and musical structure. One hears the term 'counterpoint' in music and thinks of the counter aspects of a play. I'd hate to have to spell out the relation really.

*Certainly, existentialism has had quite an effect not only on the arts but on our way of life. Could you tell us in this connection what do you think of Sartre as a dramatist?*

ALBEE: Not much.

*As a philosopher?*

ALBEE: Interesting. Important ... certainly important and fairly interesting. Same with Camus, who was of course not a very good playwright but a damn good novelist and an important philosopher.

*What do you think of the situation in the European theatre as compared with the American theatre?*

ALBEE: I suppose they're a little better off, only because they've had a theatre longer. It has become ingrained into their nature. I mean in Europe it's the natural thing for a person to go to the theatre. Here the natural thing to do is go to the movies or stay home and watch television.

*Are you now, then, satisfied with your own work for itself?*

ALBEE: It's not a question of being satisfied with the work for itself. It's merely something coming into the conscious area of the mind. Probably something that I've always felt. But the experience, basically, does end with the *writing* of it. The exhaustion is sufficient there, and complete. And the emotional involvement is over. The rest is just work that one has to do. It's considered part of the responsibility of the theatre. At the same time I don't like to see my plays produced unless I have been involved in the production. One of the most painful things is to see a terribly distorted production of one of my plays.

*Have you seen any such productions?*

ALBEE: Many.

*Could you give us an example?*

ALBEE: No. . . . Poor people, I wouldn't do that.

*Without any names, of course.*

ALBEE: They know who they are.

*It has been a source of amazement for many that, in a play like* Virginia Woolf, *not being married yourself and not having completed college, you could capture the atmosphere of the 'college crowd' and the 'married crowd' both so well.*

ALBEE: In fact, I never even *saw* a teacher while I was there (at college). I did go to prep school, though, and I saw a number of teachers there. And they're exactly the same type of people, except a little nicer, I suspect. No, I meet a lot of people and I look and listen. I'd much rather do that than talk.

*Someone has said that if you really want to understand* Virginia Woolf, *you should buy the recording, listen to it at* 2:00 A.M. *and every time a character takes a drink you take one and by the time the sun comes up you'll know what it's about.*

ALBEE: If you know *anything*. I do think that is the ideal time for the play to be put on—at two o'clock in the morning. But don't forget, they're fairly established heavy drinkers and they know what they're about. And after all, they're teachers.

*It would seem that something like* Virginia Woolf *might be akin to something that Ibsen might have done, perhaps from the opposite direction . . .*

ALBEE: More Strindberg than Ibsen, I think. Ibsen approached things from a much more sociological point of view, rather than psychological.

*What do you think of Ibsen?*

ALBEE: Less than I think of Chekhov and Strindberg. I'm glad Ibsen happened because he helped free a lot of playwrights from artificial conventions. But I do think too many of our playwrights are limited by imitation of Ibsen. No, I will not name them. . . . *They* know who they are.

*What do you hope to accomplish by your writing in the future?*

ALBEE: I don't concern myself with that. Maybe I'll discover it after I've stopped writing.

*Ionesco once said that while watching one of his plays, he couldn't believe he had written it. Do you feel this kind of separation from your work?*

ALBEE: Well, after a certain point it's impossible to remember the act of writing. One is fascinated, detached, objective. At the same time, curiously enough, I do know that I could recite if I had to every one of my plays line perfect. Even now . . . all of them. Whatever that proves.

*Have you any plans for rewriting any parts of any of the plays?*

ALBEE: I might want to make a few changes in *The Death of Bessie Smith*, possibly; change one or two lines in *The American Dream*; unclarify *Tiny Alice* a little more, not much, though.

*Is there any one of your plays that you regard as your favourite?*

ALBEE: *Sandbox*. *Sandbox* is a perfect play. Fortunately it's short enough so that I can't make any mistakes in it. It's . . . a very good play . . . a *damn* good play. It's a good fourteen minutes.

# Friedrich Dürrenmatt

THIS INTERVIEW is one of a series of 'workshop conversations' with contemporary German-language writers tape-recorded by Horst Bienek in 1961. It was broadcast on West German radio and is part of Bienek's *Werkstattgespräche mit Schriftstellern*—a book issued by Carl Hanser Verlag of Munich in 1962. Translated by Corliss E. Phillabaum of the Department of Theatre Arts of the University of Wisconsin-Milwaukee, this interview followed immediately after production of Dürrenmatt's *Frank V*. Although a fair amount of the questioning relates to that play, the interview is not limited to that work and is successful because it casts light upon this playwright's basic views of life and theatre —two questions that Friedrich Dürrenmatt finds inextricably intertwined.

That welding and melding is the strength and the mystery of this extraordinary Swiss writer. Since he is interested in life, Dürrenmatt is concerned about people and the human condition. It is both puzzling and irritating to him that so many critics and reviewers on both sides of the Atlantic have attempted to show their own sensitivity and profundity by viewing his works as murky statements of existentialism or *avant-garde* theatre philosophy. In every interview that he has given, Dürrenmatt has attempted to discourage this compulsive 'hunting of symbols'— to use the phrase favoured by Edward Albee.

'I would ask you not to look upon me as the spokesman of some specific movement in the theatre or of a certain dramatic technique,' he said in a 1954 lecture on Problems of the Theatre, 'nor to believe that I knock at your door as the travelling sales-man of one of the philosophies current on our stages today—whether as existentialist, nihilist, expressionist or satirist, or any other label put on the compote dished up by literary criticism. For me, the stage is not a battlefield for theories, philosophies, and manifestoes, but rather an instrument whose possibilities I seek to know by playing with it. Of course, in my plays there are people and they hold to some belief or philosophy—a lot of block-heads would make for a dull piece—but my plays are not for what people have to say: what is said is there because my plays deal with people, and thinking and believing and philosophising are all, to some extent at least, a part of human nature.'

In an interview shortly after Dürrenmatt's *The Meteor* opened in 1966, the dramatist went on to state that 'It's a silly prejudice to say that plays have to live from plots. They live from characters. Writing a play means putting characters on the stage; of course, then they develop plots among themselves . . . Theatre has to be sensuous. A play isn't so much constructed as composed, almost musically: resonances, relationships, opposites, reversals determine its structure.'

This does not mean that the characters come easily to Dürren-matt, for in that same interview he told Urs Jenny of *Theatre Heute*, 'I have to play around, try out characters and scenes. I've written each of my recent plays something like fifteen times, differently every time, with different characters . . . sometimes the casting forces or evokes the changes.'

Dürrenmatt is a practical man, and despite his compelling concern with people (i.e. characters), he had a realistic awareness of what makes effective theatre and the dramatic benefits of a situation filled with urgency, inner tension, irony and conflict. He cannot ignore the audience or the stage, and he does not pre-tend that he writes solely to express himself. He is a working playwright with an immense sense of morality, a writer who

would shun the label 'moralist' and who often treats moral questions in comic terms. To compound the irony, this dramatist
whose sense of tragedy is so acute insists that tragedy is not his
forte and he prefers to write his extraordinary 'comedies'. One
cannot wholly disagree with the playwright's estimate of his
works. Yes, they are 'funny'—but the 'joke' is on us, all of us.
Dürrenmatt's perceptive view of the human condition is amusing
but not cheering. It is also challenging theatre.

w. w.

I NEEDN'T SAY MUCH about Friedrich Dürrenmatt. His tragicomedy *The Visit* has been seen on nearly every German stage
and was a great success on Broadway. Up to then, admittedly,
things hadn't been easy for this minister's son, born in 1921 in
the Swiss canton of Berne, who originally wanted to be a painter
or a schoolteacher. But then writing—to use his own words—
fell over him so suddenly that he never found time to finish his
studies. A rich body of literary work preceded his box-office hit
*The Visit*; there were frequent failures, but also a number of
encouragements. The paradoxical fact was to develop that plays
which years before hadn't gone beyond a problematic first production subsequently won a place on the stage and proved their
quality.

Perceptible from the very beginning were his intense devotion
to the theatre, his gift for dramatic-grotesque conflicts, the intelligent mastery of the means of his craft, and, above all, a tragic
quality, alienated by irony and often moving into the macabre.
Representative of this are his plays *Romulus*, *The Marriage of Mr
Mississippi*, *An Angel Comes to Babylon*, *Frank V*, *The Opera of a
Private Bank*, and his most recent play, *The Physicists*. In addition,
he has written novels, short stories, theoretical essays on the
theatre, screenplays, and a whole series of successful radio plays,
all of which have established his reputation as not only a prolific
but also a versatile and always provocative writer.

Dürrenmatt lives with his family in Neuchatel in French Switzerland. He has bought a house there on a lonely height a bit outside the city. His workroom is a regular writer's workshop. An immense table strewn with layer upon layer of papers and books, to the side a brand-new electric typewriter. Behind him, compass, telescope, chronometers, and old physics instruments, virtually a miniature observatory, which may point to scientific inclinations on the part of the author. On the chairs, on the floor, everywhere, phonograph records—mostly recordings by Kreisler or Oistrakh. I ask him if he's particularly fond of violin music, but he demurs. 'I'm writing a play,' he says, 'that will be called *The Physicists*. It takes place in a madhouse, there's a man there who thinks he's Einstein and fiddles all day. So now I have to listen to violin music all the time to work up that sort of atmosphere.' As it seems—a typical Dürrenmatt situation. After *The Physicists* had its brilliantly successful premiere at the Zürich Playhouse in late February 1962, E. Brock-Sulzer wrote: 'Dürrenmatt is on a new road here, and he has reached a new goal. His first classical play. Unity of Place, Unity of Time, very few main characters, concise language, theatre in its purest form—all this he has really achieved.'

Perhaps the most beautiful part of this large workroom is the view: it looks out over dark wooded slopes, over tightly clustered rust-red houses, on to darkly shimmering Lake Neuchatel. The chains of peaks of the Swiss Alps shine in the background, white and three-dimensional. It is summer, and the silence here seems mighty, as though Nature were holding her breath. Repeatedly, even while we are recording the conversation, our gazes wander over the sun-drenched, seductive landscape, which Dürrenmatt loves so well and without which he says he might have to stop writing.

The conversation took place in summer 1961.

HORST BIENEK

*Mr Dürrenmatt, I'd like to begin our workshop conversation with your stepchild,* Frank V. *You'd just gained an enormous reputation among the critics with* The Visit, *then with* Frank V *you were rejected, sometimes quite violently. For the most part the reviews started from the premise that reality, the real world, simply isn't the way you see it. In your commentary in the book edition of the play there's a statement about this which seems to me to lie right at the heart of your work. It says, 'Once we drop the requirement that the world of the theatre and that of reality have to agree, we gain a new freedom.' Could you explain that more precisely?*

DÜRRENMATT: My statement means—and I hope I'm interpreting myself correctly, we're often our worst interpreters—that I don't feel I'm capable of reproducing reality by means of a play. I think reality is too violent, too offensive, too cruel, too dubious, and above all, much too opaque for that. I don't represent reality in a play, I present a reality to the spectator. You see, I think a play is always real for the audience in a completely naïve sense; to the audience, what's on stage is real killing, burying, loving, swindling. The audience is always naïve. Even today, especially today, thank heavens. Theatre can't exist without this assumption. The audience accepts its play, joins in it, instinctively, wants to play along. This participation alone makes a dramatist's freedom legitimate, his freedom which consists of the right to present a fiction, to create his own worlds, personal worlds.

A dramatist has to take advantage of his freedom. If he dares to do it decisively, the spectator always goes along with it, is never left up in the air, because no matter how grotesque a play is, no matter how far removed from every reality—it's still impossible for it to fall completely out of reality, because every play is nourished, is inspired by reality. Every play's aim is to play with the world. And so, for me, theatre isn't reality, it's playing with reality, transforming it into theatre. I don't believe reality in itself is ever comprehensible, only its metamorphoses.

*In* Frank V *you tell us not to kid ourselves—things are no more honourable in business than they were centuries ago in the Battle of the Teutoburg Forest. Do you believe that tragedy today shouldn't deal with history anymore, but rather with current economic conditions?*

DÜRRENMATT: As a young man I loved to draw pictures of battles, the most grandiose patriotic brawls. In 1933 I received my first prize for one of my bloodthirsty pictures; since then I find business battles far more important, and I also think they're bloodier. Now, every play has its sociological background; the big mistake a lot of drama makes—even a lot of modern drama—is to show people only as individuals, out of context as it were, or at most in a conventional frame. But man is a *zoon politikon*, and the political pen he stays in, has to stay in, in which he's more or less well fed and in which he develops his habits, this political pen determines him too. Classical tragedy, for example, could still use the family to symbolise human society, the state; the state was still the 'father-city,' later the fatherland. All right. But we don't necessarily still live in antiquity. We have to look for other fundamental patterns for our existence in the state. Perhaps banks, firms, corporations provide far better fundamental models for our states, which aren't unquestionably fatherlands anymore and for which we no longer necessarily find it sweet to die.

*Is* Frank V *symbolic for you, or is it just an amusing 'banker's opera', the way Brecht once wrote his 'beggar's opera'?*

DÜRRENMATT: It's possible that *Frank V* is symbolic. I can't stop thinking man, the reflective spectator from drawing parallels. Nevertheless, I don't aim for something symbolic. It isn't my primary intention. The stage only interprets the world unintentionally; on the other hand, it intentionally and—I freely admit— rather maliciously takes advantage of the comic possibilities the world offers, offers daily. Malice is a part of every author's dramatic duty. We haven't to be positive, we have to be honest. As for *Frank V*: the world's gone so much to the dogs that I stumbled on my flatulent gangster bank involuntarily. Besides, I don't like your term 'amusing'. In German culture, humour is something second-rate. Wit is expressed either with great pathos or in a strange awkward fooling around that's found only in these parts and is obviously supposed to pass for *esprit*. The comic element is suspect, it isn't accepted or taken seriously.

But I can be understood only from this angle, from humour taken seriously. My love for tragicomedy is showing in this paradoxical statement. I go from the comic element, from a comic idea, to do something quite uncomic: namely, to represent man—perhaps that's how I could define my art. For me man is a being who can only be represented through paradoxical, comic means, forms, because man can't be balanced like a set of books, and when he is balanced that way the books have certainly been juggled. To put it another way: comedy is my *dramatic*, I'd almost say my *scientific* method of experimenting with mankind, by which I get results which often astonish even me.

*Your name is constantly being mentioned in connection with Bertolt Brecht. People try to establish things in common between you. How do you feel about Brecht?*

DÜRRENMATT: I don't refer to Brecht, Mr Bienek, but people want to tie me to him—there's a difference—the same way they always play me off against Max Frisch, or *vice versa*. German critics, and even French critics now, imagine that a German playwright reads nothing but Brecht, writes nothing but Brecht, etc. I have a very high opinion of him, but I have a very high opinion of other great playwrights too, I'm glad they exist, and when, for instance, Frisch writes a new play, as he has just recently—*Andorra*—I get in the groove again—speaking sportingly; feeling the need to make a spurt can be stimulating in writing too, not just in sports.

*Let me ask you this: what author, what dramatist has made the strongest impression on you?*

DÜRRENMATT: My great literary experience was Aristophanes, a dramatist who can be read only with imagination and can't be produced at all anymore. Otherwise, to get back to Brecht, I just can't afford to occupy myself with Brecht—I have to write myself, after all, and when I'm writing, every other writer bothers me, even Aristophanes, even Shakespeare, all of them. Anyway, I'm spending less and less time on literature, I make some of my own, unfortunately and besides, you don't make literature by spending time with literature but by overcoming the world. Writing is overcoming the world through language.

*You call* Frank V *'The Opera of a Private Bank'. Why didn't you write tragicomedy, like your successful* The Visit? *What led you to use songs all of a sudden?*

DÜRRENMATT: A man has to keep trying something different, something new, and then too the songs were there before the written play. They developed very quickly, in a couple of weeks' work with the composer at my home, words and music were written simultaneously.

*Then you didn't invent the actual plot of the play till afterwards?*

DÜRRENMATT: Oh yes, I invented the plot with the songs. That is, I imagined the scenes where the songs would appear as high points, and then wrote down the songs, but not the scenes.

*Did you think more of Brecht or of Ionesco as you were doing it? Please don't take that as a catch question.*

DÜRRENMATT: I wasn't thinking of those two at all. I was thinking of Shakespeare.

*Why Shakespeare specifically?*

DÜRRENMATT: I'll explain. I made the decision to write a bank story in 1958 in Paris when I saw the English production of *Titus Andronicus* directed by Peter Brook, who later directed *The Visit* in New York and London. *Titus Andronicus* is a horror play according to the dramatic fashion of its time, one of Shakespeare's early plays, his first play, if I'm not mistaken. Now, I was interested in transferring the possibilities of the Elizabethan theatre to the modern stage—that is, in planning, as they did then, a dramatic structure that aims at stringing together a series of basic conflicts like on a chain: setting children against their parents, showing a lover who has to murder his beloved, etc. All of them basic dramatic scenes *in nuce*, in primitive form almost.

That's why *Frank V* is modelled on a chronicle play—I want to show a society similar to Shakespeare's, but a contemporary one, and therefore I have to turn to some collective other than a monarchy—that's important. I'm not representing an ordinary bank but an evil one, an evilly run one, the story of an evil banker who is succeeded by his efficient son.

*Frank V* is an experiment in pure drama. The idea of using songs came to me from one of the original scenes of the play. I don't know if you remember it: the villains tell each other stories about honest people during their coffee breaks, the way honest people often tell stories about villains during their breaks... That could only be expressed musically. The songs don't generalise the play the way they do in *Threepenny Opera*; they make it bearable. In *Frank V*, the bearable things are the lies, the excuses, the specifically poetic atmosphere that bathes the play. People sing in *Frank V* when they're lying—in *Threepenny Opera* they sing when they're telling the truth.

*That reminds me of something Verdi once said: 'When the emotion turns sentimental or false, then you have to put it to music.'*

DÜRRENMATT: I've never heard that, but it fits exactly.

*About* Frank V *again, don't you feel that you've been somewhat misunderstood in it?*

DÜRRENMATT: I don't feel misunderstood. I don't think this play has actually been realised yet. It'll have to sail for a long time yet under the false colours of *The Threepenny Opera*—that's its fate. It's being done next in England—I can't wait to see what happens there.

*Let me tell you about a chat I had after the Frankfurt production with the director, Harry Buckwitz. I said that the play ought to be played straight through as a sort of swindler show, without a curtain, without an intermission. It ought to be a paradistic carousel spun in front of the spectator that makes him dizzy. Buckwitz answered, 'That's just what Dürrenmatt doesn't want—for him it's a social protest.' Should* Frank V *be a sort of critique of capitalistic society?*

DÜRRENMATT: I'm not representing a capitalistic society, but rather an authoritarian system. Non-capitalistic authoritarian systems can act this way too. *Frank V* is a fictitious model. If you analyse the collective that's represented on the stage with its own special characteristics and laws, you come up—in connection with the world—with various questions, such as: is a gangster democracy possible? Given serious consideration, this is a very important question. Freedom is the real problem of the play, anyway, and not justice as it was in *The Visit*. But you can't do anything with freedom, especially in the West, by no means just in the East, above all you mustn't discuss it, people don't want to discuss it; it's used as a value which is beyond criticism and which shouldn't even be touched on any more.

*For Brecht, theatre was social-critical action. Ionesco, who's notably anti-Brechtian, said once that theatre has to depart from reality entirely and demonstrate a reality of its own. Does it always have to be a social reality, as in Brecht? Can't it be a fantastic or even a surrealistic one, without any intention or moral? Ionesco certainly rejects every hint of didacticism.*

DÜRRENMATT: Once, when the Moscow Satirical Theatre wanted to produce *The Visit*, the director told me that he was very impressed with my play but that he didn't understand how I could believe that everybody is corruptible. I wrote back that for my part I didn't understand how he could get that out of *The Visit*: if *The Visit* is a satire, then the statement of the play is satirical too, and so it couldn't be 'everybody is corruptible' but rather: 'watch out that you down there don't turn out the way we up here on stage have!' After that, they didn't produce the play in Moscow.

*I'm not surprised.*

DÜRRENMATT: I share Ionesco's opinion that theatre doesn't have a didactic purpose, *mustn't* have a didactic purpose, but I think this idea applies to the writer and not the audience. As a writer I couldn't write at all if I had to assume the pose of a world-teacher in the process. Even the word 'poet' infuriates me, and I can't tolerate the word 'message' at all. The worst thing I can imagine is to see a book displayed in a show window sometime: Get your consolation from Dürrenmatt.

But just as the audience by its very nature is basically naïve, it's also helpless: it's looking for help, it's oppressed by current problems, by fear, it's looking for answers—that's understandable. The audience actually creates the connection between theatre and reality; it finds its own world in ours, whether we like it or not. Everything to do with a moral, everything didactic should happen unintentionally in drama; I can only answer the questions of someone who finds the answer himself, only console someone who himself has courage: this is the cruel human limitation of art. In itself it's powerless, not a consolation, not a religion, just an indication that occasionally amidst the general despair there's someone who hasn't despaired. I can't give anything more than this indication. A writer can only fulfil his moral obligation if he's—let me use this expression—an anarchist. He has to attack, but not be engaged. His only proper place is between two stools.

*Your play* The Visit *is your best, your most successful, in fact the most successful play of any German-language author since the war. You invented a really solid plot there. Do you find that a play's success or its effectiveness depends mainly on the plot?*

DÜRRENMATT: I'm convinced of it.

*And do you think that the trouble with German drama now can be traced to the fact that younger authors are so dominated by the craze for an original form that they disregard the theme more and more?*

DÜRRENMATT: That's possible, somewhat my conviction.

*I'd like to know how you got the idea for* The Visit, *for example?*

DÜRRENMATT: At first I had the basic idea for the story. I tried to write a novella. Title: *Eclipse of the Moon*. It took place in a mountain village, an emigrant came home from America and took revenge on his old rival. That was the first phase. Then the second: the emigrant turned into a woman, the multibillionairess, Claire Zachanassian. The mountain village became Güllen. Now here I can sketch the play's development more exactly. Dramatically the first problem that came up was this: how can I show a small town on the stage? At that time I was frequently travelling from Neuenburg, where I lived, to Berne. The express train always stops once or twice at little tiny stations. Next to these little buildings there's a small comfort station. It's a very typical sight at a small railway station then; it can be used very well as a stage picture. Now, the railway station is the first place you see when you come into a town, that's where you have to arrive. The spectator comes into Güllen with the railway station, so to speak.

Then there was the dramatic problem to solve: how do I represent poverty now? Just letting the people run around in rags, for example, wouldn't be nearly enough; the whole place has to be impoverished. And that's how I got the idea that I'd make a point of not having the express train stop there anymore; it used to stop but not anymore. So the town has sunk. Now there was the further question: how does a billionairess arrive? Does she take a local train? Of course I could have had her come in a special train, but naturally it's much more elegant if she pulls the emergency cord. Billionairesses can afford that. But then, if I'm having a billionairess come by train, why by train at all? Why didn't she come by car? And here, from this tight spot— since I wanted to have the railway station at all costs as milieu— I came on the idea that the billionairess is coming by train because she once had an auto accident and now has an artificial leg and can't drive anymore. You can see from these examples how elements of the play derive from theatrical necessities, concrete necessities of the stage, and just seem to be simply ideas.

*So an idea isn't theatrical at all to begin with, but the moment you transfer it to the world of the stage it necessarily becomes subject to dramatic standards?*

DÜRRENMATT: ... and takes a hand right in the play then, too, changes the play, changes characters, creates new characters.

*This must be a typical dramatist's attitude. A novelist would surely find, think of different, more narrative forms.*

DÜRRENMATT: Yes, that's possible.

*How long does it take you to write a play?*

DÜRRENMATT: About a year, generally.

*And when can you write best, mornings or in the evening?*

DÜRRENMATT: Most of the time I write from ten to twelve in the morning and from two to five in the afternoon, roughly; in an office, one that's pleasant.

*That's like office hours, or like a craft worker.*

DÜRRENMATT: I think I am a worker, a craft worker. Writing for me isn't so much a matter of mood. To work, I have to be at home. I really can only work in my writing room.

*How do you feel about being a writer?*

DÜRRENMATT: I've got used to it.

*Wouldn't you rather have been a painter? You originally planned to be one, didn't you?*

DÜRRENMATT: I can't afford it. I look on writing very strictly as a profession, as my profession. I had to write a lot, because I had to earn money to maintain my family and myself: detective novels, radio plays. I've never regretted it, and I've also never denied that I wrote these things to make money.

*Wouldn't you like to write a regular tragedy sometime?*

DÜRRENMATT: I don't think I'm exactly suited for tragedy.

*What works do you have planned for the immediate future?*

DÜRRENMATT: I'm not planning at all now—I'm writing. At the moment I'm writing a new play, a new comedy, in which—something new for me—the unities of place, time and action are strictly observed. The play's called *The Physicists*. I'm also writing a novel.

*A somewhat problematic question, Mr Dürrenmatt: do you believe that a poet can change the world, or at least influence it, at least disturb it—which in itself would be quite a bit?*

DÜRRENMATT: At best disturb it, influence it in the rarest cases—change it, never.

*In your article 'Problems of the Theatre', I found a shattering statement, though probably a bitterly true one. You say, 'Today art only manages to get through to the victims, if it manages to get through to people at all anymore. It no longer reaches the mighty.' What do you mean by that? Is it resignation, despair, or simply an objective conclusion?*

DÜRRENMATT: An objective conclusion, but also a point of departure for work.

*Mr Dürrenmatt, years ago you worked in films. You wrote the screenplay for a detective movie. Now Kurt Hoffmann has made a movie of your* The Marriage of Mr Mississippi. *From what we hear, you worked on the filming yourself. Can you tell us something about your film work?*

DÜRRENMATT: It was a very exciting time, I wrote the screenplay and Kurt Hoffmann shot, filmed what I wrote. That's a rarity, you know. If the film doesn't turn out well, it's my fault. I think it's good, but then I never go to the movies, so I don't really know what I've done, what Kurt Hoffmann and I have done. I adapted my own work, that was fun. The film got a different setting than the play, and a perhaps more religiously orientated comedy turned into a political farce. I don't see this as a betrayal, but as a necessity compelled by the film medium. We mustn't be picky about this: Bach once turned an aria about sensuality into one of his most beautiful religious arias. In addition to the art of inventing, there's often the delight of making variations. In the *Mississippi* film I varied one of my own themes. By the way, I worked on this from a stage version which has existed up to now only in French and which I did too. I prepared it in Paris together with George Vidale and with the director for the Theatre La Bruyere.

*I can see, then, that you're always ready to prepare new versions when necessary. In fact there are a lot of new versions you've made of your plays. In contrast many authors will put up an energetic fight for every single sentence. Brecht very freely undertook revisions and cuts—and not just for political reasons. For him a play was a piece of work that just was never finished. Is it the same with you?*

DÜRRENMATT: A play can never be completely finished. Every time you take it up again, you get new ideas. That's perfectly natural. But then, this business of constantly having to work with it again comes from the organisation of our theatres. We can't rehearse like the Americans, who have a play performed for months before audiences out of town and rewrite it many times over before it comes to Broadway. Our rehearsal time is much too short. Rehearsals last four weeks. You can't correct a fault because there's no time for you to be able to fix it. At most you can spot it, usually at the premiere.

There are a lot of things that just have to be solved on stage and not at the writing desk. A painter has to keep stepping back too, has to be able to look at the picture from a distance, and for a playwright that just means a performance. The classic playwrights were constantly rewriting too, you know—think of the various versions of *Götz* and *The Robbers*—so why shouldn't I too, seeing as I'm a classic playwright myself—except that no one besides me has noticed it yet.

*Mr Dürrenmatt, you mentioned the American theatre. With* The Visit *you conquered Broadway, in fact all America, in a single night. Your play was the high point of the 1957–58 season. Do you think that your* Frank V *and* The Physicists *will be produced there too?*

DÜRRENMATT: It's planned. You never know how things will work out and how long it will take. At the moment they're to be produced in England.

*What sort of experiences have you had with performances of your plays
in other countries, besides that Moscow story you mentioned?*

DÜRRENMATT: Well—various. There are plays which are perhaps
better suited to certain countries than are others. For example,
*Romulus* was actually a greater success than *The Visit* in Rome,
and in France I saw a wonderful production of *Romulus*, yet in
Germany it's always dismissed as nothing but a joke. That's
simply the way things are: every country reacts quite differently.
Then you have to say that even successes, such as in America,
for instance, can rest to a large extent on—I believe—misunder-
standing. Every play is misunderstood in every country in a very
particular way, but that's legitimate too, and I generally don't
take it at all tragically.

*In the Afterword to* Frank V *there's a provocative statement, 'As a
matter of principle, I don't write for fatheads.' That evoked a bit of
annoyance from the critics; some of them may have felt themselves touched.
Do you think that the critics can be of use to an author?*

DÜRRENMATT: Possibly. Wonders can always happen. The critics
demand good plays from us playwrights, consequently we demand from them—and I think justly—good criticism. The essence
of good criticism lies in whether it gives, or can give, not just an
opinion but a well-founded judgment. Most of the critics make
the big mistake of not really identifying with the parts they
criticise, of not really reflecting; they judge purely by feel, by
personal taste. I'm not at all sure that I'm a good writer. But a
critic can't very well be a critic at all unless he imagines he's a
good critic. Every critic is convinced he's infallible.

*But you were a critic yourself for a while.*

DÜRRENMATT: Yes, I'm speaking from personal experience too.

*Even with* The Visit, *when it had its premiere in Zürich, the reviews
were generally quite good, but still hesitant, sometimes doubtful, sometimes even negative. With your play's parade of triumphs, with its
success, the reviews got better and better too, more and more emphatic,
more and more enthusiastic.*

DÜRRENMATT: There's no art needed to find a successful play good.

*You think that the power of suggestion of success impresses the critics too?*

DÜRRENMATT: I think so.

*In conclusion, Mr Dürrenmatt, let me ask one personal question, a hypothetical one: if you could award the Nobel Prize, to whom would you give it?*

DÜRRENMATT: I'm in favour of giving it to a lyric poet every time, or to an essayist. These people have the lowest income of all writers, so they need prizes the most.

# John Osborne

THIS IS AN EDITED TRANSCRIPT of a television interview broadcast as part of the British Broadcasting Corporation's 'Face to Face' series on 21 January 1962, with the questions being raised by John Freeman, who has since become the British Ambassador to the United States.

John James Osborne, who has long since been weary of being described as an 'angry young man', was born in London on 12 December 1929. Hos father was a commercial artist, Thomas Godfrey Osborne, and his mother's maiden name was Nellie Beatrice Grove. Having spent much of his youth at the edge of poverty, Osborne today is a wealthy 'loner', a passionate pacifist, a simmering enemy of the still not quite dead British class stratification, a bitter foe of hypocrisy and the Establishment, an outspoken critic of the monarchy and of the arrogance of many individuals writing in the British press. He has a colourful and interesting history of writing irate letters to newspapers, issuing political and social polemics, and suing journalists such as the *Daily Mail* writer who referred to him as the 'original teddy boy'. Osborne is a tall, lean, handsome, serious man who is guarded in interviews, flamboyant in private conversation, fond of pubs, charming with women, partial to elegant dandyish attire, and excellent company because of a quick mind and a splendid sense of humour. In an *Observer* profile published on 17 May 1959, this articulate dramatist was described as 'accessible, defensive and gentle in manner, though his voice inclines to harshness'.

It is frequently said that he has a talent for dissent, but that may be a journalistic oversimplification. He does have a temper and a gift for language. His temper and sense of self are nothing new, no mere indulgence of a *nouveau riche* theatrical personality. Authority has rarely dismayed or repressed him. When a furious teacher hit him at school, Osborne struck back without hesitation. He apparently has a gift for getting people angry, so angry that one theatre man who knew him threatened to shoot him.

He is reputed to be a man who 'lives life hard and full', and perhaps he may be a bit hard to live with as well. He has been married four times, fathered one daughter. His marriage to Pamela Lane lasted from June 1951 to August 1957, and for the next five years he was the husband of actress Mary Ure. In May 1963 he married Penelope Gilliat, a journalist and film critic who succeeded Kenneth Tynan as *The Observer's* theatre critic. This complicated things as she felt duty bound not to review either films or stage plays in which John Osborne had a hand. They were divorced in 1967 and in 1968 he married the actress Jill Bennett.

Osborne was a journalist and then a competent but undistinguished actor in repertory, and it was during his years on stage that he wrote the five plays that preceded *Look Back in Anger*. In 1950 *The Devil Inside Him* was staged in Huddersfield. Written in collaboration with Stella Linden, it is a troubled tale of a young Welshman who is suspected of being deranged because he writes poetry. Unappreciated or unrecognised literary talents are often given to such reviews of scornful society; many playwrights have turned out such works during their youthful years. Osborne also wrote two dramas with Anthony Creighton, one produced some years later (1958) at the Royal Court as *Epitaph for George Dillon* and the other staged in Harrogate (1955) as *Personal Enemy*. The latter, which dealt with the reactions of the friends and family of a British soldier who chooses to stay with his Communist captors in Korea, is reported to have produced Osborne's first clash with the Lord Chancellor's censorship—this one over a homosexual aspect of the plot. Since then, Osborne has battled with the Lord Chancellor frequently and enthusiastically and has been active in a committee advocating widespread reform of theatre censorship in Britain. He has also written *A Patriot for Me*, a 1964 Court production about Colonel Redl, the homosexual Austrian intelligence officer who betrayed secrets to Russian agents blackmailing him just before World War I. For those concerned about recent controversies over the alleged homosexual domination of the British theatre, Osborne is neither a homosexual nor a particular defender of their rights.

Nineteen fifty-six was the Year of Osborne, the beginning of a major breakthrough for British dramatists and the start of a writers' renaissance that was to revitalise the English theatre. Without belittling the other playwrights, it was Osborne who blasted open the way for new ideas expressing the current attitudes, aspirations, impatience and disappointment of postwar British youth. The bomb was set off on the evening of 8 May 1956, when the new and dynamic English Stage Company presented the premiere of *Look Back in Anger* at the Royal Court Theatre. Osborne was twenty-six, and the youthful power and protest of the play startled some of the critics.

'It is intense, angry, feverish, undisciplined,' John Barber reported in the *Daily Express*. 'It is even crazy. But it is young, young, young.' The *Daily Mail* described Osborne as 'a dramatist of outstanding promise: a man who can write with a searing passion . . . we can perceive what a brilliant play this young man will write when he has got this one out of his system and let a little sunshine into his soul.' In the *New Statesman*, T. C. Worsley noted that in the fiery soliloquies of Jimmy Porter one can 'hear the authentic new tone of the Nineteen-Fifties, desperate, savage, resentful and, at times, very funny'. There were several negative reviews as well, but the heavy hitters came to bat on Sunday. Harold Hobson's review in the *Sunday Times* was clearly affirmative, and Tynan's essay in *The Observer* was a defiant hosannah.

The often quoted Tynan critique was practically a declaration of war, concluding that 'I agree that *Look Back in Anger* is likely to remain a minority taste. What matters, however, is the size of the minority. I estimate it at roughly 6,733,000, which is the number of young people in this country between twenty and thirty. .... It is the best young play of its decade.'

The box-office response was good but not overwhelming. The Osborne drama was played in the repertory cycle until early autumn, when the English Stage Company performed it alone for ten weeks. The first eight weeks were not too rewarding financially, but then an excerpt on television generated increased interest and attendance soared. The play has been revived with considerable success, and both the Broadway production and the film starring Richard Burton were well received.

Osborne was already completing *The Entertainer* by the end of 1956. 'Whenever I sit down to write it is with dread in my heart,' he has confided, but he must have felt encouraged by the fact that Laurence Olivier was scheduled to play the leading role. Olivier delivered a brilliant performance in both the 1957 English Stage Company production and the subsequent film. Osborne had proved he was no flash-in-the-pan or one-play dramatist, and this was reinforced by *Epitaph for George Dillon* in 1958 and—to a lesser degree—by the 1959 musical titled *The World of Paul Slickey*.

During a 1 February 1959 BBC 'Press Conference', he told Lord Francis Williams that the word 'angry' had been overworked and certainly was not 'very revealing. I think that people like myself, people of my age and perhaps general outlook—what people found strange about us was a feeling of dissent and a non-acceptance of established institutions and values.' He went on to suggest that the resentment might be generated by the fact that 'dissenters are the people who have changed society, and most of the forces working today are directed towards keeping it exactly the same as it is'. Osborne, an emotional Socialist who has never quite bothered to define his ideas of Socialism very clearly, has been at war with the *status quo* and the middle-class mind for a long time. If the middle-class theatregoer is troubled by Osborne plays, it is, the dramatist contends, because of the 'inescapable fact that when the middle classes discuss experience that is not dominated by their own emotional values, they hedge and bluster with all they've got'.

The Osborne plays and films have continued to roll from his typewriter. The 1960 television play *A Subject of Scandal and Concern* was followed in 1961 by *Luther*, which won Broadway's Antionette Perry award in 1963 with a remarkable performance by Albert Finney. Osborne contributed *The Blood of the Bambergs* and *Under Plain Cover* in 1962, certainly minor works in comparison with *Inadmissable Evidence* and *A Patriot for Me*, which premiered in 1964.

Osborne has announced that he wants 'to make people feel, to give them lessons in feeling. They can think afterwards.' He has also explained that the reason he has not written overt 'social message' plays is because he prefers to treat 'personal relationships, and I think these are the things that interest me most, and I think those are the things that are vital . . . my concern principally is is with the relationships between people, how people relate to each other and to themselves.' As for presenting any plans for political or social action to remedy the imperfections of this plainly flawed contemporary life, John Osborne disclaims any responsibility for this as he believes that it is not the playwright's task.

What Osborne will do next and how he will do it is not predictable. It used to be fashionable to speak of a Brechtian influence visible in his plays, but the more recent works seem to be moving in some new direction. Although some respected critics such as Robert Brustein dismiss Osborne as a 'secondary dramatist', most people seriously concerned about theatre will be watching his next steps. He is alone; the man who made the breakthrough has no 'school', no followers. He is alone because he wants to be alone, probably because he has to be. He said it plainly in a contribution to the book *Declaration*. 'If you are any good at all at what you set out to do, you know whether it is good and rely on no one to tell you so. You depend on no one.'

w. w.

🆗🆗🆗🆗🆗🆗🆗🆗🆗🆗🆗🆗 🆗🆗🆗🆗🆗🆗🆗🆗🆗🆗🆗🆗🆗🆗🆗🆗🆗🆗🆗🆗🆗🆗🆗🆗🆗🆗🆗🆗🆗🆗🆗

*Mr Osborne, at the age of thirty-two you're one of the most successful living playwrights—you're world-famous, you're a wealthy businessman. but all this material success has come quite suddenly in the last six years. Before that things were very different. Now I should like you to look back with candour and tell me, if you will, what kind of life you had before everything was changed with the success of* Look Back in Anger?

OSBORNE: Well, when I was a child . . . my childhood is something I think about a great deal because I think it's something I can avert a great deal of the time. I remember—the war was very important to me and I think people of my particular generation, people who were at school during the war. I remember the war very clearly and it seemed very important to me and I remember it very vividly. I remember the air raids vividly, and I remember the excitement very strongly.

*Where did you live?*

OSBORNE: Well, I lived with my mother in a suburb of London . . . most of the war. . . . And then about half-way through the war I was at a rather cheap boarding school in the west of England. Most of the time I was in London, or on the outskirts of London.

*Had your father died by that time?*

OSBORNE: My father died just at the beginning of the war.

*But were your parents pretty prosperous?*

OSBORNE: No, my father was a—he was a commercial artist, and he was a copy writer, and I had great affection and feeling for him. I thought he was a man of tremendous probity and integrity; he died very early in the war, about 1941.

*When you were about eleven or twelve? And after that did the family circumstances change, were you obviously much less well off when he died?*

OSBORNE: No, not really, because my father was an invalid. . . . He was—most of his life. He was a man who—most of his life had very little control over it. He was—he had asthma as a boy and then he had T.B., and he always seemed to me, seemed to be in the control of other people. It always struck me very strongly . . . I remember he used to take me round to see his mother, for example, and she was a very nice woman, I was very fond of her, but she used to tell—they were like all impoverished middle-class people, they were obsessed with money and she used to taunt him with a story how when he was sixteen he'd won some newspaper competition and the prize was a trip to South Africa and he'd won this prize, this competition, and on the way there he'd become ill and had to be put ashore in Lisbon, and there was a tremendous bill because of this, which they had to pay—about— a hundred pounds or something. And even when he was, I don't know, thirty-four or thirty-five my grandmother used to bring this up as something that he should still be ashamed of and that he still owed her. She was a very kind nice woman. . . . He was always, there was always a shadow of unemployment one way and another because of the time . . . because it was in the Thirties and because also he was a man who was in ill-health most of the time. So that it always seemed to me his life was in the control of other people.

*What about your mother, she was very different, wasn't she?*

OSBORNE: Well, my mother was—she went to work when she was twelve years old. She was scrubbing floors. . . . And she was physically stronger and I think, on the whole, she was able to cope more with life than my father, although he was a man of tremendous strength, tremendous integrity.

*Was she also, as you've just described your father, impoverished middle class?*

OSBORNE: No, no—my mother—I don't know how one would

describe her. I described my grandmother once as being a Cockney and she objected to it very strongly to me afterwards. But I would say they were upper working class. . . . I don't know how you describe them but my grandmother worked in Woolworth's—she was the head of all the cleaners in Woolworth's, and she did this for many years, and she was a very remarkable woman. . . . Still is—I mean she's over ninety.

*Now when your father died, how did the family finances go on? Was your mother still working?*

OSBORNE: Well, my mother was working—my mother's worked all her life, from twelve until about a year ago she still worked. And at that time she was working in a seed factory, when my father died, and earning very little—though I can't say that we had great hardship, but it was difficult and we were living in rooms. There was no great hardship, but it was—she had to work.

*So you left school eventually, and then presumably it was your responsibility to earn a living—what happened then?*

OSBORNE: Well, when I left school—my school days weren't particularly happy, because—I mean I regret my school days because there was a great deal of acrimony and bitterness in them. I was, in fact, at this boarding school for some time, and when I was there I was unhappy most of the time. There was a great deal of bitterness, and it's one of the things I regret—that—during my—there's very little of my childhood that I can look back on with any pleasure. Most of it I regret, I think. When I left school I was fifteen and a half, and I didn't really know what I was going to do. I had a vague idea that I wanted to write, because it was the only thing that I seemed to be able to do—or at least the only thing that I seemed to be able to do better than anybody else. I could put a sentence together rather well, and even I knew that. But I had a very vague idea of what I wanted to do. . . . I didn't feel particularly equipped—equipped with anything, really.

*And what did you do immediately after you left school?*

OSBORNE: Well, I went—I joined a firm which published trade magazines, and I was sort of a dogsbody and sub-editor. . . .

*A journalist in fact?*

OSBORNE: A journalist, yes indeed, yes.

*Were you ever a member of the National Union of Journalists?*

OSBORNE: I was never asked. . . . I can't think why.

*And then you drifted to the stage before very long, I think?*

OSBORNE: Well, you know, my contact with journalism was a fugitive contact—I mean it was only a few months and somehow I felt that I didn't like what it represented and I didn't like the people that I was in contact with, and I drifted—literally drifted—into the stage. In the most funny way—I really did drift into it.

*And presumably, therefore, were earning very little money?*

OSBORNE: Well, as a journalist I was earning two pounds ten a week. When I first went into the theatre I was earning seven pounds a week, which I thought was very good—indeed it was. I mean digs were only three guineas a week, top, and one could live very comfortably on that.

*Did you in fact ever, during the years before you were successful, know what it was to be really poor?*

OSBORNE: Well, no, I don't think so . . . I mean I think to be really poor means that there's no final appeal, and I suppose I knew always that if—in the worse kind of extremity I could always turn to my mother and she'd send me ten shillings or a pound or something.

*Yes. Well now, all that was very suddenly changed, I mean after this short period of journalism, and then some years on the stage, the whole thing was suddenly changed in 1956 when* Look back in Anger—*which I think was about your fifth or sixth play actually, wasn't it?—was suddenly, was put on and hit the jackpot. Now since then it's all been different—do you enjoy now being rich and famous? Do you enjoy spending money?*

OSBORNE: Well, what I enjoy principally about money is the security it gives me—is that I—I mean, it cushions me and allows me to do exactly what I like and to go where I like. Most of the rest of it I don't find particularly enjoyable.

*I don't know if you understand this question, but are you used to being a pretty wealthy man—is money familiar to you?*

OSBORNE: No, never. I mean I always expect to be—I'm always preparing for financial disaster, and always expecting that I'm going to end up in the bankruptcy court or prison, or nobody's going to give me a job and I think, well, who would give me a job, where could I earn twenty pounds? I never—I don't—I'm sure I'll never really get used to having money. If I sit in a taxicab I'm always surprised that I've got the fare for it.

*Does this mean that you're not extravagant? Or are you?*

OSBORNE: Well, I think I am extravagant in some ways, but, on the other hand, I'm thrifty in a petty ridiculous way. . . . I mean I still, until quite recently I used to shove two shilling pieces and half—all my silver, when I came back in the evening, I'd put into a drawer, because I thought, well, it's all, you know, that will get me out of some kind of trouble at some point. I've stopped doing that, but . . .

*What are your particular personal extravagances—clothes, books, records, what—travel?*

OSBORNE: Well, those things mostly. I mean it's the tax situation forces one to spend money that one wouldn't ordinarily. I mean it forces one to—because it's the only way of getting what you earn, and I think I work very hard and I think I earn most of what I get, but I get very little . . . as everybody does. I mean the fact is, of course, that I'm overpaid. I mean I get much too much for what I do, but one is forced to buy things and to pay for things that one wouldn't do.

*Do you actually enjoy being a businessman, because you are a director of several companies, do you like that side of it, apart from writing plays?*

OSBORNE: Well, I'm a businessman insofar as I'm a film producer. Well, I enjoy that not because I ever expected to make any money out of it. I've been very fortunate and have, up to now, made money out of it. Tony Richardson and I formed this company, Woodfall Films, and we've been very fortunate on the whole. We've made four films, two of which have been highly successful, and, of course, Wardour Street have endorsed it as a result. I mean, we only need to make one unsuccessful film and be back where we started. But what is enjoyable about it is not the feeling of being a tycoon but of . . . of doing something that you think nobody else would do, and I don't think that if we had done that anybody else would have done it. They may have done, but we happened to be fortunate—did it at the right time.

*Let's get on to this business of being famous, which is where you're leading the conversation really. . . . Apart from obviously critical appreciation of your work as a playwright, which no doubt you appreciate, do you enjoy— have you any hankering after personal publicity?*

OSBORNE: No.

*You're quite honest enough now to have analysed yourself about this and I wonder whether conceivably you do, deep down, have a sort of desire to be a figure of hate to the public.*

OSBORNE: Yes, I know what you mean. I don't think so. I mean I think there was a time, there was a period when I courted publicity to some extent, and I think even then it was to a limited extent, because . . . one did it because, from one's sort of show-business instinct, simply because you thought it was the way to get people in, to get as many lines as possible. And then, of course, after that, a point was reached at which the intrusion into one's life became so intense and so unpleasant that one made every effort to avoid it. And I think I have . . . I mean I haven't done it successfully. . . .

*Well, I was going to say, do you in fact consider that the press tend to persecute you personally?*

OSBORNE: Well, yes, I think the press select their victims, of course. I mean their piece of real, craven Fleet Street cant always is, of course, that if one is in the public eye, then the public has a right to know something about you. Well, of course, this is such a—I mean it's based on such a simple-minded assumption that a newspaper can reveal the truth about a human personality, which it can't, of course. I mean, it's an impossibility. And also it comes out of the complete—and this is what is so wicked about it—it comes out of complete moral disengagement.

*Well now, let's just relate this to cases, because there was a case recently where complaints were made to the Press Council about intrusion into your private life, and the Press Council considered those complaints and it found—I quote its words—'that the persons concerned had been very much in the public eye and the newspapers properly regarded their activities as news.' Now that's what the Press Council said. Do you think that's an unfair observation, or not?*

OSBORNE: Well, I mean the whole thing is ludicrous, just as the Press Council is a ludicrous body. In the first place, the complaint was made by somebody, without any reference to me at all, or anyone else involved. And the Press Council allegedly investigated it. I mean, the Press Council—you know it's really rather as if the Wolfenden Committee was composed of whores and tarts . . . I mean it's as serious and as ludicrous as that. They allegedly investigated this case, without any reference to me, or any of the people involved. I sent them a cable from America suggesting that it might have been a good idea for them to have contacted me, if they were allegedly investigating it—which they didn't do at all. I mean it seems to me absolutely—and then, of course, they issued a verdict on this thing. There's no doubt about it— newspapers select their victims very carefully. I mean, for example, I would consider myself to be, well, say Mr Gaitskell's political opponent, but if, for example, he were knocking off a maid or something like that, then I wouldn't feel that I was prepared to make a moral judgment about that. And I think that newspapers have no moral content and are operating from no moral standpoint at all. And they know this, of course—have no right to make this kind of moral judgment.

*Well now, some people who wouldn't necessarily sympathise with the press at all points have said something slightly different about you personally. They've said that people like you, who set out to criticise the social behaviour of their fellow men—and I think it's true that you do this— must expect to be subjected to the same sort of criticism yourself. And I think that's a proposition that you ought to answer.*

OSBORNE: Well, I think it is, but I mean the thing is that I don't think that one should be—I've never attacked anybody on that kind of personal level myself. I've always tried to present the truth as I've seen it, but I don't think I've ever attacked anybody on that kind of trivial personal level, without any kind of moral content involved at all. I mean, I think it is shown by the fact that the victims are so carefully selected. I mean, you know this, when one talks about it in this way, there seems to be a terrible element of self-importance involved, but I mean, to anyone who has any access to the truth—I mean everyone knows, for example, that Lord Beaverbrook has what the popular newspapers call a permanent house guest but they would never dream of printing such a fact. Now these—the victims are people who are carefully selected, and the people who are outside society. And I think to say that simply because you criticise English institutions, that you are therefore fair game for any kind of malevolence and maliciousness, misses the point altogether.

*Let's just go on then and see some of the things that you do criticise. I've tried to look at your published work and see what are the themes which really inspire it. Now would I be right in saying that it isn't Socialism—you may be a socialist, but it isn't Socialism that you're writing about so much as non-conformism, is that true or not? I don't mean in the religious sense, of course.*

OSBORNE: No, I know what you mean. No, I don't think it is.

*Tell us what—is there a continuing theme, then?*

OSBORNE: I don't think there is a continuing theme really. I mean I think it's very easy to construct one, but there isn't one that I could pick out myself. No, I couldn't.

*Do you have any vision in your own mind of the just society which isn't a completely abstract one? Do you look round the world and see any social order which corresponds to your own vision?*

OSBORNE: Well, I mean, I can think of a form of political programme that I might support, but I mean I don't consider myself to be a social critic, which I'm not.

*Well now, when you wrote your—can we talk in shorthand and let me call it your 'Damn England' letter—was that a sudden impulse of fear? It was written, you remember, about the time of the Berlin crisis—or does that, months' later, represent your considered view of British politics?*

OSBORNE: No, I don't think it does. I mean it was written in very special circumstances. . . . I mean I think perhaps the background of it might be a little interesting. . . . I wrote it—when I wrote it I was staying in the South of France, which, of course, afterwards everybody, you know, brought up as an example of sybaritic high life, ignoring the fact that thousands of people, ordinary English people spend weeks every year in the South of France. In fact, I was working rather hard, and one day I picked up the *New Statesman* and in it there was a—I think in the form of an advertisement an appeal by Bertrand Russell, and it was cogently argued and reasonable and sane. And I was moved by it and I thought, the spectacle of this old man being concerned with the survival of everybody else, I found it very moving and disturbing and I thought, well, those kind of arguments are going to go on sanely and logically, and decently in magazines like the *New Statesman* or *The Spectator* or *The Observer*, week after week, and nothing is going to happen, and I felt that I had to make some kind of act of repudiation and to couch it in a particular form and I chose it very carefully, and I chose the form of metaphor, and—I'd done it before with a similar piece when I got so over-bored by the tedium, the thought of reading about Prince Andrew's first tooth being cut and Princess Margaret's wedding, and I wrote a piece called 'The Epistle to the Philistines', which I thought was rather successful but which *The Spectator* didn't. And so, anyway, I sent this piece which I very carefully constructed, almost like a poem, and I sent it to *The Tribune*—to *The Tribune*, and ... it was strange because ... I was ... I felt that it was something that ... this kind of metaphor was something the English people would respond to, because I think English people are violent, and I think they respond to this kind of poetic content, and in fact, to my surprise, they did. I mean to an extent —I mean *Tribune* has a circulation—I don't know, ten thousand people—and I mean the thing that emerged, of course, was that nobody read it, and the popular papers picked out pieces of it and I mean they said: 'Damn you, England', for example, and they ignored the fact that I had quite carefully specified whom I meant—I meant the people who were in control of our lives. . . . I said, you know, the men who were, you know, leading us into the situation ... I mean they quite deliberately traduced it.

*No doubt that is true. It was, I think, misrepresented but also it was misunderstood and perhaps this is partly your fault. Let me therefore give you a chance now, as a last answer in this programme, because we've come to the end of it, obviously the 'Damn you, England' letter didn't represent all that you have to say about your country and your fellow countrymen. Now could you imagine now writing what I might call an 'England, I love you' letter—and if you could, what would its theme be?*

OSBORNE: Well, I don't know. It would be very difficult. I would like to be able to do it, and in fact that's what I would set myself to do as a writer, because I believe that the function of a writer is not to appear on television at all, and do this kind of thing, or justify their work, because their work should justify itself. I think that, for example, somebody once said about the French nineteenth-century historian, Michelet, that he wrote history in a style in which it's impossible to tell the truth. Well, I would like to be able to learn to write in a style in which it was impossible to tell anything else.

# William Inge

▣▣▣▣▣▣▣▣▣▣▣▣▣▣▣▣▣▣▣▣▣▣▣▣▣▣▣▣▣▣▣▣▣▣▣▣▣▣▣▣▣▣▣▣▣▣▣▣▣

SHORTLY BEFORE his comedy-drama *Where's Daddy?* opened on Broadway in March 1966, playwright William Inge faced the editor of this book and a Wollensak tape recorder in a New York City rehearsal hall. Mr Inge, a large, soft, gentle, thoughtful man of serious demeanour, had come east from his California home for the premiere of his newest work. The interview had been scheduled for magazine publication in April, but when it became apparent that the prize-winning dramatist's current play would not be a Broadway success the publisher decided that William Inge was 'not timely'. This dangerous commitment to over-simplified journalistic concepts of current news is a wide-spread and recurring problem in the mass media; only a few un-inhibited magazine editors and broadcasters have ignored it. Most have not, however, so they treat theatre figures—even the most celebrated—only when a new project is about to be launched or has just succeeded. Unless and until he has a new play opening or he makes a speech or gets arrested, a dramatist can expect little attention.

It is unlikely that this bothers William Inge, as he is a quiet, self-contained man who enjoys his privacy and does not seek publicity. The 'what have you done for us *lately*?' philosophy of the Broadway audiences and the press is not unfamiliar to this

Kansas-bred bachelor, for Inge was a journalist himself. William Inge was born in the small city of Independence, Kansas, on 9 May 1913. He was the youngest of the five children of Luther Clayton Inge and the former Maude Sarah Gibson. William Motter Inge's passion for the stage blossomed early, as is set forth in the interview that follows, and one published biographical sketch reports that he lost a year of school when he took a leave to tour with a troupe that performed under canvas.

Inge was considering a career as a teacher when he graduated from the University of Kansas in the Depression year of 1935, and he apparently still had this in mind when he finally completed his M.A. in English at Peabody Teachers College in 1938. He spent the next five years on the faculty of Stephens College for Women in Columbia, Missouri, teaching drama in a department headed by Miss Maude Adams, who had retired to the academic world from Broadway.

In 1943 soft-spoken William Inge—whom his friend Tennessee Williams has often called the Gentleman from Kansas—left teaching for the livelier atmosphere of journalism. He became the drama and music critic for the St Louis *Star-Times*, and it was in this capacity that he met Williams in January of 1945. *The Glass Menagerie* had just opened in Chicago *en route* to New York, and Williams had come home to see his parents 'as a refugee from the shock of sudden fame'. Inge telephoned the Williams' rented home in the suburbs to request an interview, and they met a second time when Inge went up to Chicago to see *The Glass Menagerie* before it departed for Broadway. After the performance that night, the two men strolled back from the theatre to Williams' hotel and it was during this walk that Inge abruptly and frankly confided that his dream was to become a successful playwright. Williams encouraged the young critic to go ahead with his writing, and later helped get Inge's 'first' play to an agent. That work, *Come Back, Little Sheba*, was the initial Inge work produced on Broadway but was actually preceded by a play titled *Farther Off from Heaven* written in 1945. After revision, *Farther Off from Heaven* was later produced by Saint Subber and Elia Kazan and

opened at the Music Box in New York, on 5 December 1957, as
*The Dark at the Top of the Stairs*.

After a 1949 summer tryout in Westport, Connecticut, and
some rather considerable cast problems that everyone would
prefer to forget, *Come Back, Little Sheba* opened in New York on
5 February 1950. Despite splendid performances by Shirley
Booth and Sidney Blackmer, plus generally good reviews, the
Theatre Guild production ran less than six months. Inge's next
work was the hit *Picnic*, which opened in New York on 19 February 1953, and played for 485 performances. It also won the
Pulitzer Prize, the Drama Critics' Award and the Donaldson
Award. *Bus Stop* had its premiere on 2 March 1955, was warmly
received and ran for thirteen months. As already mentioned, *The
Dark at the Top of the Stairs* followed in 1957; it was also a hit.

The three plays that have been produced since then have not
been successful either artistically or financially. *A Loss of Roses*
(1959), *Natural Affection* (1963) and *Where's Daddy?* (1966) did not
impress the critics as having the power or the focus of his earlier
works. The fact that he won an Academy Award for the best
original film script of 1961 with *Splendour in the Grass* may have
been some consolation, but hardly enough for a serious dramatist
who fared so well with his first four works. Some observers
have suggested that the further he has gone from his own experiences and the types of people he knew in his youth, the more
difficulty Inge has faced as a creator.

Today there is a lack of unanimity as to whether Inge is to be
'a major American playwright' or simply a gifted naturalistic
dramatist for our time—a man with a sensibility and sensitivity
for the lonely, the troubled, the sexually frustrated or the afraid.
The 'young tigers' among America's theatre critics now show
little interest in him, for they find his work lacking in boldness or
not fierce enough in its soul-searching. Interestingly enough, the
professional soul-searchers—the psychiatrists and analysts—
find Inge's work quite sound and several of them have said so.
Inge, who has been psychoanalysed, is reported to have shown the
*Come Back, Little Sheba* script to several psychiatrists who read

and approved it *before* production. In his study titled *Freud on Broadway*, W. David Sievers later referred to *Picnic* as an example of 'the most mature level of American drama in the fifties, able to draw upon Freudian insights without succumbing to the obvious or the trite, able to extract ever fresh and original patterns of human relationship from contemporary life and to view with psychological as well as aesthetic perception the life around us.'

Inge himself has commented on the great impact that Freud has made upon every conscious contemporary writer's awareness of himself, has acknowledged his own debt. It is interesting to note that other playwrights have also applauded Inge's theatrical use of 'motivation', among them Tennessee Williams. Williams has written of Inge's 'true and wonderful talent which is for offering, first, the genial surface of common American life, and then not ripping but quietly dropping the veil that keeps you from seeing yourself as you are. . . . It's just what you are, and why should you be ashamed of it?'

William Inge is not ashamed of who he is or what he has done, including the three most recent plays that did not succeed. He was no 'boy wonder' dramatist, for the first of his plays to be produced in New York was not staged until he was thirty-seven. By today's standards he was a late starter. He may also be a late finisher.

w. w.

*Mr Inge, if such a question is answerable, how do you write a play? Where do you start?*

INGE: I doubt if any two playwrights go about this in the same way. I don't know exactly what happens, except if you are a playwright you think and see life in a certain way. You think in terms of being a playwright and see life through the eyes of a playwright, and I think you have a tendency to convert your life's experiences, when you reflect upon them, into theatre. I think you cannot help but try to see them transformed into theatre. It's as if you go through life trying to digest it, and put it into some theatrical form. So, of course, you make many false starts and you're always playing with ideas and concepts and then suddenly something happens, something clicks inside and you know you have a hold of something. I suppose it's like the fisherman when he feels the fish biting his bait.

*Simply, you feel this is right for you?*

INGE: Yes, and you know you've got a hold of something that you can make something of. That you can create into something, and then you work it out.

*Perhaps a mood or a memory of the feeling at some time in the past— or a character who seems to you to be compelling?*

INGE: Yes . . . or it may come out of memories or it may come out of one's desires to deal with experience. To get it down on paper. The writer, maybe, just feels he wants to be honest with himself in some way. To face something in an honest way.

*That is your pattern in all of these plays?* Come Back, Little Sheba?

INGE: I suppose . . . yes.

Where's Daddy? *is a comedy?*

INGE: Yes.

*Your first full comedy?*

INGE: I think *Bus Stop* is a pretty complete comedy, even though there are some serious matters in the play and the play itself, I think, has meaning. I've always regarded *Bus Stop* as a comedy and I've always regarded *Picnic* as a comedy too.

*Is there any time of a day that you write?*

INGE: Yes, morning, preferably morning. Right after breakfast. I'm a very early riser. I'm usually up around six, and I'm almost always at the typewriter by eight and I write until twelve or one, usually.

*That is almost the same pattern that Tennessee Williams follows.*

INGE: Yes, you're right. I was thinking he wrote at night, but I guess he doesn't because I remember now him mention morning writing.

*He said the other day that he has a rather elaborate ritual which he was reluctant to describe, but apparently a martini is part of it.*

INGE: Yes. I think a martini in the morning would ruin any chance I might have of being productive at the typewriter. It certainly doesn't seem to hurt him.

*Do you evolve pretty much the whole story before you start typing, or does it grow?*

INGE: When I do feel that I've got a hold of something, I know I still have to work it out and I never try to outline a play. A play is something like a problem that I have to work out, all on the paper, with the typewriter itself. I have to work my play out as I go, and then rewrite, of course. I've never been able to outline a play before I try writing it.

*You do several rewrites like most playwrights?*

INGE: Oh yes, many, four, five, maybe many more. . . . They aren't total rewrites, just a piece here or changes here and there.

*Do you show it to anybody before it's finished?*

INGE: Yes, and it's something which at this late date in my career as a writer I realise I must not do anymore. I've always been too eager to show it to people, and I think that I'm suffering from doing that.

*That's pretty natural, isn't it, for a writer to want a little reassurance on the way?*

INGE: Yes, it's a natural thing to do, it's a natural tendency. You complete something that you're proud of and suddenly you rush to someone with it and say 'Oh, read this for me.' Well, I believe it's a mistake doing that, but you show it to a friend or your agent, a supposed friend.

*A playwright has no friends—not while he's writing anyway.*

INGE: No, he doesn't . . . and I know. I've quite often done that and evoked very discouraging results . . . and then had to come back to my work with a kind of new determination. I know I've got something here, whether they do or not, and I just haven't made it clear yet. I haven't fully realised my concept yet on the paper, and I've just got to work more.

*Do you find that directors have been helpful in interpreting this, or have directors at any time substantially altered or changed anything you've done or tried to do? I know you've worked with Mr Kazan, who has a reputation of being a very strong director.*

INGE: Gadge is a strong director. Because he is a fine director and a strong director, people think of him as being an autocratic director. He isn't bossy at all. He does not dictate to the playwright, ever. As a matter of fact, he works closer with the playwright and, as a director, depends more on the writer than any other director I know.

*More than Mr Clurman?*

INGE: No, no . . . not more than Clurman.

*He's a very close worker?*

INGE: Yes, Harold respects the writer very much. But Gadge will keep you right by his side every minute; he wants the writer's concept of every line that has been written. And some directors, as soon as they get a script, will just turn their back on the writer and want to get off on their own as soon as possible and forget the writer even exists, and I think that's a mistake. Well, you know I've seen directors mess up good plays very badly by doing that.

*Your own, or other people's . . . without mentioning names?*

INGE: Let's just say that I've seen it happen.

*What other directors have you worked with?*

INGE: Oh, I've worked with Daniel Mann, was the first director I've worked with. He did a very good job with *Come Back, Little Sheba*, and I worked with Josh Logan on *Picnic*.

*Is he a strong director?*

INGE: Josh is strong, yes. Josh has to do a play in his own way, and he can be very creative, if you can do it as he sees it. You do get Josh's concept of the script sometimes more than you get of the script of the play itself. So you give a script to Josh or you want to work with Josh only when you can agree on the script, when you do see it together. But, you know, he certainly did a beautiful job with *Picnic*, and I think I've said before I didn't want anything to be different but the ending.

*What other ending did you want?*

INGE: I saw a less dramatic ending on it, and yet I could see that once Josh takes over a play it kind of has to be his own and he kind of has to make it his play if he's going to do anything with it at all. And so *Picnic* was, well, part of it was Josh. I don't say that with any regrets or recriminations at all. I thought he had, at least, got the essence of what I'd written and he had created a beautiful show and so I was happy, pleased, even though I did complain from time to time when I thought this should be different or that, but he did a job that I certainly could never regret.

*Who did* Bus Stop?

INGE: Harold Clurman did *Bus Stop*, and did a beautiful job with it. *Bus Stop* was produced almost exactly word for word. I really don't remember having to make a single change. I'm sure I must have made some when we went to rehearsals, but I don't remember any. There were certainly no big rewrites after each rehearsal, none at all.

*Were you involved with the film* Bus Stop? *Did you do the script?*

INGE: No.

*The only film you've written is* Splendour in the Grass?

INGE: No, I did an adaptation of a novel, *All Fall Down*, by James Leo Herlihy. I did that, and then I later did an original that kind of got messed up—and I took my name off it.

*Do you think of yourself as a film writer?*

INGE: No, no, I'm not a film writer. I can write a good film once in a while, but it has to be something that I like or something that I feel some real desire to do or an original. Unless I feel some liking, some identification with this story itself, I can't— I'm not a good enough craftsman just to sit down and take a novel or a piece of work that's meaningless to me and make a film of it, just for the money; I wish I could, but I just can't.

*Well, some playwrights seem to do a play every year or two. You have not followed that pattern in recent years. Is that because there hasn't been anything that has hooked you, that has compelled, that has touched you?*

INGE: No . . . no, I had a play on about three years ago, *Natural Affection*, and then I do a play every two or three years.

*Are you writing almost constantly?*

INGE: Well, I've always got something in progress. I am working on a novel now too. I've been working on the novel for a long time, making many false starts and going back and making new ones. But I do keep working on it, simply because it's a story I feel I have to tell in some way, and I don't know, it may be eight or ten years I'll. . . .

*Is it also a story with its roots in your own life and experience?*

INGE: No, it's a story of kind of an unusual rape case that happened back in my home town years ago; it had quite an unusual story element that fascinated me.

*This would make a better novel than a play, you think?*

INGE: I couldn't see it as a play. I could see it as a movie but I choose to write it first as a novel.

*Is the story of your newest play,* Where's Daddy?, *also rooted in some experience or feeling of your boyhood?*

INGE: No, *Where's Daddy?* is the first play that I've ever been able to write with a New York setting, and strangely enough I was never able to write about New York until I moved away from New York. I live in California now, and while I was living here I guess I was too close to New York life to see it clearly, to have any reflections about it and it wasn't until I had moved to California that the life I had known in New York began to distill itself, so to speak, and that I could reflect about it. And so I've written my first New York play; this play is set in New York, and it's about New York people, and for the first time I've been able to write of New York as part of my own life and experience, out of my own life as an experience.

*Frank Gilroy said that he finds that he is always writing things about twenty years after they happen.*

INGE: Yes . . . yes.

*Does that make any sense to you? It takes you a decade or two to let it work its way down? Then you bring it up again?*

INGE: No . . . no.

*Do you find that there are any playwrights whose works you really think have influenced you? I know you were helped in the beginning or encouraged by Tennessee Williams, but I'm talking about through the ages, way back to the Greeks.*

INGE: No, I've never been influenced by the Greeks; I feel most affiliation, I think, with the Irish writers—Synge particularly, and he's not a very popular writer now, but I feel closer, I think, to Synge and some of the early O'Casey. And Chekhov—a great experience for me, I mean really opened up the whole world for me when I first began writing as a student back in college. There is something about Thornton Wilder's work that makes me feel; I have been influenced somewhat by him and also some by Tennessee, but I think my viewpoint—whatever viewpoints I have—are quite separate from these men.

*Tennessee has been quoted as saying that his plays reflect 'Man's struggle between good and evil.' Is that relevant to your work? We're all concerned with that as human beings, but do you think it's a particular theme in your work?*

INGE: No, not so much. It seems to me that I'm usually concerned with Man's realisation of himself, with his place in the universe.

*Do you have any religious feeling?*

INGE: I'm a religious man, yes.

*Do you go to church, or not go to church?*

INGE: I don't regularly go to church. I'm not that disciplined. Yet, I have quite a few friends among clergymen, Jesuits, and it took me a long time to realise that I am religious. I didn't fight being religious, I just never realised that I do have a belief in God. One day I just admitted it to myself. However, I don't see Him as a man; I don't see God in a very personal way. I see him as a force in life, who does not control the individual life but the individual lives of men. I see God as a force to help us to face the difficulties of life, not as a great Father to remove the difficulties of life.

*Then you wouldn't place yourself with the existentialist playwrights?*

INGE: I don't think we understand the existentialists, but maybe we all understand them all in our own way. I feel in my way I am an existentialist. Of course, there are many religious existentialists. Certainly the early existentialists, Kierkegaard and Pascal, were very religious men of the cloth. It's been only some of the contemporary existentialists, mainly the French, who have been atheistic. I think we misunderstand existentialism if we feel or think of it as saying that life is worth nothing. Camus's philosophy of the absurd does not mean to me that life itself is absurd or that Camus takes it any less seriously. I think we have to accept many of the happenings in life as absurd ... and absurd in the sense that they mean nothing. But if a man's wife or sweetheart or dear one is killed by a truck in the middle of the street, that is an absurdity in the sense that it was not planned that way—it did not have any personal meaning in the happening. It's an absurdity in that it had no planning or no purpose and Man must develop, I think, that new personal regard towards life in order to live it peacefully at all.

*Are you reasonably confident about your work? A number of established playwrights to whom I've spoken said, 'Yes, success is fine. Prizes and money and glory are fine, but every time I put a piece of paper into that machine, I'm quite tense and nervous.'*

INGE: Yes, that's true. I don't think any real writer ever has a confident ego. I don't think he can tell himself, 'Well, I know I can do this or I can do that.' I don't think any serious man in any field safely has that degree of ego confidence. Any man who tells himself, 'Sure, I can go out and do this or take on some Herculean task and get it done,' that's vanity.

*Almost every play is a Herculean task, isn't it?*

INGE: Yes, even though when you are writing it you have the greatest faith in it. You cannot write a play without faith. Yet, after the play is finished, you cannot possibly tell yourself, 'I know this is going to make a big hit,' or 'I know people are going to like this.' You have to face the fact that its future may be a very unpleasant thing.

*Does the current American theatre 'hit or disaster' situation trouble you?*

INGE: Oh, yes. It's a very discouraging theatre to write for, a theatre that has no sure audience. The New York audience is a constantly shifting one, from whom you can expect no loyalty. Mostly, if we depended upon just New Yorkers alone, those who are interested in going to the theatre, a play would run two or three months, and that would be all. A play that has a run of a whole season or a couple of years does that on out-of-towners, people who come and go and who can be expected to hold any loyalty for the theatre itself in New York.

*When a play comes in, a play written by a playwright whose work I've seen and enjoyed, my tendency is to go and see it even if the reviews are disastrous. But I don't suppose very many people do that.*

INGE: No, no, not very many people do. They don't take an interest in the playwright unless he's got a hit. There is no interest in the playwright's career as such.

*Do you think the audience has changed since* Come Back, Little Sheba?

INGE: It was pretty bad even then. The theatre has been that way, I think, certainly ever since World War II. I think there was a more devoted audience back in the Twenties; there undoubtedly was and probably in the Thirties too.

*And that was an audience which was more interested in theatre than in what some of my friends call a social experience.*

INGE: I think so, but maybe I'm wrong. I wasn't in New York in the Twenties. I didn't come to New York until 'Thirty-nine, and I made a visit then, in the summer of 'Thirty-nine. Certainly the theatre was very prosperous then, and a good play had a chance to get seen on Broadway and to have a run without being a hit. It's strange, but when you look back upon most of the plays that we regard today as American classics, they were plays that did not pay off.

*I've noticed plays from my teen-age period, plays which I recall with great esteem, ran 80 or 100 performances.*

INGE: Today that can't happen. I think that even *Our Town* had a very short Broadway run, didn't it? I know *The Time of Your Life* had a short run, and not a very profitable run; I'm pretty sure that's so.

*Do you think that the critics contributed to this? Do you think our critics are different, worse, or better than they used to be? Or are they catering to this audience?*

INGE: I don't know if it's the critics' fault or if it's the audience's fault for interpreting critics as they do. I wouldn't know. There now seems to be something so negative in the atmosphere; when I read reviews of plays it's somehow as though no one has expected the play to be good in the first place. You read about failure after failure coming along now, a kind of sickening monotony, and there is a feeling of hopelessness about the theatre generally now. Very discouraging.

*We do have a 'theatrical explosion' all over the country, with these resident repertory groups.*

INGE: Yes, I think they're coming as a result of the decline of theatre on Broadway. We've come to realise that our audience must be bigger than New York, that original theatre in a country this size must exist somewhere else other than New York itself, where the audience is restricted and where the nature of theatre is necessarily restricted too by that audience. I think that we are coming to realise our theatre must be bigger than that; it must be bigger than New York. It must be a theatre that reflects the whole country.

*Do you travel much? Do you go to Europe?*

INGE: No, I am a very provincial man. I have never been abroad.

*You don't still think of yourself as a Midwesterner, do you?*

INGE: Yes, I do. Rather stubbornly now. I kind of cling to my identity as a Midwesterner almost as members of small minority groups cling to their identity. When I was a college student I thought of myself as a much more cosmopolitan person than I do now.

*You didn't think of yourself as a Midwesterner then?*

INGE: No, I was very embarrassed to be a citizen of the rural 'backward' state of Kansas where people had no sophistication and so forth . . . then I felt myself to be a much more cosmopolitan person. Actually I wasn't, I was just a hick putting on a show. But I did start acting when I was a child. . . .

*Was that in grade school or at home or what?*

INGE: In grade school. It was just something that happened spontaneously and I just started giving recitations and monologues and . . . to entertain the classroom and so I became kind of a prodigy when I was seven years old. Then I continued acting.

*You acted at college too?*

INGE: Yes. Then I acted with a couple of summer theatres.

*Now, at college did you work at any of the college shows, their musicals?*

INGE: Oh, yes, sure.

*Did you enjoy that?*

INGE: Oh, I loved it. I lived for it. I hated my classes, did very poor school work.

*And then when you taught, did you teach drama? Writing or English?*

INGE: Yes. I started out teaching English and then I went to drama.

*You had written your first play before you had met Tennessee?*

INGE: No, I wrote my first play after I met him. I was thirty years old at the time I wrote my first play.

*And he helped get it to an agent?*

INGE: No, he helped get *Come Back, Little Sheba* to an agent, but it so happened that when I wrote my very first play his friend Margo Jones was just beginning at the Dallas Theatre. He was visiting here at the time, and I called them and told them that I finished a play and they said 'Send it to us.' They liked it and Margo asked me if she could do it.

*Are you still friends?*

INGE: Oh, we are friendly, yes. We rarely see each other; I am on one side of the country and he is on the other, but I still have great regard for him.

*He shares a hobby of yours. He is also a passionate swimmer.*

INGE: I know. We do share that one recreation. I know I go two or three times a week to the athletic club here for a swim and a steam and enjoy it very much, and I think that he does the same.

*Do you still sketch and paint?*

INGE: Occasionally.

*And also collect paintings?*

INGE: Well, I buy pictures. I am not a big collector. I have a small collection of which I am pretty proud.

*What sort of paintings do you have in your collection?*

INGE: Well, I have two Giacomettis now. I have a beautiful oil that is now in the Modern Museum's show. It is travelling all over the country. I also have a bronze that I bought years and years ago before he became very well known. I also have a big de Kooning woman and a small Klein abstraction. I buy pictures because I like them, not because they're considered very good buys. My collection is very personal. I also have a couple of Piccaso drawings, Matisse, and a couple of small Rodins and a Giacometti bronze, and I have a Degas bronze, a beautiful ballet dancerwoman.

*Do you go to the theatre very much when you are in New York?*

INGE: No, not anymore. It is as if I had fallen out of love with the theatre, not just because the theatre has fallen into such decline. I am fifty-two years old now, and I don't like much to go out at night. I like to stay home. I listen to music and read and watch television. Quite often I will go to a movie in the afternoon, but I see very little theatre. I have seen only one show since I have been in town, and that was *Sweet Charity*, which I enjoyed very much. I intend to see some other shows, but I keep putting off going.

*Do you read plays at all?*

INGE: Not much. I try and read plays that I think are new or particularly interesting.

*Do you read Albee and Schisgal?*

INGE: No, I go to see their plays and enjoy them very much.

*Do you think we have some promising playwrights?*

INGE: Of course. With all the decline in the theatre generally, there have been some really first-rate playwrights appear in the last ten years. Albee and Schisgal are both marvellous playwrights, and I am interested in seeing anything that they do.

*How about Osborne and Pinter? Do you see their work?*

INGE: Yes, Osborne's early plays. I have never seen the later ones. Pinter's *Caretaker* moved me profoundly. Just the mere fact Albee and Schisgal have appeared on the scene in the past ten years is significant; you can't expect many gifted dramatists to appear in a decade. I think we are fooling ourselves that we are going to suddenly find, or that we have a right to expect, a large number of gifted playwrights. No culture ever did have more than a few at a time.

*How about novelists? Do you read a lot of them?*

INGE: Oh yes, I read lots of novels—but let's stay with the theatre for a bit. The state of the theatre generally can improve. We should have good repertory companies doing classics and doing some of the early American plays that we shouldn't forget. We should remember it as a part of our culture. I think we should have a theatre somewhere that would make us conscious of the dramatic literature that we do have in this country. Yes, I read novels too. Right now I am rereading a novel that came out in the Thirties.

I read it when it first came out—Santayana's *The Last Puritan*. I read it when I was quite young, found I had forgotten what it was about, so I am rereading it now with great interest. It is a beautiful piece of work.

*Do you find that the violent harshness of our time disturbs you?*

INGE: Yes, I do now, and it is just beginning too. I think it has been disturbing me since I reached my late forties. I find now for instance when I first discovered the music of Bartók I was very excited by it because I heard there a contemporary sound that was new, that was part of our time, and Poulenc, and I still am very fond of the music of these men. Today I find myself playing much more Schubert and Brahms and the Beethoven quartets.

*You don't write anything political?*

INGE: No, I am not what you call a social-activist writer at all. I think very little in political terms.

*Do you have any particular feeling about Arthur Miller's refusing to go to the White House?*

INGE: Do you mean Robert Lowell?

*No, I mean Arthur Miller has also come out against the Vietnam policy . . . I don't know whether he was invited or he simply came out against U.S. policy.*

INGE: I have often wondered about Vietnam, and I honestly don't know what to think. I don't know if I know enough as an individual to form an opinion. One day I will think we should be out of there, and another day I think, well, maybe we shouldn't.

*You don't write about social controversy such as the civil-rights movement?*

INGE: No, but I think that in a subtle way *Where's Daddy?* has something to do with civil rights. I wanted to see integration happening onstage, and so I write about a Negro couple and a white couple living in the same apartment building without any friction at all.

*Did you find that after the string of successes that you had that there was a lot of bother? People like me coming along to interview you, television, et cetera—did you find that it wasted a lot of your time or deflected you in any way?*

INGE: No. An interview usually makes you stop and think and reconsider.

*Your early plays had a family theme to a large degree. Has your family been a major factor in your thinking and feelings and beliefs?*

INGE: I guess so.

*Are you still in touch with your family or are your parents deceased?*

INGE: My parents are both deceased, but I have a sister living, and some cousins.

*Do you think you appear at all in any of these plays? For example, I reread* The Dark at the Top of the Stairs *the other night and I had the thought that the little boy was somehow connected with your experience.*

INGE: Yes, I guess I was the little boy. However, it was not an autobiographical play, but I did kind of base a piece of fiction around the members of my family. But they are only very vague resemblances to my family.

*If you have written this current play concerning integration, among other things, I assume then integration is one of the things that concerns you now?*

INGE: Oh yes, very much. I think it is something that has to go through. I think we all have to live as one people. If I want to sound religious about it I'll say that is the problem that God gave us to solve, and I think we have got to solve it. I don't think it will be easy, but I think enough progress has been made since I was a boy so that we have a right to hope.

*Speaking of living together, closeness, do you find that your friends, the people that you spend most of your time with are other writers or are musicians or movie directors or whatever they might be?*

INGE: I have a few writer friends, not many. Oh yes, I have several good writer friends. Well, Jim Herlihy is one.

*Do you spend more time with non-writers than you do with writers?*

INGE: Yes, I think so. Out in California I know several painters and a few directors and very few actors. Actors don't always make very good friends.

*Speaking of actors, would you have any complaint about the quality of actors we have available today?*

INGE: It is harder now in New York and it gets harder every year to cast a play well.

*You mean because the good ones have been taken by the big money to the West Coast?*

INGE: Yes, I saw a couple of productions last year in which I was really shocked at the level of acting—straight productions. They were European plays, and I found that the only actors in them that were really good were the Europeans, the British. The American actor for some reason finds it very difficult to appear at home in a foreign play. I wish that were not so. I don't think it has to be so.

*When they did the television series* Bus Stop *were you involved in that much?*

INGE: Not at all.

*You just sold the title, that's all? Have you done any TV work or doesn't it interest you?*

INGE: Yes, it interests me very much. I love television as a medium. I think the medium is marvellous. Television has come out with the best production of *Hamlet* I have ever seen, *Hamlet of Elsinore* with Christopher Plummer and another first-rate

English actor, Robert Shaw. It was the best one I had ever seen in my life. It is the only *Hamlet* that ever made me forget that I was watching a classic and become so involved in the human conflict I had forgotten that I had seen the play before. I think it is a marvellous medium. I had a play done on the Chrysler Show last fall, an hour show, and it came off quite well.

*You had written that especially for television?*

INGE: It was a one-act play that I had that I adapted for TV, and I thought it came off pretty well. There are, however, many disadvantages to the medium as it stands now. You have to work on such a tight time schedule. Sometimes a play is hurt by time. You have to get finished at a certain time, so sometimes you are finished before the play is really done. It is now a difficult medium for the writer, but I would love to be able to do two or three 'hour shows' a year because I love the hour medium, the hour form. I would like to write more or be able to write more in an one-hour form, but there is just no market for it.

*You spoke about going to the films more than you go to the theatre. Do you think this is becoming a more exciting medium?*

INGE: Yes, there is little in the theatre that could come up to Fellini's 8½. Very little. That was one of the great masterpieces of the century. The theatre has to depend on literary values; the film can depend on pictorial or visual values but it has many more values to employ. The Fellini picture was just like watching a three-ring circus. There was so much going on and it was so filled.

*How about American films?*

INGE: Well, they are kind of disappointing. I think we have to admit.

*You are not a compulsive moviegoer?*

INGE: I don't go unless it's really something I want to see.

*And when you watch television, do you watch anything special?*

INGE: TV is the great passive indulgence in our lives today, but there are a few shows that I have watched with a lot of interest. I think the Dick Van Dyke show is really first-rate. Beautifully done, beautifully written and with a wonderful clean humour that was very contemporary without being dirty at all. Not that I am such a purist in theatre or entertainment.

*Do you think our theatre has got a little 'dirty'?*

INGE: I have never been offended in the theatre, although I know at times I have given offence. I know lots of people were offended by *Natural Affection*.

*Why?*

INGE: Well, I don't know. They just told me they were. The critics wrote about it as though they had been offended. I think I take offence at very little culturally. I think we are at a time in our cultural life when we are trying to realise that many of these things are not dirty, when we are trying to find a new freedom and so when we do use a four-letter word we want the audience to feel that this is not dirty. I know I had a great experience when I went to see LeRoi Jones's *The Toilet* out in California. Buzz Meridith did a beautiful production of it out there, and Al Freeman, Jr., played it beautifully along with Shirley Knight, and I went only out of a feeling of responsibility. I thought this is a new play and I should see it. I was fascinated by it and when I went out of that play I realised that nothing in it had been dirty at all. I had lost all my feeling about dirty language. Nothing in it was dirty. This was a part of life and I actually felt kind of cleansed. There is no such thing as a dirty word on stage; it is only the interpretation.

*Do you think there is an overemphasis on sex in our culture today? I mean items such as the topless-waitress fad out in California? Does that reflect anything in the culture, or just this new liberty we are experiencing?*

INGE: I think we are taking advantage of the new liberty since World War II; I know I was teaching right after World War II and I could tell that the returning GIs had a totally different attitude or they had a brand-new attitude. They weren't going to take any false values or false moral values anymore and I know that in the colleges at that time—I don't know whether the general public knew it or not but in most colleges and universities all over the country—there was a kind of a concern about the liberality of student behaviour that had been influenced by the GIs. There were things happening on campus that had never happened before in the parking lots and so forth, and yet I think that kind of passed after those few postwar years. I was teaching then at Washington University in St Louis, and I had one reading course for GIs in which they were able to read almost anything they wanted from world literature and report on it and get credit for it. We created this course for them simply because they had been away for years and had not been able to do much reading and wanted a chance to do some and get credit for it. So the English Department did create this course for them and I taught one section of it. I noticed the way they reported on books, on the sexual happenings, completely different, very casually and there was no shock or anything.

*What do you think of the young generation of America today? Tennessee thinks they are wonderfully courageous and adventurous and afraid of nothing but their own shadows as he puts it. He meant the civil-rights demonstrations in the South and challenging the clichés of the culture.*

INGE: Well, they are challenging the clichés of the established culture but they are creating clichés of their own. It is hard for me to define that except that I think youth has created, and not just youth but people who are maybe old enough to know better, have created such a thing of being 'in' and of being anti-cliché and being anti- so-called Establishment—that much of this supposedly social behaviour is falsely motivated. It is really more a manifestation of hostility than it is of generosity.

*Do you have any sense of being past fifty, that you are old or ageing or out of touch with these people, the young Americans?*

INGE: Well, I wonder. I don't know if I am in touch with them or not. I know I am to some extent and I know I feel with them in many ways. I will give you one example of what I mean. I met a housewife, not a teen-ager, God knows, in California. She is a notoriously unhappy woman, married to an important man in the film business, and she was taking it upon herself to drive Negro students to white schools and she was getting up early every morning to do this. I don't have to restate or test my own views on integration, but I frankly doubt the motivations of this woman. She was doing it out of hostility—not love or respect for human dignity. She was hitting out at the *status quo* because her own life in it was miserable. She enjoyed the conflict and controversy and attention, the enmity. I suppose people sometimes do worthwhile things for ugly reasons, but I find it pitiful. The thought that some of our young people may be attempting to 'improve' society for such bitter reasons troubles me. I suppose it troubles them too.

# Eugene Ionesco

THIS 1960 INTERVIEW with Eugene Ionesco was conducted by Professor Rosette Lamont of the Department of Romance Languages of Queens College, New York City. She also translated the dialogue from the French for publication in the May 1961 issue of *Horizon*—a publication of the American Heritage Publishing Company.

Ionesco, who has been so often called 'master of black humour' or 'chief representative of the surealistic *avant-garde*' that these terms are cliché evaluations, has been more accurately described by the critic Martin Esslin as 'a serious artist dedicated to the arduous exploration of the realities of the human situation, fully aware of the task that he has undertaken, and equipped with formidable intellectual powers.' He is well educated, modest, impudent and bold, a master of language, witty, imaginative, friendly and totally committed to total theatre. The fact that his first work was described by him as an 'antiplay' does not diminish his commitment.

He does not look like the *provocateur*, the menacing ogre who has aroused Paris and London critics to lengthy denunciation as a threat to good theatre. One English magazine has described him as 'a little man like a quail', and Muriel Reed wrote in *Realités* that 'he is small, round and timid. . . . He is gentle,

mischievous and good-natured. He likes to eat well and to drink
well and he looks like a sort of charming dunce. A very witty dunce,
though, who comes up from time to time with strange and irresis-
tibly funny humour. But in his joking he usually tries to make
himself the butt. He likes to laugh about his hard luck and his
failures.' In an article-interview by Luc Norin published in *Show*,
the playwright appeared as 'Two round eyes, a round nose in a
round head, a round hand that takes yours. Neither tall not short,
neither fat nor thin, Ionesco could be a character in one of his
own plays.'

Eugene Ionesco, the son of a French mother and a Rumanian
father, was born in Slatina in Rumania on 26 November 1912.
He was still a very small child when his family moved to Paris, so
French was his first language and his earliest memories are of the
great city by the Seine. In a much quoted reminiscence originally
published in his article on 'Experience of the Theatre' in the
*Nouvelle Révue Française*, the playwright has written how his
mother 'could not tear me away from the Punch-and-Judy show
at the Luxembourg Gardens. I stayed there, I could stay there,
enrapt, for entire days. The spectacle of the Punch-and-Judy
show held me there, as if stupefied, through the sight of these
puppets that talked, moved, clubbed each other. It was the
spectacle of the world itself, which, unusual, improbable but
truer than truth, presented itself to me in an infinitely simplified
and caricatured form, as if to underline its grotesque and brutal
truth.'

The family lived near the Square de Vaugirard, but shortly
after the boy reached eight he fell ill with anaemia and he and
his nine-year-old sister were sent to board with farmers in the
village of La Chapelle-Anthenaise. Separated from his mother
and troubled by nightmares and odd apparitions 'like figures out
of Breughel or Bosch', young Ionesco was a lonely, sad child.
He dreamed of becoming a saint, then decided to become a
warrior. When he returned to Paris at twelve, he wrote his first
play, which he has since described as a 'patriotic drama'.

The Ionescos did not remain in the French capital very long, and they returned to Bucharest, where the teen-ager finished high school and developed his command of Rumanian. He then studied French at the University of Bucharest, wrote poetry in both languages and produced an extraordinary pamphlet titled *No!* It contained two articles that he had previously had published, one scourging three Rumanian writers as provincial mediocrities and the other lauding them as great literary figures. This prophetic publication was designed, Esslin points out in his excellent book on the Theatre of the Absurd, 'to prove the possibility of holding opposite views on the same subject, and the identity of contraries'.

Following graduation, Ionesco taught French at a Bucharest high school and continued to write—but not for the theatre. He was not to write a play for many years. In 1936 he wed Rodica Burileano, and in 1944 their only child, a daughter, was born. In 1938 Ionesco returned to France on a grant to collect material for a projected thesis on 'the themes of sin and death in French poetry since Baudelaire'. He never wrote it, and for the next ten years the Ionescos lived on the verge of poverty. For a period his wife worked in an attorney's office to supplement their income, and his own job in the production unit of a publishing firm was rewarding neither in stimulation nor remuneration. He regarded himself as a failure, and he often joked about this with such lavish good humour that he began to develop a reputation as a wit. This was only among friends, however, for Ionesco was unknown even in intellectual and *avant-garde* literary circles.

In the world of theatre, he did not exist at all. He has recalled that in these years he enjoyed fiction, essays, films, concerts and art shows—but emphatically detested the theatre. It seemed so crude, mechanical and lacking in poetry or imagination. He has written how 'it was the presence on the stage of flesh-and-blood people that embarrassed me. Their material presence destroyed the fiction. I was confronted, as it were, by two planes of reality—the concrete, material, impoverished empty, limited reality of these living, everyday human beings, moving about and talking on the stage, and the reality of the imagination, the two face to face and not coinciding, unable to be brought into relation with each other; two antagonistic worlds incapable of being unified.'

Ionesco preferred the fiction, the imagination, and in that he chose the world and ways of the artist who imposes his own vision on nature to present the fundamentals of nature and man more profoundly and truthfully. It is his rejection of reality in deed and in dialogue, as usually presented on the modern stage, that has offended so many critics. 'M. Ionesco royally takes everyone for fools,' Parisian critic Jean-Jacques Gautier has complained, and Kenneth Tynan wrote in an *Observer* review of *The Chairs* that 'Words, the magic innovation of our species, are dismissed as useless and fraudulent. . . . M. Ionesco certainly offers an "escape from realism": but an escape into what? A blind alley, perhaps . . . or a self-imposed vacuum . . . or, best of all, a funfair ride on a ghost train. . . . M. Ionesco's theatre is pungent and exciting, but it remains a diversion. It is not on the main road: and we do him no good, nor the drama at large, to pretend that it is.' For those who keep scorecards, Kenneth Tynan had earlier written about another production of the same play that 'Here is pure theatre . . . Ionesco is more than a word-juggler. He is a supreme theatrical conjuror.'

Ionesco came to this later controversial use of language in the course of studying a language, his 1948 effort to learn English via the Assimil records. This rote learning brought him to his unique vision of language and its inadequacy as a means of communication, as well as its primitive truths. 'Conscientiously I copied whole sentences from my primer with the purpose of memorising them,' he later reported in an article published in *Spectacles*. 'Re-reading them attentively, I learned not English but some astonishing truths—that, for example, there are seven days in the week, something I already knew; that the floor is down, the ceiling up, things I already knew but that I have never seriously thought about or had forgotten, and that seemed to me—suddenly—as stupefying as they were indisputably true.'

The Assimil lessons featured an imaginary English couple named Mr and Mrs Smith who engaged in this sort of fantastic dialogue, obviously written by the same bard who created 'my aunt's pen is on the table' and other lasting works. Ionesco, who hated theatre or thought he did, abruptly found himself 'compelled' to write a play about Mr and Mrs Smith and such 'brainless' conversation filled with pseudo-truisms. It was a difficult and disturbing experience for the thirty-seven-year-old Ionesco. 'While writing the play (for it had become a kind of play or anti-play, that is, a parody of a play—a comedy of comedy) I felt dizzy, sick, nauseated. I had to interrupt my work from time to time and, wondering all the while what demon was prodding me on, lie down on my couch for fear of seeing my work sink into nothingness, and me with it.'

Ionesco's goal was a serious dramatic presentation of 'the tragedy of language', and while he had deliberately chosen this droll technique for the dialogue he was somewhat surprised when his first reading of the script to friends produced great amusement. Not quite dismayed, he took their enthusiasm as encouragement and sent this play to several important producers—including Jean-Louis Barrault. They all rejected it, but it came to the attention of the *avant-garde* group at the Theatre de Poche late in 1949, and twenty-three-year-old director Nicholas Bataille persuaded Ionesco to let him stage the new work. During the course of rehearsals in April 1950 an actor inadvertently erred in reciting a line about a blond teacher and substituted another phrase that Ionesco found much more comic-relevant to his goals. The work was rewritten to include mention of the newly invented character, and the play was renamed *The Bald Prima Donna*.

On the evening of 11 May 1950, *The Bald Prima Donna*—openly billed as an anti-play—opened at the small Théâtre des Noctambules in Paris. At the beginning, the audience laughed at the 'banal and nonsensical conversation' of the Smiths, but when the dialogue continued along the same unusual track the mood of the theatregoers chilled slowly but steadily. Although two reviews were favourable, the bulk of the critics rejected the play, and the efforts of the actors—who paraded the streets with signs advertising the play before each performance—were of little avail.

Some performances saw only three seats filled—with Mr and Mrs Ionesco in two of them—and the play closed in six weeks.

Ionesco was not defeated; indeed, he suddenly found theatre exciting, challenging, irresistible. He next wrote *The Lesson*, which was staged with a similar lack of popular acceptance in 1951. By the time his third extraordinary work, *The Chairs*, which he labelled a 'tragic farce', opened in 1952, the playwright was beginning to generate some interest, and a significant number of Parisian critics attended the premiere. Their reviews were emphatically 'mixed', to use the polite euphemism. To be sure, *The Chairs* did a bit better at the box office than *The Bald Prima Donna* had managed. There were no longer nights when only three seats were filled. Now the average was ten.

Even as indomitable and self-contained a personality as Eugene Ionesco could not help but be disappointed, but he kept coming to the theatre—'returning to the scene of the crime', a psychoanalyst might say—each night stubbornly. One evening, he recalls wryly, something different happened. As he entered the lobby he heard 'just what every playwright dreams of hearing: laughter, applause and a happy crowd. I rushed into the theatre: it was as empty and gloomy as ever. In a hall next door, a group of Zionists were holding an enthusiastic meeting.'

It is interesting to note that these three plays have all since been produced frequently and, generally, successfully in many lands. Ionesco's early works stand up. This is not very common, for it is much more usual for a writer to produce a few faltering or mediocre plays that are later forgotten when he 'hits his stride'. To resume the chronology, *Victims of Duty* followed in 1954 and *How to Get Rid of It* (*Amedée*) opened the same year. Whether it was the dialogue, the tragedy of the loveless couple or the fantasy of the huge growing corpse, this play drew audiences, and Ionesco was no longer a failure. *Jack, or The Submission* was similarly well received in 1955, and in 1956 a new production of *The Chairs* suddenly erupted as a major hit. The opening-night applause sent Ionesco fleeing from the theatre in panic, but the next day's front page of *Le Figaro* was even worse—or better, depending on your point of view. Playwright Jean Anouilh's review said 'You must see *The Chairs*. I believe that it is better than Strindberg because it has black humour in the style of Moliére, in a way which is insanely funny at times, and that it is frightful, witty, poignant and always real.'

That did it. Overnight, Ionesco was no longer 'out'; he was *the* 'in' playwright in Paris. When *The Lesson* and *The Bald Prima Donna* were revived on a double bill that summer, they ran for 300 performances. In 1957 *The New Tenant*, reportedly written in three days in 1953, finally reached Paris after earlier productions in Helsinki and London. It has been quite usual for Ionesco's plays to be preceded by an earlier published short story in which he explored the theme and story, and it has been equally common for the plays to be produced several years after they were written —often after some other play that he finished a year or two later. Even though he is internationally acclaimed, Ionesco does not follow the pattern of more orthodox dramatists such as John Osborne or Edward Albee, whose works often go into production within weeks of completion. Their theatre—their world— is much more 'orderly'.

The two Ionesco plays that have attracted most attention in the United States are *The Killer*, his second full-length work which he finished writing while in London in August 1957, and *Rhinoceros*, first performed in English and on radio on the BBC on 20 August 1959. Both plays shared the character of the almost Chaplinesque Bérenger, and some critics have said that *The Killer*, which failed in its initial New York production in April 1960, is Ionesco's best work. Yet, as Esslin pointed out, 'The era of Ionesco's international acceptance as a major figure in the theatre undoubtedly dawned with *Rhinoceros*.' Ionesco told interviewer Peter Gelbard in 1962 that 'the rhinoceros is a symbol of any kind of totalitarianism, Communism, Fascism or any collective hysteria—religion or even advertising slogans.' In a splendidly revealing talk with Vieri Tucci that appeared in *Mademoiselle* in April 1961, the playwright described *Rhinoceros* more broadly as 'a denunciation of the evils of politics, of political passions, of dreams of glory, of grandeur and imperialism. Primarily it is the experience of Nazism that is at the base of the play. It's a political play against political fanaticism, against all these slogans that assail us. It reasserts the idea of private life, of relations with other people, of how people can live together. That's the big problem: how can one live and how can people live together.'

Ionesco has explained, as John Arden does elsewhere in this volume, that it is for the dramatist to ask the provocative questions but not necessarily to try to answer them definitively. He continues to write in his own special way, a way that defies the convenient categorisation of either '*avant-garde*' or 'absurd', about the things that interest him. His way may not be quite the conventional one, but it is rooted in his reality. His vision is one that an increasing number of theatregoers accept, and Ionesco is probably correct when he says that 'The public understands what I am trying to do better than the critics do.'

He frankly admits that his work is much less complex than many so-called intellectuals seem to see it, that a few basic themes such as death and human communication recur. 'Every author has two or three problems of his own that he tries to solve in his work,' he told Peter Gelbard. 'In all my plays, the same themes and obsessions reappear—treated differently. . . . My theatre is not intellectual. It's a simple theatre, an elementary theatre of obsessions and images. I want to go beyond the "social categories" to arrive at the universal. It exists, it is true. Barriers between people are false—they must be surmounted.'

W. W.

HARDLY ANY modern dramatist has caused so much critical soul-searching as Eugene Ionesco. The problem, not at all simplified by the playwright's own whimsical and contradictory pronouncements about his writing and intentions, has been to determine whether his plays 'mean' anything beyond their glittery surface of verbal fuming, and whether it matters if they do. *Rhinoceros*, at least, had an obvious significance, critics and audience could discuss happily; the interview that follows was recorded in French shortly before the New York opening of *Rhinoceros* in July 1961.

Ionesco is forty-eight, born in Rumania, the only son of a French mother and Rumanian father. His early years were spent in France. He was living in Rumania when the Iron Guard began to gain power, and, like his hero Bérenger in *Rhinoceros*, he felt that he couldn't give in to the rise of the cult. He left his job—he was teaching French in a *lycée*—and took his bride of some months back to France, where he started working towards a doctorate in French letters. His love of language, his bizarre manipulation of it, is one of the salient characteristics of his art. He has predilection for puns and word games, and each of his plays is animated by the poetic power of ambiguity, not only in the action of his characters but also in the meaning of the words they use.

There are thirteen plays, of which the first—presented in 1950—was *The Bald Prima Donna*. They bear equivocal designations—comic drama, tragic farce, pseudo-drama—and with them Ionesco is often said to have evolved a new theatrical genre: the metaphysical farce, a twentieth-century morality play which does not preach.

The literary ancestors of this genre are the surrealists, the symbolists, the Dadaists, and, in particular, an *enfant terrible* named Alfred Jarry, who wrote the first metaphysical farce, *Ubu Roi*, while he was still in school. It was performed in 1896. In this raucous play there appears for the first time, practiced by a character called Père Ubu, a science called 'Pataphysics—a mock philosophy in which Ionesco is deeply interested. It has been described as 'the science of the realm beyond metaphysics'. In 1948 Jarry's followers honoured his invention of the science by creating the College of 'Pataphysics. It is an august body with a publication of its own, *Cahiers du College de 'Pataphysique*, and an absurdly involved hierarchy of rulers and commissions under the supervision of a Vice-Curator, six Proveditors-General, officials of the Rogation and Executive Organon, and a Corps of Satraps. The college is actually a spoof on all academies, existing forms of government, and official bodies, with particular emphasis on such trappings as honours, processionals, decorations, and titles. Ionesco claims he is very proud of belonging to the group and of being honoured with the title of Satrap. Other Satraps include Raymond Queneau, author of the best seller *Zazie dans le métro*; the film director René Clair; and the artists Marcel Duchamp and Jean Dubuffet.

Ionesco's view of the world is by no means as flippant as might be suggested by his association with the college. His plays often seem to have been written only to amuse by their clever twists of situation and language; but even a short conversation with Ionesco reveals his fundamental seriousness. His demeanour is serious, his voice slow and measured—but then suddenly one is aware of the duality: he smiles, a quick childlike smile revealing teeth the size of milk teeth; the hair at the sides of his head is usually long, surrounding his face with a fringe, like a parted stage curtain, from which he peers out, wary and amused.

R. *Lamont*

IONESCO: If I don't answer your questions right away, you mustn't mind me. Any constructive thinking one does is done at the rate of an hour per month, and the rest of the time we exploit what we have achieved in this hour of grace. At the end of two weeks the substance is drained, and we utter only stupidities.

*Let me start with a factual question, then. You have been known as a dramatist for only the last ten years. Your first play,* The Bald Prima Donna, *was presented in 1950. What kind of work did you do before that time?*

IONESCO: Employee in a publishing firm, teacher, journalist, labourer, unemployed intellectual, scholarship student in the keep of the French government, white-collar worker, bureaucrat.

*Did you ever write a play before* The Bald Prima Donna?

IONESCO: I wrote my first play at the age of eleven. It was a patriotic play.

*When were you conscious of having become a writer?*

IONESCO: I am less conscious of having become a writer than a businessman. I spend the greater part of my time calling people and receiving calls, signing contracts, fighting with my agents, running to my lawyer. For this activity, which takes a lot of my time, I've had to engage a secretary. My typist used to be a nice old lady. Now it's a bearded young man. But you know, there's something pleasant about all this fussing around. At a time of sterility, such as now, after I've dictated six or seven letters, spoken to a journalist, given a lecture I've done nothing, but at least I have the feeling I've worked.

*Do you write every day?*

IONESCO: In principle, yes. Actually, no.

*But I am speaking of a creative period in your life.*

IONESCO: For some time now I have decided I ought to work every day, so I do, even if it's only for five minutes.

*How do you and your secretary work together?*

IONESCO: I dictate. If I'm not satisfied with what I have dictated, I use the text as a rough draft for future dictation. Sometimes I make things up on the spur of the moment, and at other times I come with a written text to use as a point of reference. Sometimes I write something at home and come with it all ready for dictation. As you see, it varies a great deal.

*Do you dictate your plays because you like to hear the way a line sounds—test it out, so to speak?*

IONESCO: I wish I could say that. Actually it's because I'm far too lazy to write. I can't sit down at a table any longer. The idea of picking up a pen and writing sickens me.

*What about typing? Do you ever sit down at a typewriter to write?*

IONESCO: Yes, all the time. I sit down at the typewriter, and then I don't write because I can't type.

*What about the creative act itself?*

IONESCO: I used to have to walk, now I sleep. Many people get their best ideas at that moment in the morning between sleep and waking. I get up and write down as many thoughts as I can. However, it's become increasingly difficult. Ideas seem to flee from me. When I stand motionless, they take to their heels. When I'm lying down, I feel that today things will work out, but as soon as I get out of bed my ideas fall at my feet like broken pitchers. Nothing at all remains.

*What appears in your mind first: an image, a character, a situation, a word?*

IONESCO: It used to be a line of dialogue, as in cartoons or comic strips. You see a character saying something, and what he says appears as the caption. And so I used to see first the written words, then the characters speaking these words, then the complete picture, and it would all tie up neatly. Now all this has changed. I write with great difficulty. It takes me months and months to finish a play. Sometimes the act of writing seems meaningless to me now, absolutely meaningless.

*What you are saying reminds me that some people claim you were happier when you were less successful, when your audience was made up of three or four good friends, your wife, and your daughter.*

IONESCO: It's true that I feel that the struggle is over. Maybe I'm just getting old and weary. But of course one has to earn a living.

*How did success come to you?*

IONESCO: Raymond Queneau, the novelist, helped me a great deal. He came to see my play *The Bald Prima Donna*. It was being given in a tiny theatre, Le Théâtre des Noctambules. Queneau had just published his *Exercises de style*, and he understood perfectly the kind of word game I used in my play. He liked it, and the next day he brought Armand Salacrou, the dramatist, and later Jean Paulhan and some others. Then at a cocktail party at Gallimard, where he worked at the time, he posted himself at the door and told every one of the two hundred guests: 'Did you see Ionesco's *The Bald Prima Donna*? Well, you must.' No one had heard of Ionesco but that's how it started.

*Did any other French writer help you in starting?*

IONESCO: Yes, Jean Anouilh. By writing an article in *Le Figaro* the day before *The Chairs* was supposed to close. He gave me quite a build-up. Now he doesn't like me and Beckett. I guess we've become too successful to be safe.

*What about the title of your first play.* The Bald Prima Donna? *After all, there is no bald soprano in the play.*

IONESCO: That's precisely the point. Actually, the title used to be *English Without Toil*, because I derived the whole idea for the play from a conversation text by that name, the Assimil method. At one time I wanted to learn English, and though, as you can see, I never succeeded, I became fascinated with this textbook. In it you meet a number of people—Mr and Mrs Smith, Mr Martin—and all of them seem amazed at their own existence. They have the need to explain the simplest things, such as where they are, what they like to eat, who is married to whom. I decided to put these characters on the stage. People misunderstood my intention; they assumed I was laughing at the bourgeoisie, whereas I was trying to evolve a free, pure comic style similar to that of the Marx Brothers in the movies.

*But this still doesn't explain the title.*

IONESCO: That's a well-known story, and I've told it many times. It happened by pure accident. Nicolas Bataille, my director, did not like the original title. During a rehearsal one of the actors flubbed his lines. In the text I had something about a blond prima donna, but he said 'bald prima donna'. We all laughed, and the mistake became the title of the play. Of course, we also changed the reference within the play. This made it even wilder—which is exactly what I was aiming for.

*Would you say that* The Lesson *and* The Chairs *still belong to your first period?*

IONESCO: I would say that three plays belong to my first manner: *The Bald Prima Donna*, *The Lesson* and *Jack*. These three plays were exercises. I wanted to set in motion the mechanism of the theatre. I was trying to depict the progression of an aimless passion. In *The Lesson*, for example, comedy changes to tragedy. The play is a ceremonial of murder. It was in this play that I became conscious of dramatic structure.

*Were you aiming for a kind of purity of style?*

IONESCO: I wanted to divest the theatrical language of its literary aspects. Like the cubist painters, I wished to find the joints of my art and show them in motion.

*But what about* The Chairs? *Does that play belong to the same period?*

IONESCO: No. In *The Chairs* I tried for a kind of amplification. Objects themselves became a language. I wanted to find a visual language, a language of the stage more direct, more shocking and stronger than that of words. You see, the artist is seldom able to renew literary themes. There are few new themes. What he can do is renew language.

*What about* Rhinoceros? *It is, after all, a much more traditional kind of play.*

IONESCO: That's true. This does not mean I'm going to keep on writing this way, but everyone assumes as much. All the people who were once my enemies are now welcoming me into the fold, and my friends have turned against me. My friends want me to remain true to myself, and by that they mean that I have no right to change.

*Are you thinking of a play right now?*

IONESCO: I've been thinking for some time of a play in which I would speak of death. I wish to describe the agony of a dying man. I am thinking of putting on the stage a dying king. This monarch might represent perishing modern values. So many things go through my mind when I read the papers, and I get annoyed by what I read. Somehow it has all crystallised around a central theme, that of death, of the agony of a king. Yet at the same time I don't seem to be able to come to grips with my subject. Perhaps it is because this is the deepest, the greatest anguish of my being, and there is a kind of psychic refusal.

*Haven't you already treated the theme of death in* The Killer?

IONESCO: The theme of *The Killer* is evil, fundamental aggressiveness without reason, almost without hatred. A kind of divine principle of destruction.

*You use the same hero in* The Killer *and in* Rhinoceros—Bérenger, *a modest, frightened, yet courageous man.*

IONESCO: He is the hero in spite of himself. He's terribly frightened but he says to himself that no one seems to be doing anything, and that someone *has* to do something even if that someone is as insignificant as himself. He has the feeling that he is struggling against the whole world, that he alone can save the world. Of course he knows all along that it isn't so, but he acts as thought it were.

*Is Bérenger an aspect of yourself?*

IONESCO: I suppose so. When I was in Rumania as an adolescent I witnessed the rise of fascism. Everyone around me joined the Iron Guard. Everyone except me. Somehow, I did not espouse the reigning ideology. To this day I still don't know how it happened. All I know is that I was quite alone. It took twenty years for that to appear in a play.

*Is* Rhinoceros *then concerned with the individual's struggle against a rising political ideology?*

IONESCO: It is wider than that. It depicts a struggle against any tyrannical and dogmatic system, any ideology that becomes an idolatry, be it of East or West. It makes the Brechtians quite mad. I don't care for didactic theatre. The theatre is an autonomous system of expression. It cannot be the illustration of an ideology. Anyway, all affirmations are stupid. Only second-class minds, grade-B intellectuals, make violent affirmations.

*Would you name one such intellectual among your contemporaries?*

IONESCO: Sartre. He's a superior kind of fool. Like most intellectuals he gives in to brute force, he admires it. First he reads Heidegger and Husserl and becomes their disciple. Why? Because at that time Germany is a strong country, and political power gets confused in his mind with cultural vitality. Then, after the defeat of Germany, he becomes a humanist and an existentialist. Now, existentialism was at its beginning a philosophy of the absurd; how can it become humanistic? Still, that's the way the wind blows. Then Russia becomes powerful. So of course Sartre turns Marxist. Marxism is a religion, a mystique. And yet Sartre the intellectual, the clear, lucid mind, takes up the cult. I believe that Sartre's ideology, his noble sentiments, spring from envy and jealousy. He wants to speak to Khrushchev; he goes to Brazil to attack De Gaulle—what does it all mean? Spite. Sartre would like to be a politician or at least a diplomat. His is the case of a lost vocation.

*Doesn't he think of himself as a kind of lucid conscience in the world, a guiding prophet?*

IONESCO: Exactly—except that he's shortsighted and timid. Like all timid people he gives in to the power of historical events. Then he flies to the rescue of history. What is interesting in a man is not to know *what* he thinks but to discover *why* he thinks what he thinks. Sartre is motivated by self-hatred. Most French intellectuals nowadays are masochists. They hate French nationalism, and yet they worship all nationalistic feelings which are not French. They all hate Malraux, who's the best of them all.

They hate him because he has a cabinet post. In fact, when at the end of the first performance of *Rhinoceros* I was called out on the stage and saluted Malraux, who was sitting in his box, I was denounced bitterly. I was called a rhinoceros myself for making this gesture.

*What do you think of De Gaulle?*

IONESCO: I think he is an admirable, lonely man who wants to save France.

*And the French intellectuals are fascinated by Khrushchev?*

IONESCO: They are. You cannot imagine how excited everyone got over his shoe. When he took off his shoe at the United Nations General Assembly and started banging on the table with it, I felt as though his shoe were on *my* table, as though he were insulting me personally, but the French intellectuals were delighted. Their suspicion of the United States, its philanthropy, is to my mind one of the greatest injustices of history.

*What do you think of Arthur Adamov, who writes in the same vein as you do but is a leftist writer and a great admirer of Brecht?*

IONESCO: We used to be great friends till my plays caught on. Adamov was present at a performance of *The Chairs* when there were three or four people in the audience. He was wild with excitement. He paced the room, waved his arms, said it was magnificent. Empty seats on the stage, empty seats in the theatre. '*Ça a de la gueule!*' he shouted. As soon as I became a little more successful, he became my bitter enemy. As for his political ideology—which is as shifty as any I have ever known—I've always thought it an effect of his disappointments as a writer.

*Do you like his plays?*

IONESCO: Yes. I particularly like the early ones, *La Parodie* and *Le Professeur Taranne*.

*And Camus, did you know him?*

IONESCO: Poor Camus. We became friends about five months before he died. Before that he did not like me very much. He didn't consider that I took life too seriously. But shortly before his death he spoke of one of my plays over the radio. I was in the theatre rehearsing *Rhinoceros* the day he died. Someone called out Barrault and told him, and then Barrault walked out on the stage and told us. Simone Valère started crying, and the rehearsal was stopped. Then Barrault ordered the rehearsal to go on after fifteen minutes. The following day, however, he could not show up.

*People have called Camus' death absurd.*

IONESCO: That is stupid. The only absurd thing is life itself.

*Some people say that you criticise the bourgeoisie in your plays, while others call you a bourgeois writer. Which are you?*

IONESCO: That is the reason of my visit to the United States. I have come on a secret mission, which is to rehabilitate the bourgeoisie.

*This does not seem to go together with your membership in the Collège de 'Pataphysique. How do you reconcile the two?*

IONESCO: One can say anything about 'Pataphysics. Everything is true.

*What is the Collège de 'Pataphysique?*

IONESCO: It's a club.

*Is the whole thing a big practical joke?*

IONESCO: Oh, no, it's extremely serious. You see, 'Pataphysics has always existed. It's universal.

*Do 'pataphysicians, of which you are one, hold meetings?*

IONESCO: From time to time, for promotions, decorations, commemorations, and pilgrimages. It's all very earnest.

*Just like the French Academy?*

IONESCO: Much more. We have no uniforms, but we have insignia. For example, I am decorated with the Ordre de la Grande Gidouille [the Big Belly]. That's from Jarry's *Ubu Roi*. And I have the rank of Satrap. I'm very honoured to belong to this group.

*Who are the great 'pataphysicians?*

IONESCO: Raymond Queneau, Jacques Prévert, and Boris Vian before he died, were among them, but I believe that the actual rulers of 'Pataphysics are secret. Queneau, Dubuffet, René Clair and myself—we're a front. We're there for glory. The real head of the Collège de 'Pataphysique is a gentleman by the name of Salmon, who died recently and was reincarnated under the name of Latisane. I believe it's the same one.

*And who is Latisane?*

IONESCO: It's Salmon.

*And this Latisane, what does he do in life?*

IONESCO: He has a double who is a teacher. The Vice-Curator of the Collège de 'Pataphysique and the Perpetual President of the Supreme Council of Grand Masters of the Ordre de la Grande Gidouille is His Magnificance, Baron Jean Mollet.

*Who is Mollet?*

IONESCO: He was the secretary of Guillaume Apollinaire the poet, author of *Calligrammes* and *Alcools*. His avocation is cooking.

*How was he elected to this position?*

IONESCO: By unanimous vote, the only elector being Raymond Queneau. This is in the democratic tradition of the Collège de 'Pataphysique. Raymond Queneau wrote the name of Mollet on the ballot, cast the ballot in the urn, removed it himself, and thus the Baron was elected.

*Can 'Pataphysics be compared to any philosophy or body of thought?*

IONESCO: In my opinion, 'Pataphysics is occidental Zen.

*How do you become a 'pataphysician?*

IONESCO: One does not become a 'pataphysician, one *is* a 'pataphysician. For example, if you commit suicide, you are a 'pataphysician, and if you choose not to kill yourself, you are still a 'pataphysician. I was lecturing once to a group of foreign students, and at the end of the lecture one of them raised his hand and asked a very tricky question: 'Are you a conscious or an unconscious 'pataphysician?'

*What would you answer to such a question?*

IONESCO: I believe that the conscious 'pataphysicians are unconscious and the unconscious 'pataphysicians are conscious.

*What are some of the conscious or unconscious activities of a 'pataphysician?*

IONESCO: The best activity is to refrain from all activity. That is why one of the greatest living 'pataphysicians is the Satrap Marcel Duchamp, the painter who anticipated Dadaism and who has been living in the United States. He now refrains from painting and devotes his life to playing chess.

*Does a 'pataphysician take vows?*

IONESCO: Each one takes his own.

*And what vows have you taken as Satrap of the College de 'Pataphysique?*

IONESCO: As Satrap I am for war and tyranny. I will exercise tyranny myself. As for war, I will have others wage it because I can't do two things at once.

*You have been influenced by the surrealists, and the Dadaists, haven't you? In fact, the 'pataphysicians are, in a sense, Dadaists?*

IONESCO: All of us came out of surrealism.

*What do you think of André Breton?*

IONESCO: There are two men in France to whom you must listen without interruption. One is Cocteau, the most brilliant conversationalist I have encountered, and the other is André Breton—Cocteau because he is dazzling and Breton because he does not brook any interference, not even a question.

*Among your contemporaries, whom do you consider the best dramatist in France?*

IONESCO: Samuel Beckett.

*Are you friends?*

IONESCO: Yes. We see each other rarely, but we're good friends. Beckett is a fine fellow. He lives in the country with his wife, but we see each other when he comes in, at the theatre, in cafés, in *brasseries*.

*Do you talk about the theatre? What do you talk about?*

IONESCO: We don't talk about anything much. He is a very generous man, very loyal. Those are rare qualities. I was told that for a long time his principal occupation was to play chess by himself.

*And Jean Genet, do you know him?*

IONESCO: Oh, yes, we meet in literary salons.

*Does he still steal?*

IONESCO: Possibly, just a little to keep up his reputation. You see, after a society woman has invited him, her friends call her to find out what is missing, and she is so happy if she can answer that it's an ashtray or a fork. So Genet obliges his hostess. He's a very decent sort of fellow.

*Is he rough in appearance and language?*

IONESCO: Oh, no, he's *un homme de lettres*. In fact, he writes a little too well, don't you think? Like Giraudoux. That's his greatest fault.

*What other contemporary dramatists do you admire?*

IONESCO: Friedrich Dürrenmatt and Boris Vian. Vian wrote a very interesting play *The Empire Builders*, a play which was badly received because it was very good, of course.

*It is obvious from your Molièresque impromptu,* The Shepherd's Chameleon, *that you do not think much of critics.*

IONESCO: The trouble with most of them is that they want the artist to conform to some pre-established law of their invention.

*What is it that you mean when you speak of 'anti-theatre'?*

IONESCO: The anti-theatre is the theatre. The so-called theatrical plays are anti-theatrical. They are false, full of tricks, too neat. The language is too literary, too beautiful. I am looking for something bare, something essential.

*Who are those dramatists who have influenced you?*

IONESCO: Theatrical works have left almost no impression on me. I've read them in school, but I was completely detached from them. The works that have influenced me are works of philosophy and possibly some novels. There was a time when I liked Kafka very much; then at another time I liked Dostoevsky, Chekhov, Proust.

*Didn't you mention once that you wanted to write a play based on Proust's* Remembrance of Things Past?

IONESCO: Yes. I'm in the process of re-reading the whole thing now. I don't know what will remain. At times I am tempted by what is theatrical in Proust—the dinner at the house of Madame Verdurin, the reception at the Guermantes'. All this is fine theatre. I am also tempted by what is less theatrical about the work. But in what terms does one work out a visualisation of the passion of jealousy? It's very difficult.

*Since we're on the subject of Proust and your own interest in the novel, I would like to ask if you ever thought of writing one yourself.*

IONESCO: Yes. I'm thinking of writing a novel which would be called *La Vase* [*Slime*]. It would be a novel of decomposition and reintegration. It would happen in a ditch. I would tell the story of a man who is in the process of decomposition and who is slowly sinking in the mud. He loses a leg, then an arm, then his whole body begins to decompose, until what remains is a vague contour in the mud, a form vaguely outlined in the slime.

*This ties in with your projected play about the dying king, doesn't it? Death is your leading preoccupation, or, as you call it, obsession?*

IONESCO: That's obvious.

*Do you recall when you first became conscious of death?*

IONESCO: I was four years old, and I was with my mother in a room. We looked out the window, and there was a burial procession passing by. I asked my mother what it was, and she told me a man had died. Then I asked her how people came to die, and she said that it happened to them when they were old and sick. 'And what does it mean to grow old?' I asked. 'Does it mean that you hunch over more and more, and that you grow a white beard which gets longer and longer?' Yes, she said. 'And does everyone grow old and die?' And she said yes again. Then I started to scream and to cry. I must have cried for hours.

*Were you religious as a child?*

IONESCO: I wanted to be a saint. I went to church dutifully. Then one day a school chum offered me the first scientific refutation of the existence of God that I had heard. We were seven or eight at the time. My friend asked me where God was, and I told him that God was in heaven. 'If God is in heaven,' he said, 'then how come we cannot see the bare soles of his feet right above us in the air?' To this day his argument seems to me to make as much sense as any of the longer philosophical discussions I have read on this side of the question.

*Do you believe in an after-life?*

IONESCO: Who can tell? What I am certain of is that if it exists, it is bizarre.

*Death, destruction and old age are your dominant themes, it seems.*

IONESCO: Yes, but also beauty and sex. *Jack* is a highly erotic play, and so is *The Lesson*. Erotic possession is the hidden meaning of *The Lesson*. In *Jack* not much is hidden.

*Jack is the play about a bride with three noses. I am wondering what your idea of beauty is.*

IONESCO: The bride in *Jack* has three faces rather than three noses. She was very beautiful in the Paris production. I think that when a type of beauty appears, it always seems ugly at first because it astonishes. Then it becomes beauty. Look at the actress Melina Mercouri in Jules Dassin's film *Never on Sunday*. She's probably the most beautiful woman in the world, and yet in a way she seems ugly. She's ugly and beautiful at once. Beauty is never pretty. It surprises first and then captivates and attaches.

*Could we end with a fundamental question: What do you consider the function of theatre?*

IONESCO: The only function of the theatre, if we must speak of function, is to be theatre, to *be*. Do we ask of a flower what function it serves? It simply exists, just as existence exists. The theatre must teach people that there are activities which do not serve any purpose, which are gratuitous. Modern man does not understand that what is useful is more often than not a useless, crushing weight. Have you ever watched the inhabitants of a large city? They are harried creatures, prisoners of necessity. They run like dogs, their noses to the ground, along a well-traced course. They ought to walk like cats, aimlessly, slowly, gracefully. In our time people are terribly frightened of freedom and humour. They don't seem to realise that there is no life possible without these qualities. In that sense the theatre is a supreme game: it is free action, and in it one must find a living language, not the language of realism but one that is based on the marvellous, fabled world, which has far greater reality than the so-called real world. The theatre is the incarnation of dreams, of phantasmagoria. Bourgeois unrealism such as we find in the Broadway drama or the *théâtre des boulevards,* and socialistic unrealism as in the Brechtian plays, are the two greatest dangers which threaten the creative forces of the theatre. A work of art is above all an adventure of the mind; it is the creation of an autonomous world introduced into our world from fundamental truths—which are those we find in dream and imagination.

# *Harold  Pinter*

THE FOLLOWING is an excerpt from an interview taped by
Lawrence M. Bensky in London in 1966 for publication in *The
Paris Review.* The full text has been published in the January 1967
issue of that lively international journal, and the published transcript is the distillation of Bensky's two conversations with the
playwright in his office situated on the fifth floor of his 1820
house facing Regents Park in London. Pinter lives there with his
attractive wife, actress Vivien Merchant (whom he married on 14
September 1956), and with his son, Daniel.

Harold Pinter was born in London on 10 October 1930, son
of Hyman Pinter and Frances Mann Pinter. His father was a
Jewish tailor in East London, as was Arnold Wesker's father.
The resemblance basically ends there, for while Wesker is
'committed' to drama with some message or social cause Harold
Pinter has a much greater interest in the problem of self—the
individual human. He has often been compared with Eugene
Ionesco because of this, and criticised by the same people who
deplore Ionesco's indifference to political ideas, mass movements
and social problems. Kenneth Tynan raised this during a 1960
radio interview on the British Broadcasting Corporation's Home
Service, and Pinter then answered that he was focusing on his
characters 'at the extreme edge of their living, where they are
living pretty much alone'.

The key word, if there is one, may be 'alone', for this sense of isolation as a widespread quiet horror—as part of the human condition today—is a recurrent theme in Pinter's fascinating works. His subtly haunted plays are populated by characters who initially seem very ordinary, who struggle to avoid speaking the unspeakable but who nevertheless communicate its mysteries and terrors. Suspense, fear and expectation are so often and expertly used in his dramas that more than one critic has suggested that Pinter has been influenced by the films of Alfred Hitchcock.

Pinter finished his formal academic education at sixteen, studied acting at the Royal Academy of Dramatic Art and the Central School of Speech and Drama in London. He emerged as a respectably competent actor, and spent several years performing under the stage name of David Baron. Why he chose not to use his real name is not clear. In any case, he toured Ireland with a Shakespearean group and spent years in a great variety of roles in provincial repertory. John Osborne also developed his theatrical skills via years of apprenticeship as an actor, and both playwrights have said that this experience behind the footlights was useful.

Pinter has continued to act off and on until fairly recently, primarily in television versions of or revivals of his own works. He has also written a number of exceptionally good television plays which have subsequently been produced on the stage, and he has contributed several first-class film scripts that earned him large sums of money. It is said that fees from these film-writing assignments enabled him to purchase and renovate the Regents Park house. Harold Pinter has also directed some productions of his own plays, and in general works very closely with the director when someone else holds that position of responsibility. The dramatist recently admitted that there may be more than one way to direct a Pinter play, 'but always around the same central truth of the play'.

Harold Pinter's career has included at least one other type of work, toil of a sort that may have contributed to his writing, as Arnold Wesker's labours as a pastry cook helped with *The Kitchen*.

When the 1958 pregnancy of his actress-wife precluded their future touring the provinces, the young and then little-known writer rented a basement flat in a dreary part of London. To pay the rent, Pinter bartered his services as, yes, the caretaker.

As the interview that follows sets forth, Pinter wrote his first play, titled *The Room*, in four frantic days when he was only twenty-seven. 'Hooked' by the reaction of the University of Bristol audience to his one-act 'first-born', the dramatist promptly set to work writing a full-length play that was to be produced as *The Birthday Party*. This first Pinter work to be staged professionally in London came to the Lyric Hammersmith in May 1958 after its April premiere at the Arts Theatre in Cambridge, but it did not stay in London more than week since most of the critics ravaged it and the audiences shunned it. However, *The Birthday Party* did not politely perish, for the playwright directed another production in Birmingham in January 1959, and in 1960 a television production brought Pinter's work for the first time to a mass audience. Eventually too, the play reappeared on the London stage in a successful production by the Royal Shakespeare Company in 1964.

His next work was a play commissioned by the BBC and written for radio, *A Slight Ache*, broadcast on the Third Programme on 29 July 1959, and later redone as a stage drama at the Arts Theatre on 18 January 1961. By that time another one-act stage play titled *The Dumb Waiter*, written in 1957 and produced first in Germany before the Hampstead Theatre Club offered it to London audiences on 21 January 1960, had already attracted considerable attention in *avant-garde* theatre circles. The phase 'Theatre of the Absurd' was gaining in circulation, and more than one observer noted how prominent a star Harold Pinter might be in that galaxy.

When *The Room* and *The Dumb Waiter* were staged together at London's Royal Court, Pinter took the opportunity to answer those who had criticised the deliberate ambiguities, lack of certainty and questioning of apparent realities that are now recognised as integral to his view of life and human relationships.

'There are no hard distinctions between what is real and what is unreal, nor between what is true and what is false,' he wrote in a programme note. 'The thing is not necessarily either true or false; it can be both true and false. The assumption that to verify what has happened and what is happening presents few problems I take to be inaccurate. A character on the stage who can present no convincing argument or information as to his past experiences, his present behaviour or his aspirations, nor give a comprehensive analysis of his motives, is as legitimate and as worthy of attention as one who, alarmingly, can do all these things. The more acute the experience the less articulate its expression.'

It is difficult to ascertain whether this last sentence would apply to the dramatist's personal 'acute experience' with the Düsseldorf production of his next full-length stage play, *The Caretaker*, first performed at the Arts Theatre in London on 27 April 1960. 'I took, as is the Continental custom, a bow with the German cast of *The Caretaker* at the end of the play on the first night,' Pinter reminisced in his widely reprinted article titled 'Writing for the Theatre'. 'I was at once booed violently by what must have been the finest collection of booers in the world. I thought they were using megaphones, but it was pure mouth. The cast was as dogged as the audience, however, and we took thirty-four curtain calls, all to boos. By the thirty-fourth, there were only two people left in the house, still booing. I was strangely warmed by all this, and now, whenever I sense a tremor of the old apprehension or expectation, I remember Düsseldorf, and am cured.'

In the same month that *The Caretaker* began its year's run in London the ABC television company broadcast another Pinter play called *A Night Out*. It had been broadcast as a BBC radio drama several weeks earlier. Pinter was writing a lot of drama for radio and television during this period, and has indicated that he may do more if and when a theme or a situation seems more likely to develop fruitfully that way. He is quite different from U.S. television writers who flee from the 'vulgarity and limitations imposed by ad agencies and networks' once they have achieved some success, and joyously renounce the TV world for the greater and more open spaces and higher fees of feature films and—infrequently—the stage.

To continue with the chronology, two plays titled *Night School* and *The Dwarfs*—the latter based on his unfinished and admittedly imperfect novel—were broadcast in 1960, and then in 1961 *The Collection*, and in 1963 *The Lover*, were televised. The latter, which were later done in theatres, were a final break from the earlier works which critics had labelled 'comedies of menace'.

Certainly that phrase could be applied to his first three plays. Pinter has spoken rather freely about his philosophy of theatre over the years. In regard to the 'comedies of menace', he has observed that 'Everything is funny; the greatest earnestness is funny; even tragedy is funny. . . . The point about tragedy is that it is *no longer funny*.' He is not at all impressed with being labelled a genius of the Theatre of the Absurd, a phrase that doesn't really have much meaning and has become—to use Murray Schisgal's description of the term 'black humour'—a Cop-Out. If the phrase is an evasion, Pinter sometimes answers it with semi-evasions, as when he told the editor of this book in 1964 that 'Sometimes I feel absurd and sometimes I don't. But I know that life isn't, and my plays are not either. I'm trying to get to this fairly recognisable reality of the absurdity of what we do and how we behave and how we speak.'

Speech is one of Pinter's main tools. His characters talk in *non sequiturs*, ramble, misunderstand and generally communicate even more poorly than most people do in the confused and frustratingly imperfect contacts that mark daily life. Pinter has said that he believes he is presenting—in his shadowy tantalising and fascinatingly unrealistic version of realism—a true picture. 'I feel that instead of any inability to communicate,' he told one interviewer, 'there is a deliberate evasion of communication. Communication itself between people is so frightening that rather than do that there is continual cross-talk, a continual talking about other things rather than what is at the root of their relationship.' He has written that 'often, below the word spoken, is the thing known and unspoken. . . . There are two silences. One when no word is spoken. The other when perhaps a torrent of language is being employed. . . . The speech we hear is an indication of that which we don't hear. It is a necessary avoidance, a violent, sly, anguished or mocking smoke screen which keeps the other in its place . . . I think that we communicate only too well, in our silence, in what is unsaid, and that which takes place is a continual evasion, desperate rear-guard attempts to keep ourselves to ourselves.'

Although Pinter is regarded as an existentialist and absurdist focused on the self and has often said that he finds politics 'boring', it would be a gross mistake to view him as detached from the 'real problems' of daily life. He does not write 'message plays' or join 'ban the bomb' marches, but he has strong convictions about problems that may well be much more basic than whether the U.S. is justified in bombing North Vietnam. Pinter is a pacifist, and at eighteen risked a prison sentence for refusing to be called up—National Service was at that time compulsory. It was peacetime and the judge was lenient, so Pinter got off with a fine of thirty pounds. Pinter has a continuing and powerful passion for truth but at the same time he admits that it may be difficult or impossible to distinguish what the truth is in any given situation. His truth is not that of cold absolute fact, but of human feelings, uncertainties, needs and relationships. In that sense, he may well be the most realistic of all our contemporary playwrights —focused on realities more profound and potentially much more disturbing than those which the vast majority of people would label 'real problems'. For the record, he is a careful writer who usually does three or four drafts of a play.

Pinter, whose continuing growth is reflected in his latest drama, titled *The Homecoming* (1964), is undoubtedly a major talent. Martin Esslin has praised his many gifts 'and, above all, his ability to turn commonplace lower-class people and events into a profoundly poetical vision of universal validity' which collectively 'justify the very highest hopes for his future development'. To John Russell Taylor, 'the conclusion seems inescapable that even if others may be more likeable, more approachable, more sympathetic to one's own personal tastes and convictions, in the long run he is likely to turn out the greatest of them all.' Harold Pinter is neither rude nor unpleasant, but considerations as to whether he is 'likeable' or 'approachable' are not very significant to this playwright. 'What I write has no obligation to anything other than to itself,' he declared in a credo published in *The Sunday Times*. 'My responsibility is not to audiences, critics, producers, directors, actors or to my fellow men in general, but to the play in hand, simply.'

This is Pinter's unequivocal 'commitment'.

W. W.

---

*When did you start writing plays, and why?*

PINTER: My first play was *The Room*, written when I was twenty-seven. A friend of mine called Henry Woolf was a student in the drama department at Bristol University at the time when it was the only drama department in the country. He had the opportunity to direct a play, and as he was my oldest friend he knew I'd been writing, and he knew I had an idea for a play, though I hadn't written any of it. I was acting in rep at the time, and he told me he had to have the play the next week to meet his schedule. I said this was ridiculous; he might get it in six months. And then I wrote it in four days.

*Has writing always been so easy for you?*

PINTER: Well, I had been writing for years, hundreds of poems and short pieces of prose. About a dozen had been published in little magazines. I wrote a novel as well; it's not good enough to be published, really, and never has been. After I wrote *The Room*, which I didn't see performed for a few weeks, I started to work immediately on *The Birthday Party*.

*What led you to do that so quickly?*

PINTER: It was the process of writing a play which had started me going. Then I went to see *The Room*, which was a remarkable experience. Since I'd never written a play before I'd of course never seen one of mine performed, never had an audience sitting there. The only people who'd ever seen what I'd written had been a few friends and my wife. So to sit in the audience—well, I wanted to piss very badly throughout the whole thing, and at the end I dashed out behind the bicycle shed. . . .

*What other effect did contact with an audience have on you?*

PINTER: I was very encouraged by the response of that university audience, though no matter what the response had been I would have written *The Birthday Party*, I know that. Watching first nights, though I've seen quite a few by now, is never any better. It's a nerve-wracking experience. It's not a question of whether the play goes well or badly. It's not the audience reaction, it's *my* reaction. I'm rather hostile towards audiences—I don't much care for large bodies of people collected together. Everyone knows that audiences vary enormously; it's a mistake to care too much about them. The thing one should be concerned with is whether the performance has expressed what one set out to express in writing the play. It sometimes does.

*Do you think that without the impetus provided by your friend at Bristol you would have got down to writing plays?*

PINTER: Yes, I think I was going to write *The Room*. I wrote it a bit quicker under the circumstances, he just triggered something off. *The Birthday Party* had also been in my mind for a long time. It was sparked off from a very distinct situation in digs when I was on tour. In fact the other day a friend of mine gave me a letter I wrote to him in nineteen fifty something, Christ knows when it was. This is what it says. 'I have filthy insane digs, a great bulging scrag of a woman with breasts rolling at her belly, an obscene household, cats, dogs, filth, tea-strainers, mess, oh bullocks, talk, chat rubbish shit scratch dung poison, infantility, deficient order in the upper fretwork, fucking roll on . . .' Now the thing about this is *that* was *The Birthday Party*—I was in those digs, and this woman was Meg in the play, and there was a fellow staying there in Eastbourne, on the coast. The whole thing remained with me, and three years later I wrote the play.

*Why wasn't there a character representing you in the play?*

PINTER: I had—I have—nothing to say about myself, directly. I wouldn't know where to begin. Particularly since I often look at myself in the mirror and say, 'Who the hell's that?'

*And you don't think being represented as a character on stage would help you find out?*

PINTER: No.

*Have your plays usually been drawn from situations you've been in?* The Caretaker, *for example?*

PINTER: I'd met a few, quite a few, tramps—you know, just in the normal course of events—and I think there was one particular one . . . I didn't know him very well; he did most of the talking when I saw him. I bumped into him a few times, and about a year or so afterwards he sparked this thing off. . . .

*Had it occurred to you to act in* The Room?

PINTER: No, no—the acting was a separate activity altogether. Though I wrote *The Room*, *The Birthday Party* and *The Dumb Waiter* in 1957 I was acting all the time in a repertory company, doing all kinds of jobs, travelling to Bournemouth and Torquay and Birmingham. I finished *The Birthday Party* while I was touring in some kind of farce—I don't remember the name.

*As an actor, do you find yourself with a compelling sense of how roles in your plays should be performed?*

PINTER: Quite often I have a compelling sense of how a role

should be played. And I'm proved—equally as often—quite wrong.

*Do you see yourself in each role as you write? And does your acting help you as a playwright?*

PINTER: I read them all aloud to myself while writing. But I don't see myself in each role—I couldn't play most of them. My acting doesn't impede my playwriting because of these limitations. For example, I'd like to write a play—I've frequently thought of this—entirely about women.

*Your wife, Vivien Merchant, frequently appears in your plays. Do you write parts for her?*

PINTER: No. I've never written any part for any actor, and the same applies to my wife. I just think she's a very good actress and a very interesting actress to work with, and I want her in my plays.

*Acting was your profession when you first started to write plays.*

PINTER: Oh, yes, it was all I ever did. I didn't go to university. I left school at sixteen—I was fed up and restless. The only thing that interested me at school was English language and literature, but I didn't have Latin and so couldn't go on to university. So I went to a few drama schools, not studying seriously; I was mostly in love at the time and tied up with that.

*Were the drama schools of any use to you as a playwright?*

PINTER: None whatsoever. It was just living.

*Did you go to a lot of plays in your youth?*

PINTER: No, very few. The only person I really liked to see was Donald Wolfit in a Shakespearean company at the time. I admired him tremendously; his Lear is still the best I've ever seen. And then I was reading, for years, a great deal of modern literature, mostly novels.

*No playwrights—Brecht, Pirandello . . .*

PINTER: Oh certainly not, not for years. I read Hemingway, Dostoevsky, Joyce and Henry Miller at a very early age, and Kafka. I'd read Beckett's novels, too, but I'd never heard of Ionesco until after I'd written the first few plays.

*Do you think these writers had any influence on your writing?*

PINTER: I've been influenced *personally* by everyone I've ever read —and I read all the time—but none of these writers particularly influenced my writing. . . . Beckett and Kafka stayed with me the most—I think Beckett is the best prose writer living. My world is still bound up by other writers—that's one of the best things in it.

*Has music influenced your writing, do you think?*

PINTER: I don't know how music can influence writing; but it has been very important for me, both jazz and classical music. I feel a sense of music continually in writing, which is a different matter from having been influenced by it. Boulez and Webern are now composers I listen to a great deal.

*Do you get impatient with the limitations of writing for the theatre?*

PINTER: No. It's quite different; the theatre's much the most difficult kind of writing for me, the most naked kind, you're so entirely restricted. I've done some film work, but for some reason or other I haven't found it very easy to satisfy myself on an original idea for a film. *Tea Party*, which I did for television, is actually a film, cinematic—I wrote it like that. Television and films are simpler than the theatre—if you get tired of a scene you just drop it and go on to another one. I'm exaggerating, of course. What *is* so different about the stage is that you're just *there*, stuck—there are your characters stuck on the stage, you've got to live with them and deal with them. I'm not a very inventive writer in the sense of using the technical devices other play-wrights do—look at Brecht! I can't use the stage the way he does. I just haven't got that kind of imagination, so I find myself stuck with these characters who are either sitting or standing, and they've either got to walk out of a door, or come in through a door, and that's about all they can do.

*And talk.*

PINTER: Or keep silent.

*After* The Room, *what effect did the production of your next plays have on your writing?*

PINTER: *The Birthday Party* was put on at the Lyric Hammersmith in London. It went on a little tour of Oxford and Cambridge first and was very successful. When it came to London it was completely massacred by the critics—absolutely slaughtered. I've never really known why, nor am I particularly interested. It ran a week. I've framed the statement of the box-office takings: 260 pounds, including a first night of 140 pounds and the Thursday matinee of two pounds, nine shillings. There were six people there. I was completely new to writing for the professional theatre, and it was rather a shock when it happened. But I went on writing. The BBC were very helpful; I wrote *A Slight Ache* on commission from them. In 1960 *The Dumb Waiter* was produced, and then *The Caretaker*. The only really bad experience I've had was *The Birthday Party*; I was so green and gauche—not that I'm rosy and confident now, but comparatively. . . . Anyway, for things like stage design I didn't know how to cope, and I didn't know how to talk to the director.

*How did this affect you? How was it different from unfavourable criticism on your acting, which surely you'd had before?*

PINTER: It was a great shock, and I was very depressed for about forty-eight hours. It was my wife, actually, who said just that to me, 'You've had bad notices before,' etc. There's no question but that her common sense and practical help got me over that depression, and I've never felt anything like that again.

*You've directed several of your plays. Will you continue to do so?*

PINTER: No. I've come to think it's a mistake. I work much as I write, just moving from one thing to another to see what's going to happen next. One tries to get the thing . . . *true*. But I rarely get it. I think I'm more useful as the author closely involved with a play. As a director I think I tend to inhibit the actors, because however objective I am about the text, and try not to insist that *this is what's meant*, I think there is an obligation on the actors too heavy to bear.

*Since you are an actor, do actors in your plays ever approach you and ask you to change lines or aspects of their roles?*

PINTER: Sometimes, quite rarely, lines are changed when we're working together. I don't at all believe in the anarchic theatre of so-called 'creative' actors—the actors can do that in someone else's plays, which wouldn't, however, at all affect their ability to play in mine.

*Which of your plays did you first direct?*

PINTER: I co-directed *The Collection* with Peter Hall. And then I directed *The Lover* and *The Dwarfs* on the same bill at the Arts. *The Lover* didn't stand much of a chance because it was my decision, regretted by everyone—except me—to do *The Dwarfs*, which is apparently the most intractable, impossible piece of work. Apparently ninety-nine people out of a hundred feel it's a waste of time, and the audience hated it.

*It seems the densest of your plays in the sense that there's quite a bit of talk and very little action. Did this represent an experiment for you?*

PINTER: No. The fact is that *The Dwarfs* came from my unpublished novel, which was written a long time ago. I took a great deal from it, particularly the kind of state of mind that the characters were in.

*So this circumstance of composition is not likely to be repeated?*

PINTER: No. I should add that even though it is, as you say, more dense, it had great value, great interest for me. From my point of view, the general delirium and states of mind and reac-

tions and relationships in the play—although terribly sparse—
are clear to me. I know all the things aren't said, and the way the
characters actually look at each other, and what they mean by
looking at each other. It's a play about betrayal and distrust.
It does seem very confusing and obviously it can't be successful.
But it was good for me to do.

*Do you outline plays before you start to write them?*

PINTER: Not at all. I don't know what kind of characters my plays
will have until they . . . well, until they *are*. Until they indicate
to me what they are. I don't conceptualise in any way. Once I've
got the clues I follow them—that's my job, really, to follow the
clues.

*Do you think your plays will be performed fifty years from now? Is
universality a quality you consciously strive for?*

PINTER: I have no idea whether my plays will be performed in
fifty years, and it's of no moment to me. I'm pleased when what
I write makes sense in South America or Yugoslavia—it's
gratifying. But I certainly don't strive for universality—I've got
enough to strive for just writing a bloody play!

# Peter Weiss

W HEN PETER WEISS and his wife made their first visit to New York City in May of 1966, this interview was recorded in the Hotel Algonquin, and Weiss was already a much discussed figure in international theatre circles, for the many European productions of his provocative *The Persecution and Assassination of Marat as Performed by the Inmates of the Asylum at Charenton Under the Direction of the Marquis de Sade* had been hailed as startling and sensational. Astute David Merrick had recently imported from London Peter Brook's arresting Royal Shakespeare Company production of the work, and Peter Weiss, who had formerly been the 'private property' of the *avant-garde* and intellectual journals, had become a public figure in the United States as he already was in Britain and on the Continent. He wasn't as well known as Kim Novak or Elvis Presley, but anyone with any pretension to 'culture' was aware of this German-Swedish writer. At the time that the following interview was taped by the editor of this book, plans for the October 1966 U.S. production of Weiss's *The Investigation* had just been announced.

It is, in fact, incorrect to call Peter Weiss a German-Swedish writer. He is a citizen of Sweden, where he has lived (Stockholm) since 1939, but Weiss writes in German and very probably cares much more about German problems. He was born in Germany in Nowawes near Berlin in 1916. His mother was Christian and his father was Jewish, so when Hitler came to power the family emigrated to London and then Czechoslovakia. Weiss's father was not a very religious man and the playwright does not seem to have any commitment to any religion, but he freely expresses his sympathy with oppressed minorities and he has spoken of a sense of alienation that comes from an awareness of being an immigrant, a stranger.

Speaking about *The Investigation* to Stephen Hopkins, editor of the Swedish quarterly *Industria*, Weiss explained that he had written this docu-drama based on the trial of Auschwitz concentration-camp guards because he was—is—'interested in the human situation of oppressed people. I could as well identify myself with the situation of the Negroes in South Africa. . . . In our world, there are people who are aggressors and there are others who flee or try to. You are always on either one side or the other, and sometimes you cannot help which side you are on.'

Peter Weiss's sensitivity to oppression may well have its roots in what he saw in Germany before his family left. 'My experiences as a child—we left Germany in 1934, but there were already Storm Troopers—made a very strong impression,' he recalled in 1965. 'I was always very frightened as a child, always afraid of power and soldiers and force. I wanted to hide from these things.'

The Weiss family did not find a permanent home for five years after the flight from Hitler's Third Reich, moving through Czechoslovakia and England before settling in Sweden in 1939. Weiss has grimly reminisced how—travelling on a Czech passport—he passed through Berlin to Sweden 'during the so-called *Kristallnacht*, when synagogues were being burned down in Berlin and Jewish shops were being ransacked and atrocities were being committed'. Although the playwright insists that he has no particular interest in any particular oppressed group—that *The Investigation* is not a play about Jews—there can be little doubt that his experiences have affected his thinking and writing. At the minimum, he has been left with an enduring awareness of what it is to be an outsider. 'I think if one emigrates once, one is always an emigrant, and it's this not belonging anywhere that has been a way of life,' Weiss admits.

While a teenager and before he reached Sweden, Weiss had begun to paint and write 'at one and the same time. I still have manuscripts of things I wrote when I was sixteen or seventeen,' he told Michael Roloff in an interview published in the Spring 1965 *Partisan Review*. 'Very early lyrical novellas, lyrical prose pieces. In Sweden I always painted and wrote alternately. Only in the last few years has writing begun to dominate entirely. Breughel made the first great impression on me—was my first great master—and then from Breughel I went on to the surrealists. At twenty I was very much influenced by people like Max Ernst and Dali. At sixteen I admired Hermann Hesse very much. I began to read Kafka seriously in 1940, and by the end of the war I was pretty well over my Kafka period. Then it was Henry Miller's turn. Miller made such a positive impression on me because he presented such a wonderful contrast to the Kafkaesque world, a wonderful contrast to this entire twisted, guilt-laden, doomed and damned bourgeoisie.'

Weiss is, and has been for some time, a Marxist. A precise identification with any political *party* is not clear, but he has often expressed his belief that the capitalist nations are decaying societies and that the future lies with the 'revolutionary' or 'socialist' lands of the Communist world. In 1966 it was announced that Peter Weiss would be one of the judges at a mock-trial that Bertrand Russell meant to stage to try President Johnson for 'war crimes in Vietnam'. Weiss is somewhere on the Left, but he is not a blind follower of Red doctrine. He feels quite free to criticise the censorship and lack of artistic freedom that afflicts creators in Eastern Europe, and the fact that he has chosen to continue living in Sweden rather than any Communist state must have some significance.

Weiss speaks of himself as a 'political playwright' and explains that he could not write a play without powerful political content and motivation. In this he is almost unique among contemporary dramatists in the Western world. While the main thrust of post-

World War II theatre and literature has been away from social problems and 'messages' toward a deeper, freer and more disturbing consideration of individuals and basic human relations, Weiss and a few others write to present political and social insights or attitudes.

He was not always so political, so Marxist, so dedicated to this sort of earnest ideological and almost 'agit-prop' art. Today he urges that theatre should be 'a political form . . . working almost in the way that Agit-Prop did, playing with non-professional actors, performing in factories, on the streets, in schools'. But in the past, Peter Weiss was much more surrealist than Marxist. He told Paul Gray, whose interesting interview with the dramatist appeared in the Fall 1966 number (T-33) of the lively *Tulane Drama Review*, that 'I was a surrealistic painter, and my first films were all experimental surrealist films—quite short. Later on I went over to documentary movies, which contained the seed of the work I am now doing in theatre. During the Fifties, I worked almost entirely with films. From the beginning, everything I have done has been extremely visual—even my novels—and this is essential to the staging of my plays. I have chosen my media so that they were visual, and sometimes I have forced them to be so. Sade interested me because his work is so visual—he could have written *Marat/Sade* himself—although the scenes and situations in his own plays happen to be lifeless compared to his other works.'

Before Weiss began to write solely for theatre he wrote four prose works—including two interesting but largely ignored novels. His early writing was complicated by his efforts to write in a language that was not his native tongue—Swedish—and it was only when he returned to German that he hit his stride. Still, before the *Marat/Sade* exploded Weiss was not taken very seriously in 'cultural circles' in Sweden, where the critics viewed this restless immigrant as an ambitious mediocrity in all three media—novels, paintings, films. All that changed drastically when Ingmar Bergman selected first the *Marat/Sade* (1964) and then *The Investigation* (1966) for production at the august and state-supported Royal Dramatic Theatre in Stockholm. Today, Weiss is an internationally acclaimed success and he speaks much less about any sense of alienation or exclusion in Sweden. He is happily married to a lovely blonde second wife, Gunilla Palmstierna, who is a gifted ceramicist and who designed the costumes for two European productions of *Marat/Sade*. His 'political musical' *The Song of The Lusitarian Bogeyman*—a saga of Portugal's 'colonial war against the people of Angola'—was produced in Stockholm in 1967, and in 1968 his new documentary drama *The Viet Nam Dialogue* was staged in Frankfurt.

He is looking ahead, a little less of a Communist than the Iron Curtain propaganda ministries would like and a bit more of a Marxist than most Americans and Britons realise. Even though he explains that he prefers the East German productions of the *Marat/Sade* to the Royal Shakespeare staging because the former made it clear that the revolutionary Marat and socialism were right, Weiss cannot quite toe the Communist line. Like Jean-Paul Sartre, this gifted dramatist is probably one of those idealistic 'intellectual fellow travellers' of whom the late Senator Joseph McCarthy used to thunder. Even when Weiss explains that the Nazi concentration camps—such as that in *The Investigation*—were efficient business operations that helped the later evolution of West Germany's postwar economic boom, even when he tells a *New York Times* writer that in *The Investigation* 'It is capitalism, indeed the whole Western way of life, that is on trial,' the ideological commissars are not wholly satisfied.

They do not fully trust him.

They have learned that writers are not reliable, that their ideas are constantly evolving. Weiss is still thinking about the Vietnam struggle and has recently expressed doubts whether he would join Bertrand Russell's 'trial' of President Johnson. Still a committed Marxist, Weiss continues his efforts to grow as a writer, to remain his own man.

It is, of course, a truism that any major playwright must be his own man to achieve his full potential as a creator. The dramatists know this. Tennessee Williams speaks elsewhere in this volume of having found his 'own way', and most of the other writers included in this book have expressed basically similar views. It is also a truism that only by being his own man—above mere local or national identification—can a playwright produce works of international impact, plays for no one country or one era but rather works that touch the fundamental timeless human condition.

In a sense, Peter Weiss has achieved—or endured—this international attitude because of his forced displacement as a refugee from the institutionalised Teutonic terror and massive murder machine that was the Third Reich. Weiss is one of those exotic products of our times, an ex-German. He is no longer quite a German, and yet he is not quite anything else. In a BBC Third Programme conversation with A. Alvarez, Weiss explained in Stockholm that 'If I go back to Germany these days,' as he often does in connection with productions of his works, 'I don't feel at home there at all. So I have some good friends there and there are some circles I agree to and I can speak to. But it's not my country, and Sweden is not my country as any other country is not my country—I just live here and I think it's nice to live here, but I could as well live in France or England or America. . . . This German I write has nothing for me, no emotional feelings with the country the language belongs to. It's just an instrument. But I can play on this instrument and therefore I use it.'

But the Germans—in the two Germanies—listen with a special passion, one that Weiss sometimes finds troubling.

'When I write in German, I don't write for Eastern or Western Germany,' he told Steven Hopkins. 'Yet if I write something which opens sympathies for the Eastern side, there is a strong critical reaction from the West. If I comment favourably on some aspect of Western policy, I am immediately condemned as a capitalist by the East. I must weigh every word that I put down to be absolutely sure it is something I believe in.'

w. w.

*You have come to playwriting fairly late in your career, is that right?*

WEISS: No, I have written plays already during the war. My first play was made in 1947 and was staged in Stockholm.

*What was that about?*

WEISS: That was an experimental play. You could say it had sort of a strong surrealist tendency, and I have written a number of plays since then which were never performed—the surrealist play and some smaller one-act plays. But the first play which was staged was a one-act play called *Night with Guests*, and then shortly afterwards the *Marat/Sade*.

*Have you had any formal training or preparation for playwriting?*

WEISS: No, not at all. It just developed itself—I was at the same time a painter too. I also worked with films; playwriting was just one parallel of my whole world and it developed slowly in the years I was working. What I learned about playwriting I learned by reading other plays and going to theatre, and so on.

*What sort of plays did you find interesting or could you say might have influenced you in any way?*

WEISS: Well, Brecht of course greatly impressed me. Not only his plays but even his theories about dramatics and even, of course, the theories by Artaud, whom I admired very much. There are so many plays—even Strindberg and Beckett and Ionesco—everything which is in modern dramatics influences and one is related to it in a way.

*Was* Marat/Sade *a long play to write? Did it take you quite a while to do that?*

WEISS: I spent a very long time in doing research work for the *Marat/Sade* to build up the play in the historic sense, to really have the reality behind the story. I studied the works of Sade and I read the works of Marat, but the writing of the play didn't take so long a time. But when it was staged I changed it quite a lot afterwards, after it was staged.

*I read that you have four or five versions of the play and I think you said that the last version has an epilogue—the one that's been staged in Rostock—and that version makes it clear that you believe, if we can oversimplify a bit, that Marat was right.*

WEISS: Yes.

*In what sense would you say Marat was right?*

WEISS: You know that this epilogue was already written in the first version of the play, but we omitted it when the play was opened in Berlin in '64 because we thought everything had been said in the play anyhow, and we should leave the end open. But after quite a lot of different performances I'd seen, I thought anyhow I would like to have this epilogue in the play to make the point of Marat clear, and even to make the point of Jacques Roux and of Sade clear. They all three have a short epilogue, which is in the last German edition. It's not in the English edition.

*No, I noticed that. Would you say that the point of Marat is that there was a need for a revolutionary cleansing of society?*

WEISS: Yes, I would say so, but the play doesn't get changed by the epilogue. The impact of the play is the same. It only makes it clear—takes up the certain point of views once more, and Marat states once more his clear point of view and Sade states his state of ambiguity and his belief in the impossibility of changing society in a political way. He once more states that he is an individualist and that he only believes in the development of the mind.

*I may misinterpret the* Marat/Sade, *but it seems that one of the important factors raised in it is the betrayal of the French Revolution. You have said that you are a playwright who is a revolutionary playwright and a political playwright, and I know there's been some criticism of this play in Eastern Europe. Do you think that subsequent revolutions have also been incomplete or betrayed by their own human failings?*

WEISS: Yes, we have seen so many revolutionary countries

where the results of the revolution didn't really appeal to the original meaning and goal of revolution. Goals such as freedom of thought, the freedom of art have not been achieved in many countries in the degree in which it was planned from the original revolutionary view. This is the point Sade makes very clear in the play, that he doesn't believe in revolution as long as it does not free the individual at the same time. Revolution is his whole being, and art must free itself too. So these two points of view— Marat's absolute commitment to revolution and Sade's other view —are very clearly stated in the play, and this feeling of ambiguity is not only typical for me but I think for many modern artists and playwrights.

*You have said that you feel that freedom for the artist is a continuing problem, even in Socialist countries.*

WEISS: Yes, it is, and it is the condition if freedom for art doesn't exist. You couldn't call it a free country, from my view, if you take Socialist countries where the freedom of art doesn't exist in the degree it should exist. There's something wrong with that society.

*Now, your new play,* The Investigation, *would it be totally unfair to call it a sort of non-fiction play?*

WEISS: Well, you know, I built the whole play on realistic material. I went to the Auschwitz trial in Frankfurt which was going on for more than one and a half years, and I studied the material there at Frankfurt, and I studied what was written about the case in the newspapers and the reports from the trial and I collected this material and brought it into a dramatic shape. So one could say that it is documentary, in a way, as it develops absolute realistic material. It's not imaginary; it is built on reality, but the form of the whole play, of course, is a piece of art. It's shaped as a piece of art, and I've called it 'oratorian' to make clear that it's not meant to be realistic court atmosphere but rather reminds of antique tragedy. It's devised into eleven songs—so-called songs —and this puts it on to another level from the real trial atmosphere.

*I had the interesting experience a little while ago of reading the current version of the script. I assume that, like all playwrights, you are rewriting regularly. Do you like rewriting, by the way, or does it bother you?*

WEISS: No, I don't think I'll rewrite anything in *The Investigation* because this is actually finished. But *Marat/Sade* was much different. I didn't rewrite it, but I changed scenes and songs here and there. But this play, I think will have its constant shape. I don't think I will touch it anymore.

*It has no set design instructions—except avoiding realism.*

WEISS: Yes, that's the only thing I pointed out.

*No stage directions either?*

WEISS: No stage direction other than that there are the accused which have to be there, and there are the witnesses and the judge and two others who belong to the court: the defender and the prosecutor.

*You have indicated in the last part of* The Investigation *a certain point of view towards the victims which I think is somewhat provocative. That is—none of these words are your words; they're all taken from the transcript, but they become your words by the selection process. You suggest that at least so far as the German Jewish victims were concerned they grew up in this German society of discipline and order and obedience to the state and that is was almost an historical accident that they 'happened' to be the scapegoats this time. Is that a fair estimate?*

WEISS: No, I pointed it out as a suggestion that there are some of them who could even become, would even have the possibility of sitting on the side of the accused because there were German Jews who were Nationalists. They were for Germany and they should have joined Hitler—many of them—if they weren't Jews because Hitler was making up some 'progress' for their society. And they looked down on the Jews from the Eastern countries. There were the highly educated Jews from Germany who weren't absolutely in solidarity with the Jews from the Eastern countries.

So there were very difficult situations between them. But, of course, they were chosen to be the victims and they just had to follow. And most of them did in a very passive way. That's a great tragedy—that they didn't find *any* possibility of fighting against the sort of pressure which was put.

*In the camps they were inexorably moved towards the death process.*

WEISS: But that's only one thing; it's not the main point in the play. The main point in the play is actually to show this big machinery, how it worked, and to show the possibilities of human beings, either to let themselves be suppressed and exterminated; and on the other side, the possibility of the accused now slowly to develop this mentality of mass murderers which they weren't born to be, but they develop possibilities which nobody could think of in a normal society. And this absurd small society, which develops within this camp, develops special psychology too, and this is what the play takes up too.

*What small society do you mean? Do you mean the prisoners?*

WEISS: Yes. The prisoners—the society within the concentration camp with all the sort of hierarchy and the special order—the special, strange, perverse normality which was there.

*You said at one point that many of the people in the German armies, which conquered and raped Europe, were boys that you went to high school or grade school with.*

WEISS: Yes, exactly.

*And you couldn't be sure of what you might have done if you'd stayed in that society.*

WEISS: Exactly. I left Germany as a schoolboy in '34, and later either all my friends went to war as warriors, and I don't know what happened to the rest of them. There might have been some who had been close friends to me who worked in concentration camps. I don't know, but the possibility is there. And if it hadn't been that my father was a Jew—well? I asked myself very often what would have happened to me if I had stayed there. Of course, I had no other choice than joining the Army, and of course it's a question of great moral difficulty to decide if one could have had the strength for fighting against something which one found out to be wrong. And this moral problem is in the play too. There's one song about a man called Hans Starke, who is one of the accused, who was a guard in the concentration camp at the age of twenty, and how he developed to murder. He had to shoot prisoners and he did it because he was a soldier and he had to obey, and this is the eternal problem of the soldier who has to do what is wanted of him. And when he has started once he is going on and going on, and after a while he shoots twenty people, and after a while he puts 100 people into the gas chambers because it's his duty. *The Investigation* is also about this development, how people are capable of doing things which we call horrible but which are normal in their situation because they just have to do it.

*Then this is not solely a play about the Nazis.*

WEISS: No. It's a moral play—it's about the possibilities of what human beings are capable of, both in the good and in the bad way. It even shows how they could develop solidarity and it shows the people who kept a human attitude. This is a very specific point in the play, that very often it points out that this and this man or woman really have been showing human qualities. And this, I think, is very essential.

*Of course, these mass slaughters of people have been carried out in other societies. Stalin did this kind of thing, and I'm sure at some point the Japanese have done this sort of thing, and the Christians when they came to Mexico treated the Indians similarly.*

WEISS: Well, what happened in South Africa is very closely related to it; the South African Negroes live in a sort of concentration camp.

*But they're not being massacred.*

WEISS: They're not massacred, but if one imagines a revolution there they would be massacred there the same way. They are kept as slave workers. And because of that I didn't call the play Auschwitz. The word 'Auschwitz' never gets mentioned, and not the word 'Jew' either. So it's not entirely a play about the extermination of the Jews in the special Auschwitz camp, but it's a play about suppression of people because of another race or another political view.

*It would be a misinterpretation of what you wrote to say that it was merely an historical accident that the Jews happened to be caught in this, because, after all, this historical accident has been recurring to the Jews for thousands of years.*

WEISS: Yes.

*Is there some special reason, do you think, that the Jews have been victims?*

WEISS: I don't know. Of course, if one reads Jewish history, one of course can analyse the situation which led to massacres and one can perhaps even understand in an historical way why it happened. But the extermination of the Jews during the German Nazi regime was so enormous and so well organised that it had a very special aspect, almost in the way of a factory. How human beings lost their identity and just were thrown into a state of inhumanity and the accused there treated them as just sort of objects. There were no human beings for them, either.

*Now these guards and the people involved in this murder machine, this extermination factory, are they in any sense rare specimens? Or are they uniquely German?*

WEISS: I don't think they are special German types. They are very ordinary people, not very strong characters, I should say, and perhaps their characters were quite weak. *Uber ich*, I think you will call it, the Freudian term of the—

*Super-ego.*

WEISS: Super-ego, yes. Who very easily are led by others and follow demands and carry out what others want of them. But you find it, I think, in most armies. In what has happened in the French war in Algeria and in Vietnam, and even what happens in Vietnam now. I think they are psychological realities which are not only special German qualities. You find it everywhere. You find them in the Soviet concentration camps and the Ukrainian soldiers during the war were especially cruel, and you found them even in Norway among the Quislings. I think it is a human psychological thing which develops under special circumstances where the ordinary values disappear, so the negative values will grow in special people. In other people these special circumstances can even develop very positive qualities as you found in the French Underground war where certain people you never expected suddenly became heroes.

*How was* The Investigation *received in Europe? I understand there were some difficulties.*

WEISS: Quite controversial. But in West Germany, of course, there were so many theatres that put it on, and it was broadcast on the radio and they made a television show. There was a great interest in presenting the play and very great response to it, especially the young generations wanted to know about the facts because in school in West Germany there is very little taught about the German past.

*Do they accept the responsibility, the young Germans?*

WEISS: I think many do, yes. Many want to know, anyhow, about it. They want to get the explanation *why* it *could* happen, and they ask the generation of their fathers how they could have done it. In East Germany there is much more done in education about this time. In schools they are having many more lectures about this time of the Fascist period.

*Were there any demonstrations or scenes?*

WEISS: No. Well, I got some letters which threatened me even with death and murder and things like that. But that's nothing special. The positive reactions were much greater.

*And how did the Jewish community take this?*

WEISS: Well, you know in West Germany the Jewish community is very small, and it will be shown in Israel, too, the play, so it will be very interesting to see how the reactions will be there. Some thought that I should have mentioned more that this was something which happened to the Jews, but I just wanted not to specify exactly on the Jews and have it more as a human tragedy.

*Will you continue to write plays of this semi-political, semi-sociological nature rather than personal plays?*

WEISS: Yes.

*That's your style, that's your message?*

WEISS: Yes, I have more and more developed this, and for me this consciousness of the world around is so great, and there are so many things, so many problems which involve you so you have no other choice—you have to take them up. So for me it is very difficult to imagine to write only about a small, private sphere and I find the most stimulating dramatic ideas in the conflicts which are going on just now in the whole world. And because of that, the new play which I am about to write will be in a more wider sense, regarding the whole world situation today, in a political way and a psychological way, too. The divided world—the struggle which is brought out by the different points of social structures which exist now.

*Literally, how do you write? You live in Stockholm, correct? Do you write at home?*

WEISS: I have a studio in Stockholm and I go every day there—a half an hour from our apartment where we live, and I work all day, day and night. I think the older I get the more I get involved with writing and with the material I am about to write. So I'm always occupied with it. Even if I don't write I make my notes and I think about it. I write with a typewriter.

*You work every week, almost every day?*

WEISS: Almost every day, yes. Only now when we've been in New York for a month, and this was for me so stimulating in an intellectual and human way that I, of course, didn't do any writing here. But I got very many ideas for my new work, and saw new possibilities again. I find it enormously stimulating here in New York.

*You said at one point you weren't sure you'd be admitted to the United States. Is that because you're a Marxist and you thought you'd be excluded on that basis?*

WEISS: Yes, you know some years ago it was much more difficult and they inquired very thoroughly before when I wanted to go to the States. But this time there was no problem at all. I got a visa within ten minutes in Stockholm so that there was no difficulty at all. And I think this is because in the United States there are so many different points of view developing now and the strong opposition to the Vietnam war, which we in Europe join, is so strong even in the United States that our point of view is nothing which has to be omitted in the United States just now.

*You don't take an active role in politics in Sweden?*

WEISS: No, no, not at all.

*With any party, or writing speeches, or that kind of thing?*

WEISS: No.

*Arden said the same thing a little while ago. He is out of politics. He said he thought he was much interested in Marx but unlike Brecht he wouldn't call himself a Marxist, although he draws on the Marxist point of view. Do you rewrite after a first draft?*

WEISS: Yes, and rewrite again and again. I must see what I've written when I write. I can't read my own handwriting, so I have to see the page clearly, and it even gives you another impression of the whole if you see it written down clearly on the page.

*And do you show it to anybody or do you wait until you've finished with the play?*

WEISS: Very seldom. Sometimes when I've got into it some way, then I might get together with friends and discuss it, and even read parts of it, but mostly I work for myself until it's sort of finished, at least one state of the thing is finished. Stockholm, you know, is quite a nice little city. We have very few friends there. And as I write in German there are not many there who could read what I write, and this is a special problem, too. So Stockholm is just my study where I draw myself back, and when I have the work finished, then I get the contacts with other people who might give their reactions to it.

*At one time you spoke about your sense of being an immigrant in Sweden, of being somewhat alienated in Swedish society. Does that continue or is it less so now that you are an internationally known playwright?*

WEISS: Well, because of the other language I write there is a natural isolation, but as I have my family there—my wife, my children and I are of course very closely united with the Swedish atmosphere and our friends are Swedish and I've lived there for so many years I feel at home there. This is the place where I feel most at home. But I couldn't say I had any sort of a deeper relationship to the Swedish nationality. I could imagine being at home in New York, too, because there are here many people who I could consider to be my friends. And I can work where I have friends, where I have the possibility to get into human contacts and live within a group of people who are having the same point of view towards life and community. So it's no great problem, this belonging anywhere. For me it is a question, I could belong where I find friends, where I find an atmosphere where I can work.

*You don't really then have any special roots in Sweden. You're not against Sweden in any sense?*

WEISS: No. No, not at all. On the contrary, I like Sweden, in many points. There is a social justice, a clean human atmosphere in Sweden which I agree to.

*Do you think there is any possibility that when* The Investigation *comes to New York that the remarks about some of the victims could have been the guards—do you think that could be provocative here?*

WEISS: Perhaps, but I think if one really analyses the play one would come to an understanding of this point of view. Of course, if I had built the whole play on just this special point, one could say, well, it would exaggerate that point of view. But as it is only a small part of the whole I think it could just be material for discussion.

*Your new play—have you got a title for that yet?*

WEISS: Not yet, no. I'm working on it—I'm still preparing the whole thing and I don't know exactly how it will develop.

*Where is it set?*

WEISS: It's in out time. It's in this world, and it's in this time we live in and our reality and it will be quite a long, big play—I suppose in three acts—but I don't know exactly the shape it will take.

*The* Marat/Sade, *I notice, has had several different shapes. I saw it in Copenhagen and it was even more dramatic, I thought, than the celebrated Peter Brook production.*

WEISS: Yes, even in Stockholm it was very dramatic. It had different shapes and the shape in East Germany was entirely different again, because they didn't work very much with the atmosphere of the madhouse there. The inmates were more sort of prisoners in a sort of concentration camp almost.

*And to go back to* The Investigation, *does it have any special application to the situation in which we find ourselves now, would you say?*

WEISS: I should say yes, because we thought that after the war, after the concentration camps, where we got to know about the facts, we thought this would be over forever, that it could never happen again. But since then we've seen it happen many times again. And it's still going on. The possibilities are still there and because of that this play has a great actuality still for me.

*And as a playwright you cannot ignore this terrible potential?*

WEISS: No, never. I could never ignore it.

# Tennessee Williams

TENNESSEE WILLIAMS flew up to New York in January 1966 from his home in Key West, Florida, for the production of *Slapstick Tragedy*, and it was during the first week of rehearsals that this interview was recorded in the playwright's pleasant apartment on one of the upper floors of an ultra-modern 'co-op' monolith on West 72nd Street. The questions were put by the editor of this book; a very brief edition of the interview was published in the March 1966 number of *Playbill*.

The success of Tennessee Williams is of longer standing than any of the other playwrights in this volume. He is a genial, intense, slightly plump man who remains remarkably shy after more than two decades of world-wide acclaim as a major dramatist of the twentieth century. Fame and wealth and literary honours do not appear to have brought either complacency or even solid self-confidence to this remarkably talented man; he is still trying, still reaching. He has written of the problems of surviving 'the catastrophe of Success' and of 'the vacuity of life without struggle' in a poetic essay in the drama section of the 30 November 1947, issue of the *New York Times*. Williams is, by the way, a gifted poet.

His name at birth that Palm Sunday morning of 26 March 1911, was Thomas Lanier William. His father was Cornelius

Coffin Williams, a scion of an old Tennessee family, and his mother was pretty, elegant Edwina Dakin Williams, daughter of an Episcopal clergyman and descended from aristocrats who had been Tories during the American Revolution. The couple was to have three children. A girl named Rose had been born two years earlier in 1909, and a son christened Walter Dakin Williams followed in January of 1919. Rose Williams had a tragic history of emotional disturbance that culminated in an apparently not wholly successful lobotomy in 1936; she has been institutionalised for more than twenty years. In her perhaps partisan family reminiscence-autobiography written in collaboration with Lucy Freeman, the playwright's mother suggests that her husband was at least partially responsible for Rose's deterioration and final withdrawal from reality. *Remember Me to Tom*, a poignant and sometimes chilling volume that Putnam published in 1963, portrays Rose as a lovely, delicate, auburn-tressed child traumatised by the harshness of a niggardly, boisterous, insensitive, hard-drinking and sometimes violent father. If Edwina Dakin Williams had been trying to write a very poor imitation of a Tennessee Williams play, she could not have succeeded better than with her touching but almost stereotyped literary portraits of (1) the dramatist's father as an anti-intellectual, burly, six-foot businessman who 'meant well' but couldn't communicate tenderness or much else to his family—and who was away a lot as a travelling salesman; (2) herself as the loyal, loving, high-born, long-suffering, beauteous Mississippi belle; and (3) the shy, physically weak, sensitive and poetic son who would rather read and write than play sports with the cruel and vulgar lads who abused and even persecuted him at school.

It is all as if life were—with embarrassing naïveté—copying art. In recent years the playwright has defended his father on several occasions. Poet Gilbert Maxwell quotes Williams as saying of his father that 'He was a hard man to live with, but I know now he loved us and that he was deeply in love with Mother.' The 4 May 1958, *New York Post* included a letter from the dramatist complaining about a series of articles that seemed to present his father 'in a terrible light. He was not really that bad. Since his death about a year ago, I have changed my feeling towards him. After he quit "the road" my father was a terribly unhappy man who could only escape his unhappiness through the bottle, poker, and through the great affection and esteem of the salesman who worked under him. In his favour I would like to make these points. My father was a totally honest man, he was never known to tell a lie or take unfair advantage of anybody in business. He had a strong character and a sense of humour. He lived on his own terms which were hard terms for his family, but he should not be judged so long as he remains the mystery that he is to us who lived in his shadow.

'Maybe I hated him once, but I certainly don't anymore. He gave me some valuable things: he gave me fighting blood, which I needed, and now he has given me, through the revelations of my psychoanalysis, a sense of the necessity to forgive your father in order to forgive the world that he brought you into: in my opinion, an important lesson which I hope I have really learned. Forgiving, of course, does not mean accepting and condoning, it does not even mean an end to the battle. As for his being devoted to money, as my younger brother is quoted as having said of him, all American businessmen seem to have that devotion, more or less, mostly more, and I think it is a sort of reverse sublimation. Disappointed in their longing for other things, such as tenderness, they turn to the pursuit of wealth because that is more easily obtainable in the world. My father got little of either.'

His father's somewhat shaky career as a businessman appears to have altered the family life drastically. Shortly before the playwright was born, Cornelius Coffin Williams—C.C. to his friends— lost his job as manager of several small telephone exchanges in Gulfport, Mississippi. 'He never told me why, and I didn't inquire too closely,' the dramatist's mother confided primly in *Remember Me to Tom*. Not too long afterwards, C.C. became a travelling salesman of men's clothing—operating out of Columbus, Mississippi, where his family stayed with Edwina Dakin Williams's father, who was the local minister. Tennessee Williams's first home was an Episcopal rectory, and the little boy spent a great deal of time with his grandfather, whom he loved deeply, until the old man died at the age of ninety-seven. It is hardly an over-simplification to say that with C.C. away so much Reverend Dakin was a substitute father during these crucial early years in the life of the playwright.

There was little stability, permanence, strength, in the life that C.C. Williams was able to provide. The family moved on to Nashville and then Canton before settling in 1916 in Clarksdale, where the boy's maternal grandfather had been named rector of St George's Church. It was in Clarksdale that five-year-old Thomas Lanier Williams nearly died of diphtheria, and for nearly two years after he recovered from that then often fatal disease the boy had little or no use of his legs. There is some confusion as to what the medical problem was, but no doubt that it was real. These must have been a difficult two years for the child, not helped much by the fact that his father was still away much of the time 'on the road'—now selling shoes.

He did well enough at it to be made sales manager for the firm's St Louis branch, which required the Williams family to leave the Dakin parents—after seven years with them—and find their own home in St Louis in 1918. According to the dramatist's mother, her son Tom hated St Louis and the Eugene Field public school where the boys mocked him as a 'sissy' because his legs were still too weak for him to run or play games. It is reported that the local little monsters were so offended by his non-partici-pation one afternoon that they all trotted by and kicked him as they did so. There has been speculation that these dreadful experiences as the 'new boy' have left Williams permanently shy—and desperately shy—with strangers. And if all the abuse from his classmates were not enough, Edwina Dakin Williams left town for a few months to accompany C.C. on a business trip and her mother came up to St Louis to look after the children.

It is said that C.C. Williams was among those who regarded his son Tom as a 'sissy' and that he regularly referred to the boy as 'Miss Nancy'. If all this reads like one of the worst of the cliché-ridden psychiatric case histories that used to be dramatised on sentimental hour-long television plays of the 'golden' 1950s, it is not. It is not fiction. 'Home is where you hang your childhood,' Tennessee Williams has been quoted as saying. In view of his own childhood, the playwright's sympathy with and compulsive interest in the lonely, the rejected, the maladjusted, the different, the outcast—even the freak—is hardly surprising. It is a tribute to this brilliant dramatist's courage, integrity and perseverance that he has overcome the inevitable effects of this extraordinary family galaxy as well as he has.

It is hardly surprising that he turned, at ten, to something that he could do alone—write. His adoring possessive mother bought him a typewriter when he was eleven, since he was obviously committed to writing and Edwina Dakin Williams's 'only ambition' for her offspring 'was that they do what they wanted'. In 1927—shortly before he reached sixteen—Tom entered a *Smart Set* magazine contest requiring answers to the question 'Can a Good Wife Be a Good Sport?' Posing as an unhappily wed travelling salesman, the youth took the negative position and on 8 April 1927, received a $5 check for Third Prize. In 1928—his junior year at high school—he sold his first story to a national magazine. The August issue of *Weird Tales* included 'The Vengeance of Nitocris,' saga of a homicidal Egyptian queen who drowned all her foes after having got them drunk at a lavish banquet. Williams received $35, but this does not seem to have impressed his father, who is said to have complained about the teenager sitting up late writing and running up the light bill.

During this period the future playwright went to Paris one summer with his maternal grandfather and the rector apparently attempted to give the boy some inkling of the 'facts of life' by taking him to observe the voluptuous nudes at the Folies Bergère. Impact: Young Tom had been fond of—interested in—attracted to a pretty girl named Hazel Kramer, who was a year behind him at high school, and there has been speculation that this relationship might have flowered if somebody had not interfered. The somebody was, it appears, none other than C.C. Williams, who was supposed to consider his son 'a sissy'. The story goes that the two youngsters both meant to attend the University of Missouri, but C.C. feared that the girl's presence might interfere with Tom's studies. When he told this to the young lady's grandfather, who worked under C.C. at the shoe company. Hazel was shipped off to the University of Wisconsin. Years later, in February 1935, Tom Williams collapsed and was hospitalised for exhaustion when he heard that she had married. That night, his sister had another breakdown.

Tom Williams entered the University of Missouri in September 1929, after graduating from high school with a 'B' average. When the university paper interviewed the freshman who was newsworthy as a 'published writer', Williams announced that Louis Bromfield was his favourite author and declared he planned to go to the School of Journalism later. He had not yet discovered Hart Crane, Edna St Vincent Millay, Rimbaud and Rilke, whose works he devoured in college.

He was now writing plays, entered a script for *Beauty is the Word* in the undergraduate Dramatic Arts Contest, and while he didn't win he was the first freshman ever to receive an honourable mention. Williams completed three years at Missouri, with average grades. In his junior year—the Depression year of 1931–1932—he failed the required R.O.T.C. course and did not return. His mother contends that this was the vengeance of his father, a former lieutenant in the Spanish-American War, but Professor Gerald Weales points out in his brief but intelligently informative University of Minnesota monograph on Williams that a lot of students dropped out that year. C.C. Williams got his son a $65-a-month job at the shoe company, a type and place of employment that the young writer hated bitterly for three years until his February 1935 collapse and hospitalisation permitted him to leave the world of commerce for a while. With his tuition paid by his maternal grandmother, he entered Washington University of St Louis to try to finish his college education. While there, he won a prize for a one-act play titled *The Magic Tower*, produced by a suburban 'little theatre' group. This was the second Williams play actually staged, for during the summer of 1935, which he spent in Memphis, a summer theatre had put on *Cairo! Shanghai! Bombay!*, a comedy written in collaboration with Dorothy Shapiro.

In 1936 he became associated with a St Louis drama group called The Mummers and wrote a number of plays for them. One advocated pacifism, another scourged munitions makers and a third, titled *Candles in the Sun*, focused upon 'exploited' Alabama coal miners. The St Louis *Post-Dispatch* reported that it treated 'poverty, degeneracy, accidents on the fifth level below ground, a strike and a brutal murder, ending with beans for everybody, hope, and the singing of "Solidarity Forever".'

It is surprising how little, if at all, theatre criticism has improved in the past three decades.

In September 1937 Tom Williams enrolled at still a third university to complete his undergraduate studies. He continued his playwriting at the University of Iowa, completing *Spring Storm* and most of *Not About Nightingales*—a saga of convicts burned alive that Williams is reported to have described as more filled with violence and horror than any of his other works. In 1938 twenty-seven-year-old Tennessee Williams—he'd acquired that nickname at Iowa—finally received his B.A. degree and set off to try to get work with the WPA Writers Project in Chicago. He was rejected because his work 'lacked social protest' and because he couldn't prove his family was destitute, so he next tried to win a place with the Writers Project in New Orleans. And again he failed; he took a job as a waiter in a Bourbon Street restaurant. Williams was eventually to run the classic gamut of jobs that so many writers have endured, including a totally unsuccessful tour as an ignored $250-a-week Hollywood scenarist. He was fired from a whole string of jobs, including teletype operator in Florida and New York hotel watchman, the latter post ending when he left open the door to the elevator shaft on an upper floor.

The latter jobs were after he made his first breakthroughs into New York theatre. In 1939 he won a Group Theatre Award (judges: Harold Clurman, Irwin Shaw and Molly Day Thatcher) for three one-act plays collectively titled *American Blues*. He received the telegram announcing the $100 prize in Los Angeles, where he was then 'picking squabs on a pigeon ranch' and sharing a cabin with a young clarinet player. One of the judges, Molly Day Thatcher, interested agent Audrey Wood in the playwright. Miss Wood, one of the great theatre agents of this century, has played a vital role in Williams's career. She helped get him a Rockefeller grant that supplied enough money to support him in New York while rewriting a drama titled *Battle of Angels* and when the play was finished Williams showed it to Professor John Gassner. Gassner and Theresa Helburn of the Theatre Guild were then conducting a seminar in playwriting at the New School in association with the Guild's Bureau of New Plays. Gassner passed the script to Lawrence Langner, guiding genius of the Guild, and the Guild produced it. With Miriam Hopkins starring, *Battle of Angels* opened in Boston on 30 December 1940.

And it closed a week later, never to reach New York.

'The play was more of a disappointment to us than to you,' the Guild wrote to its Boston subscribers, 'but who knows whether the next one by the same author may not prove a success?' The next several were short works, but then in 1944 a play he coauthored with Donald Windham, *You Touched Me!*, was performed in Pasadena and Cleveland. Then on 26 December 1944, the incredible career of Tennessee Williams in the theatre finally 'happened' in Chicago's Civic Theatre. With Laurette Taylor in the lead role of Amanda and Julie Hayden as the crippled daughter named Laura, the Eddie Dowling production of *The Glass Menagerie* opened to overwhelming critical acclaim. It was similarly hailed when it reached the Playhouse in New York on 31 March 1945, ran for a year and won the Drama Critics Award, the Donaldson Award and the $1,500 Sidney Howard Memorial Award.

On 26 September the Lee Shubert-Guthrie McClintic production of *You Touched Me!* opened on Broadway and fared reasonably well, although it was not the tremendous success of *Glass Menagerie*. In 1947 Williams delivered another major work in *A Streetcar Named Desire*—reportedly a revision of a film script titled *The Gentleman Caller*, which his Hollywood employers had scorned and which was later sold to the movies in its new form for several hundred thousand dollars. In 1948 *Summer and Smoke* reached Broadway, in 1951 *The Rose Tattoo*, in 1953 *Camino Real* and in 1955 *Cat on a Hot Tin Roof*. Both *Streetcar* and *Cat* each collected the Pulitzer Prize and the Drama Critics' Circle Award.

In 1957 *Orpheus Descending*—a rewrite of *Battle of Angels*—arrived, followed by *Suddenly Last Summer* in 1958 and *Sweet Bird of Youth* a year later. Then in 1960 the 'black comedy' *Period of Adjustment* opened but was not one of Williams's most successful works. *The Night of the Iguana* fared much better in 1961; *The Milk Train Doesn't Stop Here Anymore* ran fewer than 90 performances in 1962. *Slapstick Tragedy*, collective title for *The Mutilated* and *Gnädiges Fraulein*, opened in February 1966 and was to die young. Williams has also worked on six screenplays, five of these based on his theatre works; published a short novel titled *The Roman Spring of Mrs Stone* (1950) and a collection of poetry and two volumes of short stories.

Williams is now completing another pair of short plays for New York production, still striving to make contact, still struggling to communicate his truth and his vision and his hope, still reaching so that he will not remain the isolated outsider. He set his goal quite clearly in the introduction to *Cat on a Hot Tin Roof* when he wrote, 'I still don't want to talk to people only about the surface aspects of their lives, the sort of things that acquaintances laugh and chatter about on ordinary social occasions, I feel that they get plenty of that, and heaven knows so do I, before and after the little interval of time in which I have their attention and say what I have to say to them . . . I want to go on talking to you as freely and intimately about what we live and die for as if I knew you better than anyone else whom you know.'

W. W.

*How do you literally write a play; where do you begin? Does an idea germinate within you for a long time? Do the characters come first and then the story?*

WILLIAMS: It is almost impossible to pinpoint the start of the play, at least for me. I think that all plays come out of some inner tension in the playwright himself. He is concerned about something, and that concern begins to work itself out in the form of a creative activity. Sometimes I will get up in the morning and feel a little more energetic than usual and I will just start writing.

*With a pen or with a typewriter—how do you work?*

WILLIAMS: Typewriter—I typewrite very rapidly.

*You were saying that sometimes you get up in the morning and start to write dialogue.*

WILLIAMS: Yes, something on a page or two pages of dialogue will spark in the way of characters or situation and I just go along from there. I am a very wasteful writer. I go through several drafts, as many as four or five before I finish a work. I am sure that any playwright would give you practically the same description.

*Albee said to me that he writes a play when it becomes more painful not to write than to write it.*

WILLIAMS: That's a very good way of putting it, you know.

*Then the subject literally forces itself out?*

WILLIAMS: Yes, some people accuse you of being too personal, you know, in your writing. The truth of the matter is—I don't think you can escape being personal in your writing.

*Impossible.*

WILLIAMS: That doesn't mean that you are one of the characters in the play. What it means simply is that the dynamics of the characters in the play, the tensions correspond to something that you are personally going through—the concerns of the play and the tensions of the play are your own concerns and tensions at the time you wrote it. I have always found that to be true.

*I have noticed that in many of your plays there is poetry or one of your characters is a poet, and I have heard from someone you know, the former drama critic of the St Louis* Post-Dispatch, *that you began or have done a great deal of poetry writing, and yet you don't write much poetry now. Why have you given up poetry? I have read your poetry and it's excellent.*

WILLIAMS: I found that I had written enough poetry—I mean in the form of poems; I think plays can be just as lyrical as a poem can be; you can use just as much personal lyricism in a play as you can in a poem; and also I have noticed as writers get older—that is, poets—they tend to write less poetry. I think actual poetry is a medium more for the young than for the middle-aged.

*I think the question of age is an interesting one because in the introduction to one of your plays, I think* The Rose Tattoo, *you mention 'the continual rush of time that deprives life of dignity and meaning'. Does this question of ageing trouble you now that you have turned fifty? Is it something that you are going to be writing about?*

WILLIAMS: I think I have always written quite a bit about it. We were having a poker game up here last night and at one point the game got too mixed up and somebody knocked a glass off the table accidently; there was no violence involved; and suddenly all at once I began to talk about age. I said, 'I can't believe it, I am fifty-four years old now, and I think the reason it is so incredible to me that I have suddenly reached this age is that each year is not another year to me—it's a play.' And sometimes three years are a play and my life seems to be chalked off not in years but in plays and pieces of work, and so I am taken by surprise by how much time has passed and my being as old as I am.

*I am stunned, myself, when I read your biography this afternoon—to see the numbers—your age; but I have no sense of the writing of this being the work of a man of forty or fifty or any age. I have read them as plays;*

*none of that has come through, although some of your recent plays have been concerned with older people, such as the* Slapstick Tragedy, *which is about to open now.*

WILLIAMS: There is no particular age in that.

*There are elderly women in it.*

WILLIAMS: It seems to exist outside of any specific time and, no, they are not elderly women. We are not going to age the women in the plays; they are going to appear the same ages as the actresses actually are playing. Well, the play is so 'way out' that it will not have to be pinpointed in time.

*The question of pinpointing them in plays is also an interesting one. Most of your plays, I believe, are set in the South, where you grew up, do you consider yourself a Southern writer, because the questions you raise seem to be universally applicable to me?*

WILLIAMS: I think I am becoming less associated with the South than I was originally. I was a Southern writer because my parents were Southern and I was born in the South. Now, my father was from Tennessee and my mother from Ohio, so it was a sort of split between. Would you say Ohio is the North?

*Well, I guess you would say that it is on the verge of the South.*

WILLIAMS: She was from southern Ohio but she went to East Tennessee when she was a very young girl, so she grew up to be a Southerner.

*Why did you take the name of 'Tennessee'?*

WILLIAMS: Because my father's family were Tennesseeans. They were very active in the making of the State of Tennessee.

*And everyone calls you 'Tennessee' now?*

WILLIAMS: No, I prefer people to call me 'Tom', my real name. Of course, you know in professional meetings people call me 'Tennessee'.

*Your good friends call you 'Tom'.*

WILLIAMS: People whom I am closer to, I always ask them to call me 'Tom'; it's easier and I like the name 'Tom'.

*You are the grandchild of an Episcopal minister?*

WILLIAMS: Oh yes, he was almost my closest relation.

*Are you still actively involved in any discernible religion?*

WILLIAMS: Well, I keep a Russian icon by my bed. It was given to me by a dear friend in London for my birthday. It is a very beautiful Russian icon and I don't suppose I would keep it there if I didn't have some religious feeling; it is obvious that I do have religious feeling. It may seem ingenuous to have religious feeling to a lot of people but to me it seems necessary.

*Could you define this religious feeling?*

WILLIAMS: Well, it isn't associated with any particular church. It's just a general feeling of one's dependence upon some superior being of mystic nature.

*Does God or religion come up much in your plays? I haven't seen it specifically.*

WILLIAMS: Oh, yes, I notice the word 'God' occurring several times in the recent disaster.

*In one of your interviews you said that in only a few moments of life is there really human contact. Does that mean you feel it is basically a rather lonely existence?*

WILLIAMS: Now, that is probably some quotation that is not an exact quotation, because I certainly don't feel that. I feel that in many, many moments in life there is almost continual contact; under what circumstances I said that I can't imagine, because it isn't what I feel—at least not what I feel *now*.

*When you were a child, I heard an anecdote told that you once were out in the back yard digging.*

WILLIAMS: Oh yes, that was one of my mother's favourite stories.

*What were you digging for—devils?*

WILLIAMS: Yes, she said—I am sure she was telling the truth—it was quite a funny story. She found me digging in the back yard. She said, What are you digging for? I said I was digging for the devil.

*In a sense, do you still think you're digging for the devil in these plays?*

WILLIAMS: In a sense, yes; but I am also digging for the opposite of the devil.

*For the angels?*

WILLIAMS: For God.

*In one of your comments you state the plays represent a struggle between good and evil—of man's struggle between good and evil. How would you define good and evil in our contemporary society?*

WILLIAMS: I don't think it needs definition. It is so obvious. We all know—when I look at the papers that arrive every morning, it is just incredible what is going on; you know that so much is fantastically abominable going on. This whole Vietnam bit is so incomprehensibly evil to me.

*You mean the killing that is going on there?*

WILLIAMS: Yes, the naphtha—what is that?

*Napalm.*

WILLIAMS: The way they burn people alive and the way they spray chemicals over the rice fields so they will starve; I don't need to list the instruments . . .

*You are talking about the cruelty of modern weapons rather than the political connotation.*

WILLIAMS: Yes, they are incredibly cruel and, believe me, nothing that will be won out of this war will be worth the life of a single man who died in it, in my opinion.

*Do you have equally strong feelings about the civil-rights movement in the South?*

WILLIAMS: Yes, equally strong.

*Because you haven't touched that much in your writing, or do I do you an injustice?*

WILLIAMS: I always try to write obliquely. I think the closest I came to writing directly was in *Orpheus Descending* about my feelings about what goes on in certain parts of the country.

*I have found it interesting that a number of the Southern writers, such as yourself and the late Mr Faulkner, didn't really comment too directly on this question. They were primarily concerned with human struggles of a more general nature.*

WILLIAMS: I don't see the difference between them. I think they were so closely interrelated that I don't see how you can divide the two things.

*Do you think that you would ever write directly on this question?*

WILLIAMS: I am not a direct writer; I am always an oblique writer, if I can be; I want to be allusive; I don't want to be one of these people who hit the nail on the head all the time.

*Have you always been this sort of writer—I mean as a child? By the way, did you write as a child?*

WILLIAMS: I started to write around twelve.

*And did you start writing in this allusive manner then, or probably less so.*

WILLIAMS: Less so, of course, because children are more simple.

*I hate to keep bringing up your past remarks as if to belabour you with them, but in one of the interviews you gave you spoke of the depravity and bestiality in life and went on along those lines—is this a current concern of yours?*

WILLIAMS: I think it is of anyone who pauses to think and who has some perception.

*Now, on the question of perception, I recently read a critical study of your plays that made reference to the obvious influence of Freud on your work. Is that a fair statement? Have you read a lot of Freud?*

WILLIAMS: I looked into maybe a book or two of Freud but I never read any of it.

*You observed it in life?*

WILLIAMS: To the extent that I have any connection with Freud—I think Freud did illuminate many dark areas in the human unconscious, and I think I write mainly from my unconscious mind.

*And do you write day or night? Is there any special time you write?*

WILLIAMS: I find it almost impossible to write any time but the morning, when I have more energy to write.

*Is it early morning, or after breakfast?*

WILLIAMS: Immediately after breakfast.

*And do you require any special conditions?*

WILLIAMS: Oh, yes, I require many special conditions. I have quite a ritual.

*Tell us about it.*

WILLIAMS: Do you want to know about the whole ritual? I think that should be a secret of my own. I think that should be my secret . . . whatever makes it possible for me to work, I should do, because I must work. Up to 1955 I found it much easier to work, and after 1955 I was conscious of a certain fatigue, and now, well, when I get up in the morning . . . let me give you a few little clues—I have anaemia, which is rather a problem. I don't know how severe it is, or if anaemia is the right word for it, but it is the word that is used; and I have to get up in the morning and give myself an injection, which peps me up sufficiently to get to the goddam desk. And combined with the shot, there's also the two strong cups of coffee; and then I always have one of these martinis on my writing table; I don't take more than one. But I found after 1955, specifically after *Cat on a Hot Tin Roof*—that I needed these things to give me the physical energy to work; and the intelligent thing might have been to stop working, to rest. But I am a compulsive writer. I have tried to stop working and I am bored to death. . . . I don't know what I am here for . . . what is the purpose of my being here.

*I am pleased that you are so compulsive . . . and we all benefit from it every year or two.*

WILLIAMS: Well, occasionally I hope that somebody gets something out of it.

*Do you have any sense of being isolated now or lonely? I have heard somebody say that, that because one or two of your plays haven't been received as some of the earlier plays, that this has troubled you.*

WILLIAMS: I have never been without terrific anxiety about all of my work. You know, it's constitutional with me to be anxious as all hell about all of my work. I'll never get over that and I never hope to; I just have to live with it.

*I guess that's the nature of being a writer—you put your head on the block every time you put a piece of paper into the machine.*

WILLIAMS: Yes, of course you do, and it takes a physical toll of your nervous energies. You've got to do all kinds of things to try to make yourself stand up under it. Now, I am not a self-destructive person; I try to keep myself going. Every afternoon I go to the YMCA and I will swim sixteen or twenty lengths of the pool; that is when I am in New York. When I am in Key West I will swim, I would say, about half a mile in the sea.

*Do you do most of your writing in Key West or here?*

WILLIAMS: I enjoy writing in Key West more than I do here; but I have to be here right now.

*Now, about the other playwrights—first of all, which playwrights do you think have interested you or influenced your work in the past?*

WILLIAMS: Strindberg and Chekhov—if you are talking about master playwrights of the past.

*And which of the current playwrights interest you, American or foreign?*

WILLIAMS: American or foreign—nobody now, because I have my own way which has crystallised for me and nobody influences me anymore.

*Which playwrights interest you rather than influence you?*

WILLIAMS: Interest me? They all interest me if they're good. I think in America Edward Albee is by a good margin the most interesting of the new American playwrights.

*Do you read much in the way of novels?*

WILLIAMS: I don't have much taste for fiction recently—that is, in the last ten years or so, I prefer to read journals and books, collected letters of writers and other people's biographies. Right now I am reading *The Diary of Anais Nin*, who is one of our very fine writers.

*You don't travel as much as you used to; does this mean you are settling down more in America, you are more at ease in America?*

WILLIAMS: It means, I think, mainly that I don't have the energy to bat around the world like I used to. I went around the world once and lived a good deal of my time during the last fifteen years or more in Rome, Italy, and I saw most of the interesting cities in Europe, cities interesting to me, but now I don't know whether I can resume that sort of travelling or not; I am rather dubious that I can.

*There are two more questions that I would like to ask you. One, you have stated in an earlier interview that you found the state of contemporary society terrifying.*

WILLIAMS: That I am sure I have said because I really do find it so.

*What sort of things do you particularly find terrifying to you?*

WILLIAMS: All the things you see on the front page of the morning paper.

*Violence, cruelty, dishonour?*

WILLIAMS: All those things—the senseless wars going on; you know, so many things—the struggle for civil rights . . . I'm not a person dedicated primarily to bettering social conditions, because I am not able to, except through my writing, and I doubt whether people will pay enough attention to writing for writing to have any effect.

*You said one more thing. You said, 'I don't think America must settle for its present state; you must go forward and be unafraid.' In what areas must we go forward, do you think; on what areas must we move?*

WILLIAMS: I think we are moving in some good areas now. We were just talking about the civil rights.

*That's important?*

WILLIAMS: That's very important and we are making progress—not as fast as we might hope for—and there is some very ugly opposition to it; but it seems to me we are making some remarkable progress in that direction. I feel that finally American people have a sense of justice. It may take them a while to formulate it because there are so many false leaders—you know, politicians like Senator Dirksen and Mr Nixon; and there was the late Senator McCarthy; there are so many people like that who are impeding the spirit of American people—their understanding, I mean.

*On the question of the spirit of American people, do you have any particular feeling about the young people today?*

WILLIAMS: I love what the young people of today are doing. They don't seem to be scared of anything, except their own shadows, maybe, and that's wonderful. It's wonderful how they can go out and face police bullies in the South, Ku Klux Klan, the whole bit, and they do have that courage, and it's marvellous. I think this is one of the great generations of young people that we now have.

*Finally, you said: 'I'd rather stay an outsider than adjust to injustice.' Do you still think of yourself as an outsider?*

WILLIAMS: Outside of what?

*Outside of the main social stream, in America.*

WILLIAMS: I am very much a part of it, I hope; I hope to be always.

*So you don't feel outside anymore?*

WILLIAMS: No, I never did really, if I said that I was kidding somebody, not myself.

*I thank you very much, Mr Williams. You were very kind and generous with your time.*

WILLIAMS: I hope it made some sense.

# *John Arden*

EQUIPPED WITH one extra shirt and an engaging directness, John Arden flew to the United States in March 1966 when the Establishment Theatre's New York production of *Serjeant Musgrave's Dance* was flourishing at the Off-Broadway Theatre de Lys. He was interviewed in an associate's Greenwich Village apartment by the editor of *Playbill*; the results of that conversation appeared in digest form in the April 1966 issue of *Playbill* and—at greater length—in the *Tulane Drama Review's* special number on the English theatre (T-34) published in December 1966.

In the September–October 1965 issue of the late and lamented English theatre periodical *Encore*, Simon Trussler wrote that 'Arden remains the most consistently impressive of our contemporary dramatists, and the one whose work seems most likely to be sustained and fruitful.' In John Russell Taylor's informative book titled *Anger and After*, he declares that 'John Arden is one of our few complete originals, and for the occasional faults in his play—a desire to force a gallon into a pint pot, a tendency perhaps to overdo the gutsy, gutsy side of things just a little from time to time—there are numerous and irreplaceable merits. Sooner or later his definitive success with a wider public is assured.'

John Arden is a slim, logical, articulate and sometimes bearded

189

scion of an upper middle-class family in the northern part of England. He was born in Barnsley in 1930, attended a public elementary school before going on to a private preparatory school in Yorkshire because his parents feared that industrial Barnsley might be bombed by the Luftwaffe during World War II. He started to write plays at sixteen, most of them historical works set in the Middle Ages and few of them ever finished. One schoolboy effort written as an experiment in the style of *Sweeney Agonistes* treated the death of Adolf Hitler. During this period Arden saw his first professional productions—those of the 'rep company' at Sheffield—and essayed a bit of acting, including the title role in *Hamlet*.

By the age of seventeen Arden was interested in becoming a writer but had no clear idea as to how he might do so. He decided to go to Cambridge to study, not theatre or literature but architecture. He had been advised 'to read English, but I didn't see why that would help me to be a writer any more than anything else, and I was interested in architecture,' he recalled in 1961. 'Also to be a writer is a fairly chancy thing because there is no recognised period of training for it—you either are or you aren't, and you don't know at the age of eighteen. You can't be certain whether you are going to carry on with it. Architecture was a professional training which I found interesting for itself, and which I could drop if I found my writing developing.'

Arden studied architecture at Cambridge for three years, completed his studies with two years at Edinburgh's College of Art. He was then writing in various styles, including verse; a 'pseudo-Elizabethan tragedy on the Gunpowder Plot' was one effort that Arden recalls was 'very bad'. He also wrote a period comedy which he now finds embarrassing, *All Fall Down*, produced by the College of Art theatre group.

On graduation the future playwright knew that he still needed a year's practical work in an architect's office before he could be rated as fully qualified. He took a job with a London firm, designing large office buildings, stayed for two years. During the second year he wrote *The Waters of Babylon* for *The Observer* competition;

it was staged at the Royal Court Theatre. The English Stage Company, widely recognised as one of the most dynamic and creative groups in British theatre of the 1950s, was one of Arden's earliest and staunchest champions. His next play was *Live Like Pigs*, which ran only twenty-three performances. The story of *Waters of Babylon* had been partially inspired by a desire to satirise Harold Macmillan's Premium Bond scheme, and *Live Like Pigs* was inspired by Arden's recollection of a Barnsley incident in in which a council house had been given to a family of grubby squatters who were later besieged by outraged neighbours. Shortly before *Live Like Pigs* was completed it was 'commissioned' by the Royal Court and Arden quit his job. He never returned to architecture.

It is worth mentioning that Arden had previously—as had a number of his contemporaries among British playwrights—written works for broadcasting. He had won a prize from the BBC Northern Region radio for a seafaring drama titled *The Life of Man*, and he had written *Soldier, Soldier*, which the BBC hesitated to televise until later when *Serjeant Musgrave's Dance* was done on the London stage in 1959. Arden has suggested that the broadcasters might have either waited for the theatre production to 'legitimatise' or confirm his importance, or perhaps the BBC thought that the publicity generated by *Musgrave* would help pull viewers. This, if true, is an attitude that broadcasters in other nations also share. In fact in the United States the author of even an unsuccessful Broadway play will receive television offers because the mere production on Broadway somehow seems to stamp the writer as a competent craftsman. The notion is, of course, preposterous.

Before *Musgrave* was produced—to generally negative critical notices—Arden did a number of other plays that have never been staged. After *Musgrave* he seems to have got in his stride. However, he has continued to puzzle and sometimes irritate London critics by changing the style of each work in the manner that he considers most appropriate to the material. *The Happy Haven*, which the playwright completed in 1960 while on a year's playwriting fellowship at Bristol University, required most of the cast to wear strange masks throughout this grotesque comedy set in an old people's home. *Ars Longa, Vita Brevis,* a later short play, was written for some experimental programmes in which the director Peter Brook explored, with members of the Royal Shakespeare company, the application of Artaud's ideas on the 'Theatre of Cruelty' to modern English theatre. *Serjeant Musgrave* and *The Happy Haven* were quite formal in structure, but Arden's next work after *Happy Haven*—the television play *Wet Fish*—has been described as going 'to the other extreme with a closer approach to naturalism than he had yet attempted'. The National Theatre's staging of *Armstrong's Last Goodnight* in 1965, which starred Albert Finney as a crude, fierce, doomed Scottish warlord in the border battles, offered a powerful play with a quality not unlike that found in some of the Kurasawa films about Japanese samurai or the grittier Hollywood Westerns. In 1965 Arden was commissioned to write *Left-Handed Liberty* to celebrate the 750th anniversary of the Magna Carta. His main subsequent project, a large-scale musical about Nelson has proved abortive.

Whatever form or subject he chooses—and most of his plays deal with contemporary social problems in terms of theatre, rather than political 'message'—Arden believes in strong complex characters and in arresting theatrical presentations of the questions he raises. While not interested in sensationalism or sex merely for shock effect, he has stated that today's theatre is probably too timid—a notion that might puzzle a few recent visitors to London productions. In a 1963 interview published in *Peace News*, he observed that 'one of the prime functions of the theatre since the earliest time, Aristophanes and beyond, has been to inflame people's lusts—in something like the way tragedies produced a purgation of the spirit. Comedies and tragedies fulfill related functions in this.' He argued that a scene should 'be able to be nice and sexy, and at the same time make a serious point in the play'. Arden went on to point out that the need to make a serious point might be an unnecessary limitation, contending that it should be possible to go to a theatre to 'see a show that provides you with a sexual excitement'—such as Aristophanes's *Lysistrata*—providing that it doesn't leave the viewer 'dead and unfulfilled, which is all a striptease club does'.

John Arden wants to feel free to write as he pleases, and he agrees with the late John Whiting that 'when you write a play you don't think of the audience'. If Arden ever finds himself tempted to, he puts it out of his mind because he finds it 'depressing . . . very limiting'. Once he has a firm idea for a play, his pre-script preparations are generally limited to setting down very detailed notes for the first act or two—after which his characters come alive for him and then 'take over'. Arden is also a realist, however. He views theatre as a 'public art' and a dramatist who gets completely out of touch with the public as 'failing to practice the art properly'.

One of the main reasons that Arden goes on writing is his view of the theatre as a hazardous but irresistible challenge. He knows that writing a play that is both good theatre and says something significant is a dangerous experiment. 'But if you succeed,' he told the editors of *Encore* in 1961, 'you have done so by presenting, alive, on the stage, a tactile piece of human existence which will be recognised as true and meaningful and illuminating, and the recognition will be almost a ceremonious act between audience, actors and author—it is the possibility of this happening with any play that keeps the business going.'

w. w.

▪▪▪▪▪▪▪▪▪▪▪▪▪▪▪▪▪▪▪▪▪▪▪▪▪▪▪▪▪▪▪▪▪▪▪▪▪▪▪▪▪▪▪▪▪▪▪▪▪▪

*To start from the beginning, where and how do you write?*

ARDEN: At home. I have been living in the country, but I shall be living in London. I have a room, and the family—the children —are not supposed to come into that study. There are four children.

*Do they respect your need for privacy?*

ARDEN: Yes, they do—although sometimes as a sort of treat I let some of them come in because they like to watch me write. I write in pencil in a thick exercise book—on one side of the page only. When I come to the end of the book I turn it over and write back on the other side of the page; I do not know that I can account for this. I usually sit in a chair or lie back on a couch—rather than sit at a desk—to write. I write on the right-hand pages, leaving the left-hand pages for afterthoughts.

*Do you rewrite before you have the manuscript typed?*

ARDEN: First I mess about with pencil on the book, and erase if necessary. The advantage of pencil is that you can rub it out instead of having to cross it out. Until I have got what appears to be a final script, I may have to cross out whole pages and rewrite scenes in another book. When I've come to the end of a play and am fairly sure that it is sort of final form, I then transfer it on to a typewriter—myself, often rewriting as I type. I don't trust a typist to do it. For one thing, she would not be able to read my writing and—for another—I usually write without punctuation, which I have to put in later with the typewriter.

*Stage directions?*

ARDEN: I don't bother with stage directions in doing the pencil draft. I just get down the words the actors have to say, and later I put in the stage directions on the typewriter. My wife is the first person to see it then. She is a recognised collaborator on some of my plays—under her professional name of Margaret D'Arcy. Sometimes I work with her quite specifically in that she provides detailed ideas and helps me in the selection of material. In one early work, which has her name as well as mine on the title page of the published edition, some of the crucial ideas and some of the characters are purely her invention.

*Do you discuss a new play with her before you start writing?*

ARDEN: Before, and even in plays where she hasn't done as much

I have always read her passages of the work in progress. Usually when I have finished a scene I read it to her.

*Has she ever acted in your plays?*

ARDEN: Yes, my first television play—*Soldier, Soldier*. We were married by then. I'd been an architect and I married her partly because she was an actress and I wanted to be a playwright—so there was a sort of community of interest.

*After you and your wife have discussed it, to whom do you take your new play?*

ARDEN: That depends. I've had a number of plays commissioned by theatres, and last year I wrote a play commissioned by the City of London for the Magna Carta centenary. It was put on by Bernard Miles, who runs the only theatre in the City, the Mermaid. I used to get letters from him at very early stages of the writing asking whether I could give him a breakdown of the cast—so he could think about preliminary casting—and he wanted to know about the stage sets. I told him quite nicely that I didn't quite know what sort of characters I had in the play until I had finished. And I'm never sure till I've finished how a play ought to be set. If it's got several scenes in different places, for example, would it be better to use several sets which are changed between the scenes, or to make composite sets so that the action flows continuously? I don't usually work out this type of detail at the beginning of a new play, but try out different ideas as I go along. Finally, I seem to have got a good one—then go back to the beginning and rewrite the structure of the play to fit it. Oh—to answer your original question—if the play has been commissioned I'll obviously take it to whoever commissioned it. As for the other works, there is no rule.

*Do you associate much with other playwrights?*

ARDEN: I've spent most of the last few years living out of London, so I really only see them on the rare occasions when I come up to London for rehearsals and so forth—and even then it isn't a regular thing. I was in London for a few weeks last year for rehearsals of two plays, and I wanted to see Ann Jellicoe. I rang her; she said she was sorry she couldn't see anybody. She was working on a play herself; she wasn't able to have any social contacts until she had finished.

*Do you impose that same sort of separation when you're writing?*

ARDEN: Yes, I do. In fact, I have a house in Ireland on an island in a lake and it is extremely difficult to get there—and very difficult for me to get off. I want it that way. I've done a lot of work there.

*When you're writing, do you work every day?*

ARDEN: Every day if possible. Perhaps six days a week. It's not a bad idea to have one day off to devote to the family. Of course I usually only work in the mornings—from after breakfast till early afternoon. Perhaps have my lunch brought into the room where I'm working, and then emerge after lunch. The actual amount of writing I do varies from year to year, but it is usually not more than four or five months of work with that pencil in twelve.

*When you finish a play, do you start another before the first is produced?*

ARDEN: If the first one is going to be produced soon, I find myself incapable of starting a new play until the rehearsals are over. But if there is a likelihood that I'll have to wait a year for the production, then I will fill in the time by starting something else.

*Do you attend rehearsals?*

ARDEN: Whenever possible. On the whole, I've been very fortunate with the directors I have worked with—and in nearly every case I have had very close consultations with them. I go to rehearsals, and there are certain scenes in some of my productions that I can say—without conceit—I directed myself. I believe very strongly in the importance of the author's presence for the first production of a play. I am never very keen later when somebody calls me up and says, for instance—as recently happened—'*Serjeant Musgrave's Dance* is being done in New York. Could you please come over?' The same director, Stuart Burge, had done the play on English television, and I didn't think there was much I could tell him about the play at this late stage. Travelling rapidly around the world to attend rehearsals of a play I'd written seven years earlier is dangerous—because it might prevent or delay me from writing a new one.

*Is it true that British critics initially reviewed your plays as 'confused' or 'confusing', and these same critics are now much more affirmative and accepting?*

ARDEN: My works are now being accepted by the public on a slow process of building up, but *Musgrave* was a commercial fiasco when it opened in London. The critics said it was obscure, the public didn't come and the finances of the theatre simply did not permit them to run a play to empty houses in the hope of word of mouth spreading. They lost a great deal of money on it; it had to come off. The word of mouth began to build after that, and there were a large number of productions in universities. Now—seven years later—it is being revived in London at the same theatre, and the last that I heard it was doing good business. I've been reading the recent critical notices of my works and comparing them with what was written earlier. It's the old, old critics' dodge of damning an early play, and then when you write one later they say 'What a pity Mr Arden has not written to the standard of his first work that so astonished us two years ago.' They have conveniently forgotten their own reviews. They now write as if they recognised *Musgrave* as a masterpiece in 1959, which they didn't.

*Is it a masterpiece?*

ARDEN: No, I have a feeling that there is something wrong with the play. I have never been able to put my finger on it, and I've asked lots of people who have all suggested different things. It may be the scene in the churchyard at the end of the first act. You established the soldiers, the people in the town, the situation.

Then the soldiers and the sergeant all come on together to be alone for the first time, and the audience is expecting to be told everything. But somehow I have not balanced, on one hand the business of giving information to the audience so that they will be in a position to understand the play and, on the other hand, the business of withholding information in order to keep the tension going. There is a failure in the craftsmanship. It's an old play, written originally in a sort of very rapid flash of inspiration.

*Have you ever tried to rewrite* Musgrave?

ARDEN: Well, it is very difficult to go back and make what you might call rational corrections . . . of the shape of it. My principal fault as a writer is to get so interested in bright ideas that occur to me while I am working on a play that I forget what the play is supposed to be about. I am always doing this. Sometimes I manage to detect it; sometimes somebody else detects it and I can go back and rewrite bits—but in *Musgrave* I never quite succeeded in solving this particular problem.

*If losing story and purpose to 'bright ideas' is your weakness, what is your principal strength as a writer?*

ARDEN: I think that where I usually succeed is in the creation of historical atmosphere, and when I say historical I don't necessarily mean past history. I think a play set in the modern age must have the atmosphere of the modern age which the future historian would recognise. I am happy that in *Musgrave*, for example, I can create a sort of ambiance of English lower-class life in the Victorian period.

*Are you primarily concerned with lower-class life?*

ARDEN: Not at all. My own family background is middle class, but the town we lived in when I was a boy is really Serjeant Musgrave's town brought forward sixty or eighty years—and it was impossible to live in such a town without being very conscious that one was a member of the minority party in the 'class war'. To be brought up there in the Thirties with the aftermath of the

Depression and so forth—this class difference was impressed upon me very strongly when I was a boy. I went to the local municipal school, and I suddenly became very aware of social differences between myself and most of the other children in the class. I always remembered at a very early age, perhaps seven, realising that the little boy with whom I shared a desk smelled. It is very disturbing to a child to have a feeling of . . . well, my parents were not snobs but a number of their acquaintances were and one did develop attitudes as a child. I think I represented 'black reaction' in the social sense that the working classes and coal-mining families and their children were the enemy. They certainly thought I was the enemy. A little boy going to school in the sort of nice clothes that my mother would provide, clean shirt and tie and polished shoes, was quite liable to get attacked in the street.

*Did that ever happen to you?*

ARDEN: Yes, frequently—and to other children of my class. It took me a long time to grow out of this. I didn't really grow out of this until I joined the Army—when I didn't get any higher than a lance corporal. I then developed what you might call the private soldier's mentality rather than the officer's mentality.

*Does that still prevail in your plays?*

ARDEN: Yes, it probably does.

*Despite your family background and Cambridge education, you don't regard yourself as a member of that Establishment?*

ARDEN: No, except that having had the education of 'that Establishment' I can get along with them.

*A writer is really classless, isn't he?*

ARDEN: No, I don't think this is entirely true. Some are, but there are plenty of aristocratic writers in England. People like the Sitwells are definitely aristocratic. Evelyn Waugh has associated himself with the aristocracy, although I think his background is middle class. Writers like Wesker and Alan Sillitoe and David Storey have working-class backgrounds. I'm not so sure about Wesker; I think he's of a family of Hungarian Jewish immigrants who lived in a working-class district but belonged to a special section of the working class—and this produces its own attitudes.

*Do you yourself identify with any class or social grouping?*

ARDEN: No, but this is very interesting. We have been living for a period in a small country town in north Yorkshire. Our cottage was not in the town itself but half a mile away in a funny little collection of houses that ran along by a disused railway and a disused gas works—very odd houses that were rather squalid-looking outside but highly decorated inside with enormous quantities of vast candlesticks and things. We discovered that our neighbours were all of the class of people that I was writing about in *Live Like Pigs*. They were travelling gypsified tinkers—with gypsy blood—who had ceased to travel. Today they have scrap yards. Now about the question of social strata, I have heard that a local schoolteacher wondered aloud—in obvious criticism—'why when John Arden came to Galleymoorside he deliberately chose to live with the scum of the earth and the beggars?' Of course it wasn't a choice but an accident. However, those former gypsies accept me. They have their class awareness but they accept me as a sort of licensed eccentric.

*Licensed eccentric—is that the way playwrights are often regarded in England?*

ARDEN: Yes, but because I am sort of a licensed eccentric these people regard me as being on their side. One of the old men approached me once when his scrap yard was in trouble with the local town and country planning committee, asked me I could get his case aired on some local documentary television programme. I tried, and I felt honoured that he would regard me as a person to come to with this sort of request. I am really not very good at dealing with people. I'm shy and diffident. My wife is very free and easy, and it is really she that has made friends with them rather than myself.

*You said earlier that your friends are not generally playwrights. Who are they?*

ARDEN: In Ireland, where we've been spending as much time as I can spare from English activities, the only people we really know are a few farmers and their families. In London, actors and writers mostly and a few painters and musicians. In Yorkshire, our principal friends are a clergyman and his family, a Catholic priest—until we had a bit of a disagreement, three teachers and a beautiful girl who is a sort of upper-class debutante.

*You mentioned two clerics. Are you a religious person?*

ARDEN: I am religious but I am not orthodox. I was brought up Church of England.

*Does this concern with God and religion appear in your plays?*

ARDEN: Yes, I think there is something of it in most of my plays. I am still religious to the extent that I would never deny the possibility of the existence of a divinity, but when it comes to the actual definitions of the term 'God' I really cannot go along with any of the churches. I think they have narrowed the concept to a very close extent—except, of course, in the higher reaches of theological thought and it is, for my taste, too much broadened and becomes very abstract.

*In his book* Anger and After, *John Russell Taylor states that 'Arden permits himself in his treatment of the characters and situations in his plays to be less influenced by moral preconception than any other writer in the British theatre today.' Does this mean you're immoral or amoral?*

ARDEN: No. I have a sense of morality. What I think he means— and what I would prefer it to mean—is that because a character in a play is a swindler I wouldn't necessarily think that he was basically a bad man. It is simply a question that when I am writing a play I like to see a character, whatever he does, from his own point of view as well as from the point of view of other characters in the play and from the point of view of the audience.

*You don't have tidily packaged characters?*

ARDEN: No.

*That's important to you?*

ARDEN: I don't know whether that is important to me; it is the natural way I think of people. If I am writing a play about a really low class of character—a man who commits all the seven deadly sins . . . cheats people, kills people, seduces women and abandons them and all the rest of it—I would still want to know what there is of value in this man's character and try to express it in the play. There may be nothing. I wouldn't write off the possibility of a man being completely dominated by forces of evil, but there is a remark by Stanislavsky which actually relates to acting that I think also relates to writing a character as well. He said an actor playing a miser in a play ought to examine the character until he finds an aspect of generosity, and when he has found this aspect of generosity he should build on that so that you are always working in counterpoint and don't produce obvious type figures.

Of course, people will perhaps come back at this and say that the mayor and the parson and the policeman in *Serjeant Musgrave* are cardboard figures. They are engaged in a situation where only their public personalities come out, but I think that in the expression of their public personalities I have not caricatured them. It is caricature by omission rather than by exaggeration. I could envisage another play in which those three people appear without the coal strike and without the eruption of the soldiers. Then you would see them as rounded characters with families and so forth.

*You have used the same characters—not these—in more than one play, I recall.*

ARDEN: Yes. I have a number of plays set in England in the present day—*The Waters of Babylon*, *The Workhouse Donkey* and the two television plays, *Soldier, Soldier* and *Wet Fish*. All those plays except *Waters of Babylon* are set in an unnamed town in the north of England which is more or less Barnsley, where I was brought up. A number of characters sort of slip about between the three plays.

*By the same names?*

ARDEN: Yes, there is a character called Alderman Butterthwaite who is the kingpin of the local Labour Party. He is mentioned in the three Yorkshire plays, and he also comes up in the London play . . . the part of the time of his life where he is living in London.

*Since his portrait is less than flattering, has this offended the Labour Party?*

ARDEN: I have never heard that it has. *The Workhouse Donkey*, which is a satire on Labour Party administration in a coal-mining town, received very enthusiastic notices in *The Tribune*—which is a left-wing newspaper. I think that the sort of member of the Labour Party who would go to the theatre would have exactly the same objections to Labour Party politicians of the local type that I do.

*While we're on labour, I once said to Wesker that I gathered he wrote and cared about labouring people and asked whether England's working class went to see his plays. He replied that they don't yet have the theatre-going tradition. Is that still true?*

ARDEN: This is unfortunately true. Wesker is devoting more or less his whole life to try to modify this. I am not sure that he is entirely doing it in the right way, but he is trying and all power to his elbow. It is a very difficult problem—this. We are confronted with a largely bourgeois audience, and the solution to how to expand the audience will surely be complex and take considerable time. Efforts are being made all over the country. Some of the provincial theatres are very good—Bristol, Nottingham, Sheffield,

Manchester and such towns. The best provincial theatres are doing their damnedest now to encourage the public at large to come, and with an encouraging degree of success—but certainly nobody has found the real solution to this problem.

*Although your plays are deeply concerned with people, would you say that you are also a political and sociological playwright?*

ARDEN: Well, I think it is impossible to avoid being a political playwright or a sociological playwright. I think that man is a political animal, and everything we do is to some extent a political act—because the definition of 'politics' I take is the problem of living together in a society. The actual technical aspect of politics —as to whether one does this on socialist or conservative or general democratic principles—is a problem of the politicians, who are technicians who delegate themselves to do the work. But everybody should be concerned about it, and therefore almost any play that deals with people in a society is a political play. A book like *Lord of the Flies*—which deals with people on a desert island—is in fact a highly political book. I prefer to leave the technical side of politics to the politicians, and concentrate on dramatising the raw material for which the politicians work.

*In* The Waters of Babylon, *which was originally put on for a single Sunday night and without sets at the Royal Court, there was a key character named Krank. He has a poetic speech in which he says that 'The world is running mad in every direction. It is quicksilver shattered . . . all over the floor. I choose to follow only such fragments as I can easily catch.' It has been suggested that such may be the author's philosophy.*

ARDEN: No, that is not the author speaking. That speech evolved because I had met such a man, a disoriented Polish refugee. There was an original for Krank, and I was trying to find out what made him do what he did. I would not associate myself with that. I believe that one should be committed to public affairs, but that one's commitment depends upon one's talents. I am not the sort of man to run for office.

*Or write speeches as Günter Grass has done?*

ARDEN: Or write speeches. I have on occasion spoken at political rallies, nuclear disarmament rallies—a form of education which cuts across the existing party boundaries to a very large extent. I would not commit myself to speaking or assisting at a Labour Party rally, although I have voted for the Labour Party. There was also a shameful occasion in which I voted for the Conservatives, and another occasion when I voted for the Communists. I am a floating voter; at the moment I am not voting at all.

*Since there was a prototype for Krank, have people or situations you have met inspired some of your other plays?*

ARDEN: Yes, they have—but not quite in such a literal sense perhaps. The man on whom I built Krank was a Pole who worked in the architects' office where I worked—at the time that I wrote that early play—and he interested me very much as a person. In *Serjeant Musgrave*, the soldiers were made up of characteristics I had observed in different people when I was in the Army, but I would not say that any one of those soldiers represented any particular person I have met.

*You have said that two things—one, an actual massacre in Cyprus and, two, an American film about a Civil War raid—largely inspired* Serjeant Musgrave's Dance. *Is this how you often come to a play, or is there no special way?*

ARDEN: No special way.

*Do the characters first erupt, or does a general question or feeling arise?*

ARDEN: Even that I wouldn't like to say. In *Musgrave*, it was the general question first. The characters came afterwards. In *Live Like Pigs*, it started with reading an account in a North Country English newspaper of a riot in a low-cost housing development area. This prompted me to write a play investigating the causes of such a riot. *The Workhouse Donkey*, a play about a scandal in municipal politics, was based on my own recollections of municipal politics in my native town. I collected from my memory a whole lot of such scandals and amalgamated them. There is hardly any detail in the plot of that play that did not take place at some time or another either in my town or another one, but I sort of fused the whole thing and turned it round so I don't think I could lose a libel action on it.

*You said 'my native town'. Do you think of yourself as a Northern writer? Has living in the North Country influenced you?*

ARDEN: I'm sure it has, but I don't necessarily think of myself as a 'Northern writer'. That would be like a 'Negro writer' or a 'Jewish writer' or a 'Catholic writer'—dangerous sorts of labels to stick on somebody. Some authors actually like to assume such a label, but I prefer to think of myself as a writer who is a Northerner.

*To go on to other possible influences, it has been suggested that you have been at least somewhat influenced by the works of Brecht. Is that a fair statement?*

ARDEN: Yes, although I don't use him as a model. After I had started writing plays, I discovered that Brecht—particularly as a theatrical technician—was inspired very much by the same sort of early drama that was interesting me. That is the rather conventionalised plays of the European Middle Ages. That is the Elizabethan writers and various exotic styles such as the Japanese and Chinese theatres. I was also interested in this; I was not interested in naturalistic Ibsenite writing.

*Is that still true?*

ARDEN: Yes. I think the Ibsen school of playwriting was necessary and valuable in its time, but we need to develop further from it now. So my writing was really influenced by the same thing that Brecht was influenced by, which of course means that there is a certain similarity in style between us. But I am very different from Brecht because Brecht was a practising Communist. There is a strength of didactic dialectics in his work; any Brecht play can be subject to that type of theoretical analysis. I use Marxism as just one of many sources. There is a certain amount of Marxist analysis in *Serjeant Musgrave's Dance*, but it is by no means a Marxist play.

*Are you in some sense a Marxist?*

ARDEN: No, I am no more a Marxist than I am a Roman Catholic, but I would think that Marx is a very important figure and that nobody in the twentieth century can understand history without taking into account the Marxist interpretation of it.

*Would that also apply to Freud?*

ARDEN: I am not sure about Freud. I am temperamentally not in sympathy with Freud. I have a feeling that Freud's vision is much smaller than Marx's. I think that the Freudians have elevated a series of interesting hypotheses based on a small element of Central European society into 'natural laws'. Because Frau Von X had this and this complex, such complexes are universal and may be found in even ancient Egyptians. The Marxist point of view, on the other hand, seems to be based much more sensibly on the observation of history over a very long period of time.

*To return to the specifics of your work, do you work out your characters carefully before you write them?*

ARDEN: No, they grow as the play does.

*Both* Live Like Pigs *and* Serjeant Musgrave *were well received in the United States. How about the effects of American playwrights on you?*

ARDEN: Let me think . . . I don't know if I can actually list a great number of writers who make a personal impact. Of American playwrights, Arthur Miller has done so. Among the younger dramatists, I was very impressed by LeRoi Jones, whose *Toilet* and *The Slave* I saw in New York last year. I can't think of any other American playwrights that personally have a strong impact on me.

*How about European playwrights?*

ARDEN: Brecht, of course, although he is not quite as contemporary. Peter Weiss. Max Frisch to an extent, Ghelderode, Lorca.

The Irish people—Synge, O'Casey, Yeats to an extent. Of contemporary English playwrights, none of them precisely except Henry Livings, whose work I don't think is known in the U.S.A. at all. In a slightly earlier generation, Christopher Fry at one time left a very strong influence on me. I've since grown out of that influence, but I retain a sort of 'literary first love' feeling for him. Going back a few years in English drama, the early plays of John Masefield exerted a very strong influence. Two Masefield plays in particular—*The Tragedy of Nan* and *The Tragedy of Pompey the Great*—both plays that are rarely performed, little known but marvellous. . . . I really can't think of anybody else to list.

*Do you think that contemporary novels might influence your work?*

ARDEN: I don't read many, although I do attend a middling amount of theatre.

*To resume the compulsive transatlantic comparison, do you find American critics have received your plays differently than the British critics?*

ARDEN: No, almost exactly the same.

*Let's consider the audience. Taylor writes that you 'have a deliberate policy or tendency to do plays in which there are all sorts of conflicts taking place on stage, but the audience is never invited to participate in them— is even forcibly prevented on occasion from doing so. It is invited to experience a play as a self-contained totality and judge.' Is that deliberate on your part?*

ARDEN: No, I don't think it is deliberate. It is just the way my mind naturally runs. I do resent plays in which the audience is brought in by the author to take one side of the argument. I feel the sort of extremely involved problems that we are up against today—whether it is a question of war, sex or whatever—are so complicated that you can't just divide them up into black and white. I feel that it is the job of the playwright to demonstrate the complexity, to try to elucidate it by the clarity of his demonstration. But to go further than that and start deciding for his audience which viewpoint they should take is, I think, rather presumptuous—because if these problems were as easily solved as that, then they would *have been* solved by other people. Playwrights don't solve political problems. If I was able to give the answer to *Serjeant Musgrave's Dance*, I would be the Prime Minister —and I am not.

*And you have no desire to be.*

ARDEN: I have no desire to be.

*Although your plays have not been commercial 'hits', am I correct that there are enough productions of your works so you're able to earn a reasonable living?*

ARDEN: Yes.

*Can English playwrights today survive on income from their stageworks?*

ARDEN: Well, most of us seem to be doing so.

*But you won't get rich at it?*

ARDEN: John Osborne gets rich.

*Isn't that from films in part?*

ARDEN: The plays have been made into films, and this is one of the legitimate by-products of playwriting. As far as I know, he has only written one independent film script—the *Tom Jones* script. It seems to me that playwriting is a profession in England that is on the upgrade from the point of view of income.

*Has government support of theatre in Britain helped the lot of the playwright?*

ARDEN: I'm sure it has. I am sure the Royal Court Theatre, that has put on several of my plays, would not have survived without its subsidy. The National Theatre would not exist without a subsidy. I think that the subsidies have never been big enough, and the smallness of them is a constant worry to the theatre managements. The fact that a national economic crisis might cause a cut in them is an ever-present source of worry, but the subsidies at the moment are there and advantage has been taken of them.

*To go on to your next announced project—the musical play about Admiral Nelson—will it be humorous?*

ARDEN: Parts of it will be funny, but I hope that—by and large—it will be more of an heroic musical. The standard musical comedy seems a bit dated. I have just about completed the book, and my American colleagues are to do the songs. We are, of course, hopeful.

*We spoke of Osborne writing film scripts. Have you any interest in that?*

ARDEN: I would like to write for films, but the trouble with the Anglo-American film industry is that the writer is still in a rather inferior position. I'm not too happy about the way a film writer's work is manipulated, and if I did work for films I would like to have a lot more control than is usually possible to get.

*How about control in production of a play? Are you involved in casting?*

ARDEN: To some extent, but I am a bit cautious about that because I am really not a very good judge of actors. I have not got the sort of particular experience to be able to tell at an audition whether a man is a good actor or not. Mind you, a lot of directors have not either. It is remarkable what extraordinary casting sometimes goes on even in good theatres, theatre groups. It is in my contract that the casting must be approved by me.

*That's a standard American contract too—Dramatists' Guild.*

ARDEN: I take an even more active interest in the choice of the director. Since he has to work directly with me and he is interpreting my work to the actors, it is very important that I get the right man. I have had occasion to refuse certain directors that have been offered to me and ask for others.

*These plays contain a good deal of verse, but you don't consider yourself a poet, do you?*

ARDEN: Oh yes. Of course I don't write a lot of poetry. It is not my most important product and it probably is not very good. It is certainly not fashionable. It is rather old style, almost Victorian.

*It rhymes?*

ARDEN: It rhymes, but I have little in common with the modern poets. In England at the moment a lot of young poets are strongly influenced by the American 'Beat Generation' poets—Ginsberg and people like that. Now I know a lot of these people and I like them very much and I mix with them—but I don't like the sort of verse they write and I doubt if they would put my verse in their magazines. We just have a position of . . . sort of mutual respect . . . for each other. When I say I regard myself as a poet I mean that I think of playwriting as an offshoot of poetry. I think it is all part of the same craft.

*Tennessee Williams said that to me too.*

ARDEN: Yes, that is the old idea. In the seventeenth century a playwright was referred to as 'the poet'. This didn't mean that his plays were in verse.

*Why have you chosen to write plays? Do you have any ideas as to why?*

ARDEN: Not really, except that as a child I was always very interested in the theatre. I did not go very often because there were few opportunities in the district where I lived. I did a certain amount of acting when I was at school, and I still do a little. My wife and I occasionally put on plays—usually our own, small plays not intended for professional production. It is fruitful, for it enables us to carry out ideas without expense and without the risk of professional critics coming and damning us.

*Do you think you'll write any more plays for television?*

ARDEN: I haven't for some time, but if I have an idea that suits television I will do it.

*Has television drama in England helped the playwrights, the craft?*

ARDEN: I think so because nearly all of the interesting stage plays have been adapted for television. *Musgrave* has been done; some of my other plays would have been done on television except that the contracts offered didn't please me. An adaptation of Goethe's *Goetz von Berlichingen* was done on television. Pinter has done a great deal for television. Britain has quite lively television drama. Some years it is better than others, but it is a valid form.

*With a growing international reputation and a recent play in the repertory of the National Theatre, you should be fairly confident now. A few years ago you told* Encore, '*I see myself as a practitioner of an art which is both public and exploratory. The exploring is done in public, and is therefore full of danger.' Do you still have that sense every time you put the pencil to the exercise book?*

ARDEN: Yes, indeed I do. Henry Livings said to me just before the first night of a play of his in London, 'Keep your fingers crossed. I am going to stand naked on the stage.' I looked at him, and I thought that this was going to be some sort of protest against sexual inhibitions or something. Then I realised he was speaking metaphorically, and this statement was exactly true. The actors actually are on the stage, but the playwright himself feels that he is. And it is an alarming thought to have a theatre full of people who have come just to hear you tell them things.

# *Arnold Wesker*

▯▯▯▯▯▯▯▯▯▯▯▯▯▯▯▯▯▯▯▯▯▯▯▯▯▯▯▯▯▯▯▯▯▯▯▯▯▯▯▯▯▯▯▯▯▯▯▯▯▯▯

ARNOLD WESKER came to New York in February 1964 in connection with the production of his *Chips with Everything*, then on Broadway, and it was during that visit that he was interviewed one morning in a 45th Street coffee-house by the editor of this volume. A compact digest of that 105-minute conversation appeared as the first of the 'Playwright at Work' series published in *Playbill* between 1964 and 1966. At that time the interviewer described him as 'a small thirty-one-year-old Londoner with honest lazy eyes and a good deal to say' and 'a dapper, thoughtful, wary artist of considerable grace and even more sensibility'.

Some English critics have rated him as a 'major talent and example of the new working-class playwright' and 'the most promising and exciting young dramatist to come into the British theatre since the end of the war'. Writing a bit more warily in *Anger and After*, John Russell Taylor suggested that if the still young playwright 'can discipline his uneven talents,' then 'Arnold Wesker, hitherto by choice and on principle the most prosaic of our young dramatists, may turn out after all to be the poet the committed theatre in this country has so long awaited'.

Arnold Wesker is an avowedly 'committed playwright', a phrase which critic Harold Clurman has observed 'Americans might translate as left-wing'. There can be no doubt that Wesker is left-wing and that the term 'committed' is widely used in that context in Britain, but this dramatist is also equally 'committed' to a species of 'serious' theatre that has played a major role in the increased vitality and interesting renaissance of the British stage in the past dozen years. Not too long ago it was briefly fashionable to comment that the current crop of uninhibitedly socially and politically conscious dramatists in London was repeating the earlier American experience, and since Wesker was both Left and Jewish a few observers glibly described him as the British edition of the late Clifford Odets. It now seems clear that both of these judgments are oversimplifications, clichés and not very useful.

Arnold Wesker is not simple because, like so many of us, he is a man with *several* dreams. He is also, like so many other creative people, a product of his environment and a refugee from it. He is, however, not a defector but an exile who still considers himself 'working class' despite his literary-theatre status and his financial success. As is made clear in the body of this interview, the cultural and social improvement of the British worker is still his cause—and he is disappointed that the labour movement is not as much concerned with these goals as it is in improving wages, working conditions, pensions, et cetera. The fact that Socialist-oriented Sweden is experiencing similar difficulties in elevating the cultural appetites of its workers, at least for the moment, would be of little consolation to an idealist such as Wesker. If he is now disappointed, however, he is not defeated. He remains 'committed'.

Son of a Russian mother and a Hungarian father who was a tailor, Wesker was born into the working class, in London in 1932. He began to write poetry at twelve, initially to impress and please his brother-in-law, who wrote and who was then his boyhood hero. 'Having written that poem, I discovered impulses —so that six poems a day appeared,' he told Simon Trussler in 1966. The full text of that excellent interview may be found in a collection edited by Trussler and Marowitz, *Theatre at Work* (Methuen, 1967). Wesker continued to write but could not contemplate such a career as feasible. He never went to college, but went to work as a plumber's mate and then a kitchen porter. There was obviously a modest future in such unskilled labour, so Wesker decided to improve himself by learning the trade of pastry cook. He had earlier nurtured some dreams of becoming an actor after work with an amateur theatre group, and it is interesting to note that his career included a brief attempt to be a furniture-maker as his respected brother-in-law was.

Wesker succeeded in becoming a 'qualified pastry cook', spent four years at this in Norwich, London and Paris. This experience later contributed substantially to his first play, *The Kitchen*. While toiling in Paris, the restless young man felt himself drawn once more to writing and began to contemplate a change to writing film scripts—possibly also directing for motion pictures. He saved enough by living thriftily in the French capital so that he raised the tuition for 'the short course' at the new London School of Film Technique. In six months Wesker meant to master enough of this craft to get work in the movie industry. He never got a chance to try the film world, however, for he discovered the play competition sponsored by the *Observer* and impulsively sat down to write a short drama that he titled *The Kitchen*.

If life really were as pictured in the Hollywood films of the 1930s and 1940s, that play—which was eventually produced quite successfully in many countries and made into a film—would have been immediately hailed as a work of genius and the dramatist whirled away into temptation-seduction-corruption by the commercial entertainment moguls and their camp followers. Alas, Wesker's script was rejected even by *The Observer* on the unromantic ground that it was too short to be considered; it was not a full-length play. One might think that Wesker or any other aspiring uncertain dramatist would have given up the theatre at that point. However, Arnold Wesker went to the Royal Court Theatre one night to see the English Stage Company's production of a new play by a new dramatist, and, having experienced John Osborne's then sensational and epoch-opening *Look Back in Anger*, decided that important things could be said and done in the theatre.

As has frequently been said, it is difficult to overestimate the tremendous impact that *Look Back in Anger* had upon the course of British—and foreign—theatre. So far as Wesker was concerned, it gave him the confidence to begin a new full-length play that was eventually titled *Chicken Soup with Barley*.

While he was completing that script, he met stage-film director Lindsay Anderson outside a movie theatre and invited him to read *The Kitchen*. Although Anderson consented, the playwright lost his nerve, decided that *The Kitchen* couldn't be too good because *The Observer* had rejected it and decided to send Anderson the second longer work, when it was finished. Anderson liked it a lot, pledged that he'd try to interest the Royal Court group, which had asked Anderson to direct one of its new series of Sunday-night 'no scenery' productions. During this period all the major British television companies turned down *The Kitchen*, and Wesker's motion-picture script titled *Pools* was rejected as too expensive to produce by the British Film Institute's Experimental Film Fund.

There is some difference of opinion as to why *Chicken Soup with Barley* was produced by the young repertory company at the Belgrade Theatre in Coventry rather than the Royal Court's English Stage Company. The official explanation is that the London group sent the play to the Belgrade because the Royal Court leaders had agreed to lend their London stage to provincial 'rep' units for a month and wanted to make sure that the Belgrade did something worthwhile during the week that the Belgrade would have the London stage. Wesker has said that he doubts whether the Court had much faith in the play. In any case, the Court loaned John Dexter to the Belgrade for the production, which opened in Coventry on 7 July 1958, and had its London premiere at the Court a week later.

The play, which was partially autobiographical, as so many first works are, traced the history of the Kahns, an East End Jewish family, from 1936 to 1956. It had a passionately Marxist mother, as did the playwright, and a son who was losing his Communist convictions and political certainty. The London critics treated it respectfully but without much enthusiasm, although when it was later revived after Wesker was more established the play got much better notices. John Arden comments on his own similar experiences with *Serjeant Musgrave's Dance* elsewhere in this book.

The second Wesker work produced was *Roots*, staged in 1959. He was fairly advanced with that script when George Devine commissioned him to finish it for the Royal Court, but once again there was apparently some lack of complete confidence that the script was quite finished or ready for production. This was not the attitude of the brilliant actress Peggy Ashcroft, however, and she showed the script to the gifted Joan Plowright, who was so delighted with the role of Beatie Bryant that she said she would play it anywhere. She gave memorable performances in the initial Belgrade production in Coventry and again when the Royal Court presented *Roots* in London.

*Roots* was a success, and Arnold Wesker was no longer an unknown quantity to either stage or television producers. John Dexter directed *The Kitchen* for the Royal Court's Sunday-evening series, and Wesker had the privilege of being the rejector instead of the rejected as he turned down television offers for the play. Critic Walter Allen hailed *Roots* as 'by far the best and most faithful play about British working-class life that has appeared', and Bernard Levin wrote of Wesker's ear for dialogue as 'extraordinarily acute'.

The next Wesker drama was *I'm Talking about Jerusalem*, which completed the trilogy with *Chicken Soup* and *Roots*. Since then his writing has ranged much further from his own origins and experiences. Although he did serve in the Royal Air Force, *Chips with Everything* was a genuine break with his earlier writing about the Jewish Marxist problems that played so important a role in the trilogy, and then came *The Four Seasons*. In fact, Wesker had nearly completed *Their Very Own and Golden City* before *The Four Seasons* but *The Four Seasons* was produced a year earlier. The London critics found *The Four Seasons* a startling break with Wesker's earlier pattern of realism and naturalism, and his highly and deliberately theatrical language generated many negative reactions.

R

It was not a successful play. *Golden City*, which is treated in the interview, fared somewhat better but is not considered among the dramatist's most focused and effective works. It is, however, probably better than the reception accorded its first production.

Where Arnold Wesker is going is difficult to predict, and critics such as Robert Brustein are not yet convinced that he will be more than 'a secondary dramatist'. How Wesker will get to his goal—how he will write next year—is also not certain. His objective, at least insofar as he is a 'committed' political and social observer, is more definite. As he announced in an *Encore* manifesto, he means to address himself to all social classes—including and especially the 'bus driver, the housewife, the miner and the Teddy Boy' who have not traditionally attended the theatre in Britain. But that is not all.

'I want to write about people in a way that will somehow give them an insight into an aspect of life which they may not have had before; and further, I want to impart to them some of the enthusiasm I have for that life. I want to teach,' he wrote several years ago. He is well aware that he may not succeed, and, like other playwrights, is not yet wholly certain that his gifts are really commensurate with either the task or even the success that he has achieved. He has recently admitted that he is still struggling to adjust to the shock of being taken seriously as a dramatist, which means that he is still proving himself to himself.

This is, of course, a permanent condition with writers for the theatre—the most dangerous forum of all.

w. w.

*To start from the beginning, where and when were you born?*

WESKER: London, Empire Day, 1932. That's 24 May. I was born at Mother Levy's in Stepney in the East End.

*Mother Levy's?*

WESKER: It was a maternity home for poor Jews. It has improved some; my first son was born there. I'll have all these biographical details mailed to you.

*Fine. We can go straight to* Chips, *which I saw last night. Your picture of draftees in the Royal Air Force in* Chips *seems to reflect a profound hostility towards the military establishment and Britain's Establishment in general. Is that a fair judgment?*

WESKER: I do not regard the play as a vehicle for any hostility to specific groups or individuals, but rather as attacks on states of mind . . . states of mind that men have towards each other in many nations. It's universal. You have it here. I just presented it in the British way.

*It has been pointed out that—while your image of the aristocracy, the Establishment, the ruling class, is bitter—the lower or working class is also presented harshly and without illusions.*

WESKER: How can I have illusions about it? I came from it.

*Since so many critics have described your plays as sympathetic to labour and/or unsympathetic to the money-birth-power elite that is still so influential in Britain, do many workers come to applaud your plays?*

WESKER: No. Few workers go to the theatre. It is not part of their tradition, not yet.

*You have been called a Socialist playwright. Is that an accurate judgment?*

WESKER: Well, I have never read Marx. Nor Freud either, for that matter.

*Does that mean that psychoanalysis does not interest you?*

WESKER: I would be appalled at the idea of going to a psychiatrist or analyst myself, and I have studiously avoided books on these subjects. I wouldn't want to make any further generalisations on the possible merits or benefits of this kind of thing—other than to say that it can be degraded into mumbo-jumbo by the wrong people.

*Hasn't it influenced a whole generation of novelists?*

WESKER: Yes, that's clear enough. Hemingway and the others, I suppose. You still see a lot of it in characters some writers present.

*What about your characters? What is your attitude towards them?*

WESKER: I have an attitude to my characters that is essentially Jewish. Don't look so odd—it really is. I can't quite define it, but maybe you saw it in the relations between Pip and Charles in *Chips*. There's a sort of nagging, an almost pompous quality and a focus on basics.

*Do you regard yourself a a Jewish playwright?*

WESKER: I *am* Jewish and I *am* a playwright, but I hope that my work has a broader significance and appeal. I don't write for or about any one group.

*Not to belabour this point, I noticed that in* Chips *the only anti-Semitic remarks were made by an RAF corporal or sergeant from your lower class. Does that mean there is no such feeling among the upper classes?*

WESKER: I spent two years in the RAF, and I think I gave a truthful impression. Of course, I suppose that the upper classes have as much of that sort of bigotry but are 'gentlemanly' enough to be more discreet and less outspoken. As I get older, I seem to be more aware of prejudice. I'd say that there are still homes in Britain where I might not be welcome for one reason or another.

*Even after your international acclaim as one of your country's best young dramatists?*

WESKER: I think so. [Grins] Well, I'd imagine that some of *them* may be wondering whether *they'd* be welcome in the houses of Wesker or Osborne.

*Thanks for bringing up the next point—the allegedly Angry Young Men. Do you feel that you and John Osborne and your contemporaries writing plays with sociological comment or criticism are—in fact—a group or a movement?*

WESKER: I never think in such terms. Of course, an artist must try to make some coherent sense out of what he is creating over any period of time. Still, I don't have much contact with the playwrights you're discussing and I only see Pinter or Osborne once or twice a year.

*Whom do you see? Who are your friends?*

WESKER: Among writers? Doris Lessing—the novelist. Christopher Logue and Edna O'Brien.

*Which American writers do you admire most?*

WESKER: Arthur Miller. I share with his millions of admirers his view of the human condition. Malamud is a very fine writer. Salinger, of course, and Thomas Wolfe.

*Would you consider yourself a 'realistic' writer?*

WESKER: Well, as I've said before, I've found that realistic art is a contradiction in terms. It seems clear that art is the re-creation of experience rather than the copying of it.

*You've written in the* Transatlantic Review *that 'Some writers use naturalistic means to recreate experience, others non-naturalistic. I happen to use naturalistic means; but all the statements I make are made theatrically. Reality is as misleading as truth. If I develop, it might be away from naturalism.' Is this still your view?*

WESKER: Yes, and I think that my work shows it. After all, the plays usually speak for the dramatist better than most interviews or critical articles, don't they?

*Well, that's certainly the view of playwrights such as Osborne and Beckett. Let's turn to why you write plays.*

WESKER: I have not tried the other forms much—one bad novel— although I am interested in writing for films too. I began writing at twelve, and I think my first effort was a dreadful poem that I named 'The Breeze'. It wasn't easy for me to contemplate writing as a career. You might say that my family were working-class puritans. They believed in hard work—physical labour—and writing didn't seem like 'real work' at all to me as a boy. You mean why do I write at all? There are things that concern me enough to compel the sustained committed effort that leads to the script of a play. I once told a friend in London that my plays are efforts to continue—and perhaps win—certain arguments that I've had with people. And, of course, the plays are about people and relationships—troubled relationships that seem to demand explaining.

*To go on, people are always curious about a writer's work habits or methods. What are yours?*

WESKER: I don't have any. I write whenever I have the time.

*High noon or small grey hours of the morning?*

WESKER: Absolutely. I've been rather busy with my work at Centre 42 recently, but I sometimes take off mornings or write in the evening at home.

*I have heard you describe Centre 42 as a movement and organisation of young writers, musicians and other creators to bring the arts into the daily life of the entire population. But before we go into that, could you tell me how you work?*

WESKER: Physically, I write the first draft in longhand in an exercise book. I type the second—making changes in the process —and then go over it with a pen before retyping it again. There may be any number of drafts before I'm satisfied. I usually write in the upstairs study of our house in north London.

*Without interruption?*

WESKER: You mean the children? We have three, the oldest boy being four years old. No, they don't bother me once I start writing. They know.

*Was or is your wife a writer?*

WESKER: No, she was a waitress. She's English; I didn't know her during my days as a pastry chef in Paris.

*To continue with 'how' you create, can you define it or is it something magical?*

WESKER: Of course it's magical. That's the simple truth for every artist. Sometimes when I'm writing—or trying to write—I think back. Was I as conscious as this when I penned the first page of *Chicken Soup with Barley*, or was it a trance? I couldn't tell you. I don't know.

*Do you have any method or ritual, any set of conditions to stimulate the magic?*

WESKER: No, not consciously. In fact, I get to my characters in a different way almost every time. Yet, the moments at which I sit down and write *must* have something in common. Certainly. . . . Just as there are certain conditions that are conducive to making love—we all know that—I'd guess that there are states conductive to writing.

*Are you working on a new play now?*

WESKER: Yes, it's called *Their Very Own and Golden City*. I should finish it by the end of April

*Can you tell me anything about it?*

WESKER: I'd rather not. Don't be offended, but if I am quoted as stating that the play is about thus and so, then some critic may fling that back at me. You know—Mr Wesker says that his new drama is about thus and so but it seems to me, and so on.

*A lot of people would like to know about your next play.*

WESKER: No, only a very incestuous elite in London and New York are waiting for Wesker's new play . . . and even those will wait and see what the critics will say. They won't buy tickets for a play with bad reviews even if I write five or six immensely successful ones before that.

*You seem very aware or concerned about the critics. Have they treated you harshly?*

WESKER: On the contrary, the great majority on both sides of the Atlantic have been generously affirmative. I am not complaining.

*How do the London drama critics compare with those in New York?*

WESKER: They are not quite as influential as yours, but they certainly have an effect. There are some good ones in both cities, but there appear to be very few really sound critics with unified integrated sets of values as to what makes good theatre or good life. The others may like two completely opposite plays with clearly antithetical points of view—without realising the conflict. Most simply *intuit* without any real continuity of view or genuine standards.

*With unabashed insistence, I'd still like to hear about your new play.*

WESKER: Well . . . well, in a way it is a development of or from *Chips*. It is allegorical. It is about an architect who wants to design and build a dozen golden cities, wonderful places that shape the lives of the people who live there. He ends up building half a golden city—much less than his dream or capacity—and is knighted for it.

*I realise that you have still to finish* Golden City, *but may I ask how you feel about it?*

WESKER: I am not pessimistic, but there is every reason why it shouldn't succeed. It is certainly my most ambitious work—technically and intellectually.

*Not nearly as ambitious as Centre 42, is it?*

WESKER: No, but that's not writing. I give it a great deal of time, almost as if it were a regular job. I'm in our office at 20 Fitzroy

Square in London four or five days a week, usually six or seven hours a day.

*There's been a good deal of discussion of the 'Socialist content' of your plays. Would you comment on your political background?*

WESKER: My mother is a Communist—a member of the Communist Party—and I was a member of the Young Communist League, but not for very long. I later joined the Zionist Youth; I think that the Zionist movement influenced my development as much or more than any political group. It's no secret that my sympathy for the Communist cause was drastically shaken by *The God That Failed*. That book disturbed me so profoundly—really rocked me—that I wrote letters to Spender and Koestler and others to find out if the book was actually cold fact. Then the Hungarian uprising and Soviet intervention shook me even further. I ought to point out that merely being violently anti-Communist and anti-Soviet have not particularly helped the Left in Britain. It has splintered and debilitated it. Something more positive is necessary, some goal, some vision.

*You're not Communist but you're on the left?*

WESKER: I don't enjoy such labelling, but you could say that. My message to the ruling class—my warning that social and economic and political change cannot be halted—is rather plain in *Chips*, I believe.

*Now, please explain what Centre 42 is, and why it is.*

WESKER: Legally, Centre 42 is a limited company incorporated on 4 September 1961. It has had charitable status since 6 October 1961, as a National Charity. But what is it? It is an association of artists of every sort—jazz musicians, playwrights, painters, folk singers, poets, dancers, actors, chamber-music groups—united in the conviction that everyone has a right to enjoy the best of culture and art whether or not he can pay for it. We see the arts as basic to daily life, just as important as education or medical care.

*But education and medical care are publicly financed and controlled in Britain today?*

WESKER: We regard Centre 42 as leading towards eventual government support of a large cultural programme that will reach every citizen. At the moment, we are financing the Centre 42 series of arts festivals ourselves and with help from private contributors.

*Can you name these?*

WESKER: Well, we got 10,000 pounds—that's about $28,000—from the Gulbenkian Foundation in 1962 and somebody else has guaranteed us a bank overdraft of 50,000 pounds for two years. Writers such as Graham Greene, Terence Rattigan, C. P. Snow, Kenneth Tynan, Robert Bolt, J. B. Priestley, Alan Sillitoe and Sir Herbert Read are among our sponsors. So are actors such as Sir Laurence Olivier, Stanley Baker, Peter Sellers, Vanessa Redgrave, Dame Peggy Ashcroft and Joan Plowright, The Bishop of Coventry, the Countess of Albermarle, Sir John Rothenstein, Lord Harewood, Harold Hobson, Baron Moss, Jack Hylton, Johnny Dankworth, Sidney Bernstein, Tom Maschler—it's a long list. I've left out quite a few.

*Have you contributed yourself?*

WESKER: Yes, and I have also signed over the money from sale of the film rights to *Chips.*

*You've explained that 42 is an association or company of artists, but you have not said why it is and how it works.*

WESKER: The roots lie in the 1960 meeting of the Trades Union Congress, our national labour organisation. A delegate named Ralph Bond, who is now on our Centre's Council of Management, moved a resolution numbered 42 with a statement that 'We want all the people to have the chance to enjoy the beauty and riches of life in all its forms. Too much that is good is being cheapened and vulgarised by the purveyors of mass entertainment. We reject the idea that culture should be the preserve of an enlightened intelligentsia, and that any old rubbish is good enough for the masses.'

*What about Resolution 42, which is presumably the source of the centre's name?*

WESKER: Yes, you're right. Resolution 42 declared that 'Congress recognises the importance of the arts in the life of the community, especially now when many unions are securing a shorter working week and greater leisure for their members.' It went on to call for a special study of what might be done 'to insure a greater participation by the trade union movement in all cultural activities'.

*But Centre 42 is not a union venture, is it?*

WESKER: Hardly, although four members of our council are labour leaders. We get no official trade-union backing or support, since art is apparently far down on organised labour's list of priorities. This is a disappointment, since it remains incomprehensible to us how anyone can consider building a civilised society without giving the arts a high priority. Of course, this criticism can also be directed to industry, co-ops and local authorities.

*How did Centre 42 get started?*

WESKER: After the resolution was passed, a number of artists began to consider what we could do to reciprocate this concern for the future of the arts. We finally agreed on a plan to change the methods of presenting the arts in this country. Our scheme called for four steps. First, we would build or establish under one roof a centre to house facilities for all the arts.

*That's an approach that is spreading in the United States too—from the Lincoln Centre complex in New York to Detroit and Los Angeles. What were your other three steps?*

WESKER: Second, we would set up our own permanent acting company, orchestra, visual-arts department, dance group, jazz band and so on. Third, we would serve the immediate area around the Centre with cultural presentations and bring arts festivals to outlying areas when invited. We would accept invitations from community bodies such as a trades-union council, a tenants' association, a co-op guild or a university or some similar group. Fourth, we would encourage the local bodies to organise their own festival or event and we would simply provide the programme —the talent and selection of plays or dances or such—from the Centre's current repertoire.

*Has it worked?*

WESKER: Yes, but not exactly in that order. Before we could build the Centre, we began receiving requests from trades councils to help them mount arts festivals. We have done six, including everything from a new play by Bernard Kops to an American folk ballad on Lincoln to a sixteen-piece jazz band to poetry readings in pubs and factory canteens. We have put on *Hamlet* by the National Youth Theatre—with every actor under twenty-one—and Stravinsky's *The Soldier's Tale*. Exhibitions of children's art, photos, cartoons and sketches, works of local painters and sculptors, a jazz-dancing competition were standard ingredients.

*Has anything like this been tried in Britain previously?*

WESKER: No, there has never—to our knowledge—been attempted a venture of this kind before. A group of artists have said to the community, 'If you want to enjoy and share our work, then invite us. We will present it for you in the form of festivals and, since you are unlikely to be able to pay for it, we will subsidise the events as well.'

*Does this mean you don't charge admissions or pay your Centre 42 staff or artists?*

WESKER: Some events or exhibitions were free, but we charge five shillings—that's about seventy cents—for most and six shillings was the top for anything. Our small full-time staff that runs the Centre and organises the festivals is salaried, but quite modestly. Performers and technicians who mounted the festivals also received weekly wages, although in many cases they offered to accept and were given less than their usual salaries. Some gave their services free, and others worked merely for their expenses.

*Would you say that the festivals were successful?*

WESKER: Yes, the same communities have asked us to return and many other groups have requested our help. To quote our last annual report, '42 works; this is a fact whatever our inadequacies may be. It can indeed change the cultural pattern of this country and release and discover the nation's talent. It can also grow into a self-conscious monster providing an already status-conscious community with yet another status symbol.'

*How has the press reacted to Centre 42's festivals?*

WESKER: National newspapers either ignored us or were patronising in an ill-informed way about 'art and the people'. The provincial press leaned over backwards to greet and accommodate the festivals.

*To focus specifically on theatre, don't you believe that the commercial producers are doing an adequate job in Britain and America?*

WESKER: No, not in developing and reaching the enormous potential audience. The commercial theatre can meet only a limited part of the public need. As any businessman knows, he needs a laboratory or research unit to improve his product and expand his market. Centre 42—and many other similar centres that must follow—can meet these needs. It does not have to be some odd experimental play. It might simply be a production of a classic with a new director or a new form of set or staging.

*I have heard you say that your plan calls for developing a great public appetite for the arts and acceptance of cultural presentations as routine in daily life, like germ-free water and tax-supported medical care. Would that be, in effect, nationalising the theatre and other performing arts?*

WESKER: Roughly. Today almost all of Britain's 'new' playwrights came up through state-subsidised theatres or experimental groups. Bolt is the main exception. I'm convinced that art is the right and need of every civilised community, and should be subsidised rather than forced to pay for itself. Words and phrases like economically feasible, returns, profits or loss are meaningless when applied to art.

*Some Americans might reject your philosophy as too left-wing or Socialistic.*

WESKER: Perhaps, but Centre 42 has received grants from many British corporations and wealthy industrialists. You might tell your financiers that it was John D. Rockefeller III who said that 'box office and admission fees can never support the arts any more than hospital bills can cover all hospital costs, or tuition fees the full cost of education. Just as society has accepted responsibility for health, welfare and education, it must support the arts.'

*One final question. What are your long-range writing plans?*

WESKER: Well, I'd like to do some films. I never studied writing anywhere, but I did a production course at the London School of Film Technique and I'm certain that I'll write a film script some-day. My other project for my mature years may well be a life of Jesus.

*Thank you very much, Mr Wesker.*

WESKER: Now it's my turn to ask you a question. I've got a ten-pound bet on with my friend Christopher Logue. Tell me, do you really think that there is much chance of Goldwater becoming your next President?